Ireland's Minstrel

Watercolour illustration of *Lalla Rookh* by J.M.W Turner, commissioned for the literary album of the Whig politician, Walter Fawkes, 1822.

Ireland's Minstrel

A Life of Tom Moore:

Poet, Patriot and Byron's Friend

Linda Kelly

I.B. TAURIS
LONDON · NEW YORK

To Val

Published in 2006 by I.B.Tauris & Co Ltd
6 Salem Road, London W2 4BU
175 Fifth Avenue, New York NY 10010
www.ibtauris.com

In the United States and Canada distributed by Palgrave Macmillan,
a division of St. Martin's Press, 175 Fifth Avenue, New York NY 10010

ISBN 10: 1 84511 252 0
ISBN 13: 978 1 84511 252 3

A full CIP record for this book is available from the British Library
A full CIP record for this book is available from the Library of Congress
Library of Congress catalog card: available

Typeset in Calisto by Dexter Haven Associates Ltd, London
Printed and bound in Great Britain by TJ International Ltd, Padstow, Cornwall.

CONTENTS

Acknowledgements   vii

Illustrations   ix

Introduction   1

1   A Dublin Boyhood   7

2   Trinity College   16

3   1798   24

4   London Successes   33

5   Bermuda Bound   44

6   American Travels   54

7   The Interrupted Duel   64

8   The *Irish Melodies*   73

9   A Married Man   82

10   Meeting Byron   92

11   Mayfield Cottage   102

12   A Record Contract   111

13   'A health to thee, Tom Moore'   119

14   *Lalla Rookh*   130

15   Sloperton Days   140

16   The Blow Falls   149

17   Venice, Rome and Paris   157

18   Homecoming   166

19   The Destruction of the Memoirs   175

20   A Visit to Scotland   185

21   Negotiations   193

22   Bereavement and Biography   203

23   Irish Initiatives   212

24   Farewell to Poetry   222

25   'Oh who would inhabit   230

     This bleak world alone?'

Notes   239

Bibliography   245

Index   249

ACKNOWLEDGEMENTS

I have a great many people to thank for their help while I was writing this book, though its mistakes and shortcomings are of course my own. First, I am grateful to the staff of the British Library, the Kensington Central Library, the London Library, the National Library of Ireland and the Library of Trinity College, Dublin. I would also like to thank Dr Peter Cochrane for showing me his transcription of Hobhouse's entries in Doris Langley Moore's copy of Moore's life of Byron, now in the collection of Mr Jack Wasserman; Siobhan Fitzpatrick, librarian of the Royal Irish Academy, Dublin, for showing me round Moore's library; Professor Peter Jupp for reading my manuscript; Dr Alexis Leporc of the Hermitage Museum, for drawing my attention to Wilhelm Hensel's portrait of the future Tsarina, Alexandra Fyodovrna, as Lalla Rookh; John and Virginia Murray for allowing me to consult the John Murray archives at 50 Albemarle Street; John Murray Publishers for permission to quote from John Betjeman's poem 'Ireland's Own or the Burial of Thomas Moore'; Dennis Powney, historian of Bromham and its church, for sharing his knowledge and enthusiasm; Kathleen Tynan for the inspiration given by her singing at the concert at the Royal Irish Academy commemorating the 150th anniversary of Moore's death; my editors, Dr Lester Crook, Liz Friend-Smith and Gretchen Ladish; and my ever-encouraging agent Christopher Sinclair-Stevenson.

I am very grateful too, to friends and relations who have helped and cheered me on my way: Asa Briggs, Desmond Fitzgerald, Rosanna and Anthony Gardner, Rachel Grigg, John Jolliffe, Patrick and Kate Kavanagh, Nicholas Kelly, Nina Lobanov Rostovsky, Douglas Matthews, Suzy and Christopher Miles, Fionn Morgan, Sean and Rosemary Mulcahy, David Nice, Mollie and John Julius Norwich, Kevin Nowlan, Jeremy O'Sullivan, Valerie and Thomas Pakenham, Francis

Russell, Oliver Williams, Derek Wise, the late Robert Woof and Kyril Zinoviev. My greatest thanks as usual are to my husband Laurence, a fellow admirer of Tom Moore, for his unfailing interest and support.

ILLUSTRATIONS

Cover: Thomas Moore by Thomas Lawrence, 1829.
Courtesy of John Murray

Frontispiece: Watercolour illustration to *Lalla Rookh*,
by J.M.W. Turner, 1822. Courtesy of Christie's

1. 'The Origin of the Harp' by Daniel Maclise, 1842.   29
Courtesy of Manchester City Galleries

2. 'Breakfast with Samuel Rogers', 1815. Detail from   60
a mezzotint by Charles Mottram

3. 'First Number of Moore's *Irish Melodies*', 1808.   75
Courtesy of the Royal Irish Academy

4. 'Bessy Moore', date unknown. Drawing from a   88
notebook at Bowood by Gilbert Stuart Newton.
Courtesy of the Marquess of Lansdowne

5. 'Fare Thee Well': Byron's Departure from   124
England, 1816. Engraving by George Cruikshank.
Courtesy of the Department of Prints and
Drawings, British Museum

6. 'Thomas Moore': portrait study by Gilbert   197
Stuart Newton, 1826. Courtesy of Sotheby's
Picture Library

7. 'Sloperton Cottage', from a contemporary engraving   206

8. 'Thomas Moore in his Study at Sloperton   220
Cottage'; English School, nineteenth century.
Courtesy of the National Gallery of Ireland

INTRODUCTION

My boat is on the shore,
And my bark is on the sea,
But, before I go, Tom Moore,
Here's a double health to thee!

Byron's last lines before leaving England in 1816 pay tribute to a friendship
that is one of Tom Moore's greatest claims to fame. A hundred and forty
two of Byron's letters are addressed to him, it was to him that Byron
entrusted his ill-fated memoirs, and it was he whom Byron wished to be
his first biographer. 'He has but one fault...' Byron once confided in his
journal, 'he is not here.'[1]

At the time of Byron's farewell verses, Tom Moore's popularity as a poet
was second only to his own. Moore's long oriental poem *Lalla Rookh*,
published the following year, confirmed his European reputation; no other
poem of the period was so widely translated. He himself was never misled
by its success. 'I am strongly inclined to think,' he told his publisher, 'that in
a race into future times (if *anything* of mine could pretend to such a run),
those little ponies, the "Melodies", will beat the mare, Lalla Rookh, hollow.'[2]

Of course he was right. *Lalla Rookh* is virtually forgotten (though John
Betjeman spoke highly of it). His *Irish Melodies* are still known and loved.
For Irish emigrants throughout the nineteenth century they were the closest
imaginative link with their homeland; the sheet music for ''Tis the Last Rose
of Summer' sold one and a half million copies in the United States alone.
In other countries seeking freedom – in Poland, Hungary and Russia – the
Melodies were a rallying call. '*Votre poésie patriotique me parut, il y a bien
d années,*' the historian Jacques Thierry wrote to Moore, '*non seulement le cri
de douleur de l Irlande, mais encore le chant de tristesse de tous les peuples opprimés.*'[3]

Some of Moore's best known lyrics – 'The Minstrel Boy', 'Oh! Blame not
the Bard' – will always find their place in anthologies of romantic poetry.

1

But they only reveal their full qualities when they are sung, as Moore intended them to be, to the accompaniment of a piano or a harp. His own performances, first in Dublin, and then in the drawing rooms of the London aristocracy, were sensationally successful. With social gifts to match his talents Moore, a Dublin grocer's son, was welcomed into the strongholds of Whig society, perhaps the most powerful and exclusive, and certainly one of the most brilliant groups Britain has ever seen. Byron remarked that he was the only poet whose conversation equalled his poetry. 'I have known a dull man to live on a *bon mot* of Moore's for a week.'[4]

Moore's *Irish Melodies*, with their patriotic and nostalgic themes, were popular at every level of society. At a time when Ireland's fortunes were at their lowest, following the disastrous rising of 1798, and the traumatic Act of Union of 1801, Moore helped to create a sense of pride in Ireland's past. With music drawn from traditional Irish sources and lyrics recalling former glories, he gave Ireland a sense of cultural identity in tune with the romantic nationalism of the time. A Catholic, who had been a student at the time of the '98 rising, he had watched the fate of his fellow countrymen with anguish. He would be haunted by the débacle of the rebellion, expressing his sorrow and outrage in song after song of the *Irish Melodies*. Most moving of all perhaps is the song 'Oh! Breathe not his Name', commemorating the death of his friend Robert Emmet, who was executed for his part in another abortive rising in 1803.

Moore has often been criticised for singing his country's wrongs in London drawing rooms rather than seeking sterner action. But he was a poet not a politician (as a Catholic he would have been debarred from standing for Parliament in any case). His favoured place among the Whigs, the only party committed to Catholic emancipation, gave him an influence he would never have had if he had stayed on in Dublin after the Act of Union. Far more tough-minded than his sparkling manner suggested, he never lost sight of his early ideals. 'I verily believe,' he once declared, 'that being born a slave has but given me a keener sense and relish of the inestimable blessings of freedom, and an enlarged sense of sympathy with all those – whatever their race or creed, whether they be blacks or whites – who even with a glimmering sense of what they seek, are contending for those just rights and privileges of civilised man, without which civilisation itself, in its truest sense, can not exist.'[5]

Moore's decision to write the life of Lord Edward Fitzgerald, the leader of the doomed uprising of 1798, was an act of considerable political courage from which his friends tried to dissuade him. Like his other two biographies, those of Sheridan and Byron, it gains authority from the fact that he knew the subjects, though in the case of Lord Edward only by sight. He describes how as a student he saw Lord Edward walking down Grafton Street and how, 'on being told who he was ... I ran anxiously after him, desirous of another look at one whose name from my earliest schooldays, had been associated with all that was noble, patriotic and chivalrous. Though I saw him but once, his peculiar dress, the elastic lightness of his step and the soft expression given to his eyes by their long dark lashes are as present and familiar to me as if I had known him intimately.'[6]

Moore's biographies of Sheridan and Byron were both pioneering works. Moore had known Sheridan only in his later years – though Sheridan's dregs, as Byron remarked, were better than the first sprightly runnings of others. Sheridan's lyrics in works such as the *Duenna* had certainly influenced his own, and Moore's indignant verses against the grandees who had neglected Sheridan are some of the most stinging ever written. Byron, who delighted in Sheridan's company, encouraged Moore to write Sheridan's life, and it may well have been because of this that he asked him to become his own biographer.

Moore's life of Byron, written amidst great opposition from most of his family and friends, is still the foundation for all later biographies of the poet. Although inevitably incomplete, it offers not only the first sustained critical evaluation of Byron's work but a character study that is surprisingly modern in its psychological insights. And it is written with love and an eloquence sometimes soaring into lyricism: romantic prose at its best. The story of the burning of Byron's memoirs is one of the most painful in Moore's career: having raised money on the manuscript he was unable to control its fate when Byron suddenly died and was forced to witness its destruction without being able to prevent it. He came close to a nervous breakdown over the episode for which the biography was to some extent an act of expiation.

While Moore's biographies will always be essential reading for those studying their subjects, it is his journals that will give most pleasure to the general reader. They have long been known only from the heavily edited edition published by Lord John Russell in the 1850s at a time when Victorian prudery was at its height. The recent discovery of the original journals in the Longmans archive by Professor Wilfred S. Dowden of Rice University, Texas, has provided a wealth of new material, not least Moore's account of the destruction of Byron's memoirs, excluded for reasons of discretion by Lord John. The task of editing the journals, in twelve copy books of varying sizes, often badly damaged by water or defaced by Lord John's crossings-out, was an arduous one but the last of the six-volume edition was published in 1991. Racy and shrewd, and often very funny, they bring the whole brilliant world of Whig society to life. A celebrity himself, Moore knew almost all his great contemporaries, but despite a certain childish delight in any praise that came his way, he never over-estimated his own importance or tried to hide his failings. In their honesty and decency, as well as their gaiety and intelligence, they are one of the most enjoyable records of the time.

There have been a number of biographies of Moore: an excellent short life by Stephen Gwynn in the English Men of Letters series, 1905, and another by Seamus McColl in 1936. Two full length lives of Moore appeared in 1937: L.A.G. Strong's *The Minstrel Boy*, and in America *The Harp that Once* by Howard Mumford Jones. They were followed in 1975 by the American scholar Hoover H. Jordan's two-volume life of Moore, *Bolt Upright* (the reference is to Moore's unflinching political stance), published by the University of Salzburg. Exhaustive and scholarly, its chief disadvantage is its inaccessibility to the general reader: it is not available in any of the London public libraries, and it was only with the greatest difficulty that I was able to track down a solitary copy in Canada. The most recent biography of Moore by Terence de Vere White was published in 1977, a delightful book, full of insights into Moore's very Irish character, but conceived as a portrait rather than a comprehensive life.

Although Moore's *Irish Melodies* have never lost their popular appeal his own reputation has suffered many ups and downs. For the militant nationalists of the later half of the nineteenth century, he was considered too elitist, too conciliatory, to be of relevance to their cause. For Yeats, perhaps unconsciously discounting Moore's anticipation of the Celtic Twilight, he was a social climber, a 'cringing firbolg'; out of all Moore's poetry, Yeats admitted to liking only two lyrics. Since then, he has been championed by poets as various as John Betjeman – 'even Byron,' he once wrote, 'did not compare as a love poet to Tom Moore'[7] – and W.H. Auden who included Moore's 'Meeting of the Waters' in his anthology *A Certain World* and for whom the Byron of *Don Juan* and the Moore of *The Fudge Family in Paris* were the most 'Popean' in spirit of the early nineteenth-century poets. But with the exception of George Saintsbury, who gives a sympathetic assessment of Moore's work in the *Cambridge History of English Literature*, he has been consistently belittled by literary critics and historians. He himself never claimed to be 'one of the great guns of Parnassus'[8] (though there are some who might argue the point) but given the extent of his fame and influence in his lifetime, it seems extraordinary that he barely rates a mention in most twentieth-century histories of romanticism, or that a recent biographer of Byron, Phyllis Grosskurth, should dismiss him merely as 'a rather endearing little snob'.

Fortunately there are signs that attitudes are changing. After over a century of neglect, Moore's importance as one of the leading figures of the romantic movement – far more widely read at the time than anyone but Scott or Byron – is beginning to be recognised. His influence on Byron and the inter-connectedness of their poetry and politics is the subject of a fascinating new book by Professor Jeffery Vail, *The Literary Relationship of Lord Byron and Thomas Moore*, a major work of rehabilitation as far as Moore is concerned. In Ireland above all, where the National University of Ireland, Galway, is planning a complete edition of his poetic, musical and prose works, to be published in the form of an electronic hypermedia archive, Moore is coming into his own. His songs, so unforgettably performed by John McCormack in the early twentieth century, are once more being revived as the works of art they are: among others, by the Dublin-born mezzo-soprano Ann Murray in her collection of Irish songs, *The Last Rose of Summer*, and by the Irish American tenor, James Flannery, whose recordings of the *Irish Melodies*, with their accompanying study of Moore's work, *Dear Harp of My Country*, advance Moore's claims, in the words of Seamus Heaney, 'with an ardour that would surely have delighted Moore himself'.[9] Meanwhile the latest play by Brian Friel, *The Home Place*, begins and ends to the strains of 'Oft in the Stilly Night', and references to Moore's songs recur throughout the play; Tom Moore, declares one character, is 'the finest singer we have; the voice of our nation'.

Stocks in Moore are rising. It seems a good moment for a fresh look at his many-faceted career, taking into account the new material available and concentrating on the areas that seem to me most relevant: the *Irish Melodies* and their place in the romantic movement; the relationship with Byron, still largely unexplored; the ground-breaking work of his biographies; the charm of Whig society so brilliantly recaptured in his journals; above all the sense of purpose behind his butterfly exterior, which, at a dark time in its history, made him one of Ireland's most eloquent and persuasive advocates.

I

A Dublin Boyhood

There are few greater blessings than a happy childhood. Tom Moore would have his share of tragedies in life but he would always count himself lucky in his beginnings. It was not that he was specially privileged in a worldly sense. As a Catholic in an Ireland dominated by the Protestant Ascendancy, as a grocer's son in a world where wealth and power still belonged to the aristocracy, he began from a relatively modest start point. But the sunny temperament and zest for life, which he owed to the kindly circumstances of his youth, would last him almost to the end. Well into middle age we find him writing, or rather singing, for the poem was one of his *Irish Melodies*,

> They may rail at this life – from the hour I began it,
> I found it a life full of kindness and bliss;
> And until they can show me some happier planet
> More social and bright, I'll content me with this...

Tom Moore was born in Dublin on 28 May 1779, above the grocer's shop at 12 Aungier Street, a few minutes' walk from Trinity College and St Stephen's Green, where his father had set up business the year before. Revisiting Dublin long afterwards, at the height of his fame, Moore was moved to find the shop was virtually unchanged: 'the small old yard and its appurtenances, the small dark kitchen where I used to have my bread and milk; the front and back drawing rooms; the bedrooms and garrets...only think, a grocer's still!'[1] He stopped to drink a toast with the new owners before moving on to dinner at Viceregal Lodge.

The Dublin of Moore's childhood was in its eighteenth-century heyday. It was a prosperous, fast growing place, proud of its position as the second largest city in the British Isles, its self confidence reflected in the grandeur of its public buildings and the classical elegance of its spacious squares and terraces. In 1782, three years after Moore was born, the Protestant gentry of Ireland, having raised an army of 80,000 volunteers against the threat of French invasion during the American War of Independence, coerced the English government into granting them a separate Parliament. Ireland was now a nation, in the words of Grattan, the leader of the Patriot party, and though political power still lay with the Protestants, many of the worst discriminatory laws against the Catholic majority had been removed. A rising Catholic middle class was beginning to play a major role, both cultural and economic, in the nation's life, and Moore's parents, though never well off, were very much part of this trend.

Moore's mother, Anastasia Codd, came from the town of Wexford – the name was originally Welsh, deriving from the little group of settlers who came to the south-eastern corner of the county in Norman times, and who until a hundred years before, still spoke their own Welsh-Norman dialect. Her father, old and gouty when Moore knew him, kept a grocer's shop-cum-weaver's in the Corn Market and despite his humble calling, wrote Moore, 'brought up a large family respectably and was always, as I have heard, much respected by his fellow townsmen'.[2]

Of his father's family, the Moores or O'Moores from Kerry, Moore knew very little. He could not remember his father saying anything of his parents or their station in life. One uncle, Garret Moore, was a member of their family circle when Moore was young, though in later years, after he became famous, a host of Kerry cousins came forward to claim the relationship.

Moore's father, John Moore, was a handsome, rather severe looking man who liked his glass of whisky punch in the evenings. He was considerably older than his sociable young wife who used to refer to him jokingly as quite an old bachelor when she married him. Tom, their eldest child, was born a year after their marriage; other children followed, of whom only two daughters, Kate and Ellen, survived into adult life. Tom, as the first and only son, was the apple of his mother's eye. He was an exceptionally bright and clever little boy, very small for his age, who soon became something of a show child. One of his earliest memories, when he was not quite four years old, was of reciting some doggerel verses against Grattan whose patriotic credentials had been temporarily marred by his acceptance of a grant of £50,000 from the Irish Parliament:

Pay down his price, he'll wheel about
And laugh, like Grattan, at the nation.

From the beginning Irish politics formed part of Tom's consciousness.

Although not highly educated herself Mrs Moore had great ambitions for her son. She seems to have had much of the charm that would be one of Tom's outstanding characteristics and she used it to the utmost to smooth her children's way through life. Tom's first school, in the same street as theirs, was kept by an odd, wild fellow called Malone who wore a cocked hat and spent most of his evenings drinking in the local pubs. He would come in much the worse for wear at noon and work off his bad temper by beating the boys all round. Tom escaped, partly because he was the youngest boy in the school but chiefly, he wrote, 'from the plan which then and for ever after my anxious mother adopted, of heaping with all sorts of kindness and attentions those who were in any way, whether as masters, ushers or school fellows, likely to assist me in my learning'.

Leaving Malone's school – with a silver medal awarded for history – at the age of eight, Tom moved on to Dublin's leading grammar school, in Grafton Street, run by a celebrated schoolmaster, Samuel Whyte. The fact, which Moore does not even mention, that Whyte was a Protestant, shows how easy social relations between the two faiths had become in the latter part of the century. Whyte was an enlightened figure, a great believer in education for women, and in the importance of studying English history and literature, rather than concentrating solely on the classics. He was also an accomplished poet, much involved in the literary life of Dublin, contributing verses to various literary magazines, and composing rhyming prologues and epilogues for the stage. In this he was merely following the fashion of his time: it would be difficult, as Moore remarked, to find any public man of the age, with the sole exception of William Pitt, who had not tried his hand at writing verse.

Related by marriage to the Sheridan family – the young Richard Brinsley had briefly been his pupil – Whyte was passionately interested in the theatre. As well as teaching acting and elocution in his school, he also coached young actors and aspiring amateurs for the stage. Tom, with his natural gifts for recitation, was a pupil after his own heart. He was soon singled out as a star performer on the school's open days, his diminutive size making his performances seem still more wonderful. 'Oh, he's a little old crab,' said a rival mother crossly on one such occasion, 'he can't be less than eleven or twelve years old.' 'Then madam', said a man sitting next to her, who knew the family slightly, 'he must have been four years old when he was born.' This riposte, when reported to Tom's mother, endeared the speaker to her ever after.

At the age of eleven Tom made his first stage appearance, when he spoke the epilogue at a performance of the tragedy *Jane Shore*, in which Whyte's daughter played the heroine, at the private theatre of a certain Lady Borrowes. In the fragmentary memoirs – 'begun many Years since, but never, I fear, to be completed,'[3] as he wrote in 1833 – which are our chief source of information on his childhood, he proudly transcribes the playbill in which his name first appears in print. The key line was as follows: 'Epilogue, *A Squeeze to St Paul s*, Master Moore.'

It was an exciting experience, which worried his mother who, anticipating a relaxation in the laws forbidding Catholics to study law, had mentally destined him for the bar, and feared he might be tempted by a stage career. But Tom had other enthusiasms to pursue. From as early as he could remember, he had delighted in rhyming and writing verse. The walls of his little cubicle, partitioned off from the bedroom he shared with his father's two clerks, were pinned with poetic inscriptions of his own composing and his room mates were cajoled into joining a literary and debating society of which he constituted himself the president. In 1793, his first published verses, daringly entitled, 'To Zelia on her charging the author with writing too much on Love', appeared in a short-lived literary magazine, the *Anthologica Hibernica*, founded by the Trinity bookseller Mercier. The last lines give the flavour:

> When first she raised her simplest lays
> In Cupid's never-ceasing praise,
> The God a faithful promise gave,
> That never should she feel Love's stings
> Never to burning passion be a slave,
> But feel the purer joys thy friendship brings.

The Zelia in question was an old maid called Hannah Byrne – old at least in the eyes of the fourteen-year-old author – who often came to his parents' house, and with whom he exchanged poetic effusions. 'Poor Hannah Byrne!'

he wrote, 'not even Sir Lucius O'Trigger's *Dalia* was a more uninspiring object than my *Zalia* was'[4]

For the next two years, till the magazine foundered for lack of money, Tom continued to be an occasional contributor to its pages, encouraged by Whyte, to whom he addressed a poem in the March issue of the following year beginning, 'Hail! heav'n taught votary of the laurel'd Nine!' Not many schoolmasters are referred to in such terms by their pupils, but Whyte was no ordinary schoolmaster. Years later, in his biography of Sheridan, Moore paid this tribute to his former teacher: 'To remember our schooldays with gratitude and pleasure is a tribute at once to the zeal and gentleness of our master, which none ever deserved more truly from his pupil than the writer of these pages, who owes to that excellent person all the instructions in English literature he has ever received.'[5] It was a far cry from the brutality of most English public schools at the time, and from Sheridan's lonely and neglected schooldays at Harrow.

Poetry for Moore would always be closely linked with music, 'the only art,' he wrote, 'for which in my own opinion I was born with a real natural love'.[6] When he was still quite small, his father happened to have an old lumbering harpsichord left on his hands as a debt, on which his mother arranged for him to take lessons. Since his teacher was the local piano tuner's assistant, only a little older than himself, they spent most of their time romping and jumping over the tables and chairs in the drawing room, and the lessons were left off before he could do more than play a few tunes with his right hand. Later, however, the harpsichord was sold, and with much scrimping and saving, a piano was acquired for his sister Kate. Tom, 'from shyness or hopelessness of success', at first refused to learn to play. But his sister's teacher, Billy Warren, who had soon become an intimate of the family, was a constant visitor to the house. 'The consequence was that, though I never received from him any regular lessons in playing, yet by standing often to listen when he was instructing my sister, and endeavouring constantly to pick out tunes – or *make* them – when I was alone, I became a pianoforte player (at least sufficiently so to accompany my own singing) before anyone was in the least aware of it.'[7]

As a little boy, with an agreeable voice and a taste for singing, he had often been called on to sing at his parents' tea and supper parties. Later, with the arrival of the piano, he would take part in more elaborate musical entertainments. Mrs Moore sang songs like 'How sweet in the woodlands' in a soft clear voice, Tom showed off his talents in popular ballad airs by

Dibdin. Other singers included Joe Kelly, brother of the great Irish tenor Michael Kelly (who sang in the first performance of *The Marriage of Figaro* in Vienna) and Wesley Doyle whose 'sweet and touching voice' was much in demand at musical evenings. Mrs Moore loved entertaining, and the two small drawing rooms above the shop were 'distended to their utmost dimensions'[8] on such occasions.

Despite his successes in the grown-up world, Tom never felt different or cut off from the company of other children. Every summer his parents would take lodgings at the seaside towns of Irishtown or Sandymount just outside Dublin. Here, he and his sisters joined a troop of the children of his parents' friends, taking part in all their various games and theatricals, and as they grew older in 'those little love-makings, gallantries and rivalries which in their first stirrings have a romance and sweetness about them which never come again.'[9] Even here, he seems to have been a pet. When he had to go back to school before his sisters, his father provided a pony for him so he could ride down to join them on Saturday nights: 'and at the hour when I was expected there generally came my sisters with a number of young girls to meet me, and full of smiles and welcomes, walked by the side of my pony into the town'.

It was an idyllic childhood but it had its weaknesses. Visiting Walter Scott, some thirty years later, he allowed himself to regret his lack of manly training – the field sports and open air life of Scott's upbringing – and to wonder if his poetry would have been more vigorous had it not been for the 'sort of *boudoir* education' he had received. 'The only thing indeed,' he added, 'that conduced to brace and invigorate my mind was the strong political feelings that were stirring around me when I was a boy, and in which I took a most deep and ardent interest.'[10]

In the last twenty years of the century it was almost impossible not to be involved in Irish politics. Catholic aspirations were high, supported by the more enlightened Protestants in Parliament: it was a question, said Grattan, of whether Ireland should be a Protestant colony or an Irish nation. The French Revolution, by throwing the established order aside, made everything seem possible. Later, when France declared war on Britain in 1793, and it became important to conciliate Catholics at home, many of the remaining penal laws were lifted. A Catholic seminary was endowed by the government at Maynooth, Catholics were allowed to practise law, to hold commissions in the army (though only up to the rank of colonel), to take long leases on property, and attend university. Those with properties rated at over 40 shillings could vote in parliamentary elections, but full emancipation, that is, the right to stand for Parliament and hold public office, was still denied.

For Moore the immediate result of the relaxation of the penal laws was the chance to enter Trinity College and to follow his mother's treasured wish that he should study law. To catch up on his Latin and Greek, a vital requirement for entry, he took lessons with Whyte's Latin usher, Donovan, 'an uncouth, honest, hard headed and kind-hearted man'.[11] Donovan, whom Tom's mother, pursuing her usual practice of conciliating her children's teachers, had made a family friend, was a passionate Irish patriot. As well as teaching him Latin and Greek, he infused his pupil with his own enthusiasm for Irish liberties and hatred of British oppression. Moore was never the strictest of Catholics; he abandoned the practice of confession, which he found irksome and humiliating, soon after entering Trinity. But he was indignant at the laws that made him, as Burke put it, a foreigner in his own country. The concessions made to Catholics in 1793 had come too little and too late, merely underlining the injustice of a system that denied them any share in public life. Even in the narrower Protestant sense the independence of the Irish Parliament had proved to be largely an illusion. Corruption was rife. Two thirds of the members owed their seats, directly or indirectly, to the Crown, and were thus merely the tools of the Ministry in London. Despite some concessions, Irish trade was still hampered by British restrictions, while for the great mass of the rural population, living under conditions worse than almost anywhere in Western Europe, the imposition of tithes to support the alien Anglican Church was the last straw in their miseries.

The French Revolution, which at its outset was the protest of the rising bourgeois and professional classes against an aristocratic elite, was welcomed almost immediately by their Irish counterparts. The bloodstained excesses that followed, the execution of the King and the declaration of war on Britain caused many early sympathisers to draw back. In England the followers of Charles James Fox, the most outspoken advocate of the Revolution, dwindled to less than fifty in the House of Commons. But the seeds had been sown in Ireland, where a group of Protestants and non-conformists from the north, led by a young lawyer named Wolfe Tone, had banded together in the association known as the United Irishmen, inspired by French ideals and dedicated to Catholic emancipation and political reform.

A sense of Irish identity, long submerged by the Penal Laws, was beginning to make itself felt. In Scotland, the Ossianic forgeries of

Macpherson, harking back to a legendary Gaelic past, had provided an alternative to the classical terms of reference which had for so long dominated European literature. The romantic movement was stirring, and it found its reflection in Ireland in a revival of interest in the country's ancient history and language and the bardic traditions of the wandering minstrels through whom its poetry and music had been transmitted. In 1792 a great harp festival was held in Belfast at which nine of the country's last remaining harpists played, and a young Belfast organist, Edward Bunting, began what would be a lifelong task of collecting and transcribing traditional Irish melodies. The festival, for which Wolfe Tone, a passionate enthusiast for Irish music, composed an anthem, was held between 10 and 13 July as a run-up to the celebrations for the fall of the Bastille: politics, music and a non-sectarian nationalism combining in an event whose significance went far beyond its brief duration. It was, as Moore wrote later, 'the last public effort made by the lovers of Irish music, to preserve to their country the only grace or ornament left to her, out of the ruin of all her liberties and hopes…But for the zeal and intelligent research of Mr Bunting, at that crisis, the greater part of our musical treasures would probably have been lost to the world.'[12]

In June 1794, having passed his classical examinations with distinction, Tom Moore was inscribed as a student at Trinity College. 'I most heartily congratulate you on the success of your incomparable boy', wrote Whyte to Tom's father, 'for in the Course of thirty one years experience; I have not met one that has done equal Business in the time.'[13] Tom's triumphs cast reflected glory on his teacher.

Although Catholics were now admitted to Trinity, they were still excluded from any scholarships, fellowships or financial prizes. Money was short at 12 Aungier Street and for a brief moment Tom's parents toyed with the idea that he should change his faith. They quickly rejected it as unworthy, his mother as a simple but devout believer, his father, more sceptical about such matters, from reasons of patriotic pride. For some reason, perhaps a mistaken initiative of Whyte's, his name was entered in the College books as 'T. Moore, Prot.', but the authorities were never in any doubt about his religion, and three years later, when he won an exhibition, the prize money was withheld. 'How welcome and useful would have been the sixty or seventy pounds a year, which I believe the scholarship was worth, to the son of a poor struggling tradesman – struggling to educate his children – I need hardly point out,' wrote Moore in his memoirs; 'nor can anyone wonder that the recollection of such laws, and of their bigoted though sometimes conscientious, supporters, should live bitterly in the minds and hearts of all who have, at any time, been made their victims.'[14]

At the time, however, he was too delighted with the prospects before him – unthinkable only a few years before – to worry about such drawbacks. The university term did not begin till January 1795. He spent most of the intervening holidays staying with a school friend, Beresford Burston, son of a wealthy Dublin barrister, at their country estate near Blackrock. It was a social step up for a grocer's son, which specially pleased his mother, always eager to see him get on in the world. But even at this early age, Moore gave as much, or more, than he received. He was an enchanting companion, brimming over with fun and good humour, with that 'readiness to please and be pleased',[15] which, in Walter Scott's opinion, was one of his most attractive characteristics. Despite his academic triumphs there was never any trace of pedantry about him. Burston, more interested in sport than books, would have laughed down such pretensions. They were linked by their high spirits and the patriotic aspirations that Burston, a Protestant, felt as strongly as himself: Burston's father, one of Dublin's most distinguished lawyers, was a leading advocate of Catholic emancipation.

The summer and autumn went by in a haze of pleasurable expectation. 'If I were to single out the part of my life the most happy and the most *poetical* (for all was yet in fancy and promise with me),' wrote Moore in his unfinished memoirs, 'it would be that interval of holidays.'[16] Burston's sisters played the harpsichord; he would always associate his stay there with reading Mrs Radcliffe's novels to the sound of Haydn's music and had only to play over certain tunes to bring back the memory of his youthful hopes and dreams.

2

Trinity College

Tom Moore was sixteen when he entered Trinity College, a diminutive figure (only five foot high), with a tip tilted nose and a cherubic countenance topped by a mop of brown curls. No longer Master Tommy Moore, the juvenile contributor to the *Anthologica Hibernica*, he was proud of his new status as Mr Thomas Moore of Trinity College, Dublin, and of belonging to an institution that had produced such great names as Congreve, Burke and Oliver Goldsmith. The college, with its noble classical buildings, parks and quadrangles, was one of the crowning glories of eighteenth-century Dublin, a forty-acre oasis of peace and learning in the heart of the city. As at Oxford and Cambridge the education centred mainly on the classics; till as late as 1845 students taking their degrees still had to make two declamations, one in Greek and one in Latin, as well as disputing in those languages. Tom, however, was soon disillusioned by the teaching, the Fellows in general, he discovered, knowing little more of Latin verse than their pupils. But he made an exception for his tutor, the Rev. Robert Burrowes, a distinguished classicist and wit, well known as the author of a popular comic song, 'The night before Larry was stretched', and for the Provost, Dr Kearney, another distinguished scholar whose house, where Moore became a frequent guest, was 'the resort of the best society in Dublin'.[1]

Having brought a great reputation from his school, it was generally expected, especially by his anxious mother, that Moore would distinguish himself equally at college. But perhaps she had pushed him too hard; more probably he felt, as he wrote of Byron, 'that antipathy to the trammels of discipline which is not unusually observable among the characteristics of genius'.[2] Whatever the reason, he paid the minimum of attention to his studies, having decided after his first year to confine himself to such parts of the course as suited his own tastes, though as has been said, he entered for and won an exhibition of which, due to his religion, he could not enjoy the benefits. He was also awarded a prize for some English verses that he had put forward for an examination in Latin prose, and which instead of being rejected won him a handsome copy of the *Travels of Anarcharsis* – 'the first gain,' he wrote, 'which I made by that pen which such as it is has been my sole support ever since.'[3]

Meanwhile, thanks to his friendship with the son of the librarian, Dean Craddock, he had obtained permission to use Bishop Marsh's library out of hours, a privilege of which he was not a little proud. A favourite haunt of Swift's, this exquisite small library, a counterpart to the magnificent main library of Trinity, had been founded at the beginning of the century, and though housed outside its precincts, formed part of the university. 'To the many solitary hours which I passed, both at this time and subsequently, in hunting through its dusty tomes,' wrote Moore, 'I was indebted for much of the odd, out-of-the-way sort of reading that may be found scattered through some of my earlier works.'[4] He read voraciously, not only in English but in French and Italian (picked up respectively from an émigré French school-master and an obliging local priest), but his chief interest was in the literature of the classics, above all in the odes attributed to Anacreon, a Greek lyric poet of the sixth century BC. His poems, translated by poets as various as Ronsard and Tasso, had been sung to the lyre in ancient times; the combination of music and poetry already held a special attraction for Moore. As early as 1794, he had published a paraphrase of the fifth ode in the *Anthologica Hibernica*, and he had now acquired the notion of translating all the odes, whose witty construction and amorous or pleasure-loving themes tuned in perfectly with his poetic mood.

Music kept pace with poetry and reading. Since he was living at home rather than in the college, he always had a piano close at hand, and was beginning to compose tunes of his own, as well as write the words to those of others. He wrote a masque with songs, one to an air by Haydn, the others to music by himself and Billy Warren, which was performed to a great applause in Aungier Street; one of the ballads from it, 'Delusive dream' (sung by his sister in the masque), was one of his most popular party pieces in later years.

He was already becoming something of a star in Dublin drawing rooms. In a way it was a natural progression. 'My life from earliest childhood had passed, as has been seen,' he wrote, 'in a round of gay society; and the notice which my songs and my manner of singing them had attracted led me still more into the same agreeable, but bewildering course.'[5] He never sang, except to his own accompaniment on the piano, and as he far preferred the company of women to men, and was always greatly in demand at evening parties, he was saved from many of the 'coarser dissipations' of his fellow undergraduates. It is not quite clear what these dissipations would have been. Did they mean the whoring as well as the rowdiness and drinking that were commonplace among the Trinity students? Moore's memoirs tell us nothing of his love life, though if his early poems are anything to go by, he was both flirtatious and susceptible. But the conventions of late eighteenth-century Dublin, at least for unmarried girls, were relatively strict, and how far he took his romances remains a matter for speculation. Perhaps his charming poem 'Did Not' gives a clue.

'Twas a new feeling – something more
Than we had dared to own before,
Which then we hid not;
We saw it in each other's eye,
And wish'd, in every half-breathed sigh
To speak, but did not…

Warmly I felt her bosom thrill,
I press'd it closer, closer still,
Though gently bid not;
Till – oh! the world hath seldom heard
Of lovers who so nearly err'd,
And yet, who did not.

Moore's closest friends on first arriving at the university had been Beresford Burston and another school friend, Bond Hall. Neither of them were at all studious or clever, but both were so full of fun and good humour that he far preferred their company to that of more learned contemporaries. 'Indeed,' he wrote, 'such influence have early impressions and habits upon all our after lives that I have little doubt that the common and ordinary level of my own conversation (which, while it disappoints, no doubt, Blues and *savans*, enables me to get on so well with most hearty and simple-minded persons) arises a good deal from having lived chiefly, in my young days, with such gay, idle fellows as Bond Hall.'[6]

But the atmosphere of the college, and Moore's friendships, were changing, reflecting the political ferment of the day. The Society of United Irishmen, till then quite legal and open, had been suppressed in May 1794. This was in line with the clampdown on democratic and radical clubs throughout the British Isles, in response to the threat of French invasion and fear of subversion from within. In England, the combination of repressive government measures and changes in public opinion would lead to a dwindling away of radical protest; in Ireland it merely drove it underground. But there were still hopes that Catholic emancipation and reform might be achieved by peaceful means, and when in the summer of 1794 the bulk of the Whig party, unable to agree with Fox's opposition to the war, defected to Pitt, it seemed that their hopes would be realised.

The leaders of the Whig party had always been in favour of Catholic emancipation, and following their accession to Pitt's government, they were rewarded with a number of important posts. Among them was the Lord Lieutenancy in Ireland, a position offered to Lord Fitzwilliam, a liberal-minded nobleman, known for his sympathy to the Catholic cause. His arrival in January 1795 was an occasion for rejoicing, as was his dismissal of the powerful Commissioner of the Revenue, John Beresford, a determined upholder of Protestant Ascendancy. Convinced that Catholic emancipation and a measure of constitutional reform could no longer be delayed, Fitzwilliam allowed Grattan to introduce a bill along those lines. But he had exceeded, or rather misunderstood, his instructions. Pitt and the Cabinet, held back by the blind anti-Catholic prejudices of the King, did not yet feel able to carry the religious question; nor did they wish to antagonise the propertied Protestant elite at a time when the war with France was at its height. The bill was thrown out, Beresford was reinstated, and a new Lord Lieutenant, the worthy but narrowly Protestant Lord Camden, was appointed in Fitzwilliam's place.

The day of Fitzwilliam's departure from Dublin, on 25 March, was one of public mourning. Shops were closed, doors and windows were draped in black. A crowd of Dublin's leading citizens, dressed in black, drew Fitzwilliam's coach to the quayside where his ship was waiting. 'The shadow of coming calamity', in the words of the great historian William Lecky, 'cast its gloom upon every countenance.'[7]

Fitzwilliam's dismissal was a disaster for Ireland. 'Never, assuredly, was there a more insulting breach of faith flung deliberately in the face of a whole people...' wrote Moore in his life of Lord Edward Fitzgerald. 'In vain did Lord Fitzwilliam set forth the danger – and he might have added perfidy – of now retracting the boon and declare that "he, at least, would not be the person to raise a flame which nothing but the force of arms could put down". The dark destiny of Ireland, as usual, triumphed. With the choice before them of either conciliating the people or lashing them into rebellion, the British Cabinet chose the latter course.'[8]

The way to revolution was now open. Deprived of the hope of constitutional reform, the Society of United Irishmen gathered new strength and supporters, not only from the professional and middle classes but from the dispossessed and discontented Catholic peasantry. The idea of an independent Irish republic, achieved by an armed uprising, backed by military help from France, took the place of their earlier, more moderate aims. Moore, at this point, had no notion of the scope of their intentions, but he shared their anger at the dismissal of Fitzwilliam. Unmentioned in his memoirs, but recorded in those of Grattan, was an incident soon after Lord Camden's arrival, when after the Provost, Fellows and Scholars of Trinity College had been to Dublin Castle to present a complimentary address to the new Lord Lieutenant, the Scholars adjourned to a meeting at Hyde's Coffee House, where Moore was in the chair. Speaking in the name of the students of the university, he presented an address to Grattan, deploring 'the removal of a beloved Viceroy', and urging him to continue his efforts for the 'reform of those grievances which have inflamed public indignation'.[9] Shortly afterwards, possibly on the same day, he spoke in similar terms at a Catholic meeting in Francis Street, going on to denounce the idea of a re-union with England, which was already being secretly discussed in London. 'One boon I ask of Heaven,' he declared, ' – for myself, may death arrest me ere I see the day a Union takes place; for Ireland may the Atlantic close and bury it for ever in an immeasurable gulph!'[10] Bold words from the sixteen-year-old orator, which in the uneasy climate of the time, might well have led to his arrest.

Inside the university discussions were necessarily coded. Thus in the debating society, which Moore joined in 1796, it was impossible to discuss the politics of the day directly. But there was always a chance 'by a side wind of disgression or allusion',[11] of bringing Ireland and its current problems into the discussion. By far the most outstanding speaker on the nationalist side at these debates was Robert Emmet, two classes ahead of Moore in the college, and already famous for his brilliance as a scientist and his boldness as an orator. The two became friends, with an element of hero worship on Moore's side; it was an emotion that would be sealed by Emmet's heroic death on the scaffold seven years later.

Another new friend, also to suffer in the cause of Irish liberty, was Edward Hudson, an ardent enthusiast for Irish music. In 1796, Bunting's first collection of ancient Irish music was published, and eagerly pored over by the two young men. Hudson himself had made a collection of old Irish airs, which he used to play with much feeling on the flute. 'I attribute, indeed, a good deal of my own early acquaintance with our music, if not the warm interest I have since taken in it,' wrote Moore, 'to the many hours I passed at this time *tête-à-tête* with Edward Hudson – now trying over the sweet melodies of our country, now talking with indignant feeling of her sufferings and wrongs.'[12] Emmet shared their enthusiasm, and would often sit next to Moore at the piano when he was playing Irish airs. At one particularly martial tune, Moore recalled, he sprang up, as if from a reverie, exclaiming passionately: 'Oh that I were at the head of twenty thousand men marching to that tune.'[13] It was a dream that the United Irishmen would soon try to put into practice.

Some time in 1797 – he could not precisely remember when – Moore graduated from his debating club to the more prestigious Historical Society, founded by Burke and well known as a forum for debate. Here again, Robert Emmet was the dominant speaker on the patriotic side, in defiance of a strong pro-government group within the society, and the watchful suspicions of the college authorities. 'The power of Emmet's eloquence was wonderful,' wrote Moore nearly forty years later, 'and I feel at this moment as if his language were still sounding in my ears.'[14] Moore himself, according to a fellow student, was a spirited speaker on these occasions.

Meanwhile, the political situation in Ireland was becoming increasingly explosive. Wolfe Tone, in exile in France since 1795, had been working tirelessly to persuade the French government to sanction an invasion. In December 1796, a French expeditionary force of fifteen thousand men had sailed for Ireland; it was only thanks to bad weather and bad seamanship that it failed to land at Bantry Bay. The fear of a renewed attack and the growing threat of insurrection in the countryside spurred the government to drastic action. The policy of disarming potentially disaffected areas, in particular in the north, led to widespread atrocities. Unable to provide sufficient troops to carry out the searches, they gave the task to the local yeomanry, for the most part Protestant volunteers, who misused their powers outrageously, increasing sectarian bitterness by their treatment of the rural population. Houses were burnt down, pitch cappings, floggings and half-hangings inflicted on the flimsiest excuse. 'Though then but a youth in college, and so many years have since gone by,' wrote Moore in 1831, 'the impression of horror and indignation which the acts of the Government of that day left upon my mind is, I confess at this moment far too freshly alive to allow me the due calmness of a historian in speaking of them.'[15]

At the time he expressed his feelings clearly in a newspaper called *The Press*; founded by Robert Emmet's elder brother, Thomas Addis Emmet, a leader of the United Irishmen, in September 1797, it ran, surprisingly, for six months before it was closed down. 'It used to come out, I think, three times a week', wrote Moore, 'and on the evenings of publication, I always used to read it aloud to my father and mother during supper.'[16] Moore, not unnaturally, was eager to see something of his own in its patriotic columns though, knowing his mother's extreme anxiety for his safety, he kept his intentions secret. His first contribution, dropped through the paper's letter box at night, was an Ossianic imitation chiefly remarkable for its nationalistic tone. This attracted little comment, but the next, which appeared a few weeks later, was more combustible stuff. Addressed to the students of Trinity College, it was written in what Moore himself described as a 'turgid Johnsonian sort of style...seasoned with plenty of the then fashionable ingredient, treason',[17] and concluded with a virtual call to arms: 'This is not the time to express a difference of Political opinion. No, we should all have one common cause, the welfare of our country; we should all Unite, rally round her standard, and recover our Heaven-born rights, our principles from the grasp of Tyranick ministers.'[18]

As before, he delivered the article by night, confiding his secret only to Edward Hudson. He hardly expected that it would be published; great was his surprise, however, when on the next evening of publication, he unfolded the paper in order to read it to his parents and saw his own article prominently displayed. He read it aloud with seeming calm, though trembling inwardly with emotion. His parents were full of its praises while rightly judging it to be 'rather bold'. Next day, however, Edward Hudson came to call, and in mentioning the article with a significant glance at the author aroused the quick suspicions of his mother: '"That letter was yours then, Tom" she said instantly…with a look of eagerness and apprehension';[19] when he acknowledged it she begged him so earnestly never to run such risks again that Tom, as a devoted son, could only promise not to do so.

A few days later, in the course of one of those strolls in the country, which he often used to take with Robert Emmet, the conversation turned upon the letter and his authorship. Emmet, 'with that almost feminine gentleness of manner which he possessed, and which is so often found in such determined spirits', told him that though he agreed with its contents, he could not help regretting that it had drawn attention to the politics of the university, as it might alert the authorities to the good work that was quietly going on there. 'Even then,' wrote Moore, 'boyish as my own mind was, I could not help being struck by the manliness of the view which I saw he took of what men ought to do in such times and circumstances, namely not to *talk* or *write* about their intentions, but to act.'[20]

It was the first time that Emmet had alluded to the United Irishmen but neither then nor at any later date did he suggest that Moore should join them. He knew perhaps, how closely Moore was tied to his mother's apron strings, and that he was not the stuff of which conspirators were made. The only occasion, during this period at which anyone referred to the conspiracy directly, was when returning home after a lecture one evening a fellow student told him of associations being formed within the college, and suggested that he should join his lodge (the Masonic term used by the United Irishmen). Nothing more passed between them on the subject, 'but it will be seen,' wrote Moore, '…how fatal might have proved the consequences of this short conversation, both to myself and to all those connected with me'.[21]

3

1798

'Who fears to speak of Ninety-Eight?' The words of the famous ballad would echo through the nineteenth century and can still be heard in Ireland today. Whatever the degrees of blame leading up to it – did the government deliberately provoke rebellion in order to re-impose the Union, or was it merely guilty of vacillation and incompetence? – its results were a tragedy for Ireland. In the few brief weeks of the uprising more than thirty thousand people were killed, and thousands more were transported or forced to emigrate through poverty. The atrocities committed on both sides left a legacy of bitterness that has never been forgotten.

By the beginning of 1798, it was clear from the reports of government spies and informers that a huge underground army was poised for a general uprising. Its leaders included some of Dublin's foremost citizens, the barrister Thomas Addis Emmet, Arthur O'Connor, an aristocrat with strong connections among the English Whigs, and most charismatic of all, Lord Edward Fitzgerald, brother of the Duke of Leinster, and the movement's military commander. They were divided in their views on tactics, the more cautious like Emmet wishing to wait for help from France, the bolder spirits like O'Connor and Lord Edward prepared to go ahead alone. The debate was still undecided when on 12 March, thanks to the treachery of an informer, the police broke in on a meeting of the United Irishmen in Dublin, arresting fourteen delegates, among them Edward Hudson. Thomas Addis Emmet and several others who had not been present were arrested shortly after. Meanwhile O'Connor had been picked up in England on charges of sedition; Lord Edward Fitzgerald, the other leader of the violent party, went into hiding.

In the light of these dramatic happenings Trinity College (where in fact four groups, or cells, of the United Irishmen existed) became an obvious focus of suspicion. So alarmed were the authorities at the possibility of conspiracy within its walls that on 12 April the Lord Chancellor, John Fitzgibbon, recently promoted to the title of the Earl of Clare, came to conduct an inquisition of the students in his role as Vice Chancellor of the college. Some of them, Robert Emmet among them, had already prudently removed themselves; a further nineteen would be expelled or prosecuted for sedition in the course of the proceedings.

Moore knew that he was likely to be questioned. On the evening before his turn was expected there was gloom in the family circle. One of his Protestant friends, a certain Dacre Hamilton, had been questioned that day and though innocent of any involvement with the conspiracy had refused to answer certain questions for fear of incriminating others. He had been dismissed, wrote Moore, 'with the melancholy certainty that his future prospects were all utterly blasted; it being known that the punishment for such contumacy was to be not merely banishment from the University, but exclusion from the learned professions'.[1]

It was a crunch point for Moore's parents who had held such high hopes for his future, but both he and they agreed that however dire the consequences he must follow Hamilton's example if he were asked to incriminate his fellow students. The next morning, as they had feared, he was told he would be called for questioning. The interrogation would take place in the great dining hall of Trinity in which the Provost, Fellows and students of the university were assembled; Lord Clare and his assessor Duigenan sat on a raised platform at one end of the hall.

What followed is best recounted in Moore's own words; even after the long interval before he came to write his memoirs it is hardly surprising that the scene was still clearly imprinted on his mind.

'At last', he wrote,

> my awful turn came, and I stood in the presence of that terrific tribunal. There sat the formidable Fitzgibbon, whose name I had never heard connected but with domineering insolence and cruelty; and by his side the memorable 'Paddy' Duigenan – memorable, at least, to all who lived

in those dark times for his eternal pamphlets sounding the tocsin of persecution against the Catholics.

The oath was proferred to me.

'I have an objection, my lord', said I in a clear firm voice, 'I have an objection to taking this oath.' – 'What's your objection, sir?' he asked sternly. 'I have no fear, my lord, that anything I might say would criminate myself, but it might tend to affect others; and I must say that I despise that person's character who could be led under any circumstances to criminate his associates.'…'How old are you, sir?' I told him my age…though looking, I dare say, not more than fourteen or fifteen. He then turned to his assessor, Duigenan, and exchanged a few words with him in an under voice. 'We cannot,' he resumed, again looking towards me, 'We cannot allow any person to remain in our University, who would refuse to take this oath.' – 'I shall then, my lord,' I replied, 'take the oath, still reserving to myself the power of refusing to answer any such questions as I have described.' – 'We do not sit here to argue with you, sir,' he rejoined sharply, upon which I took the oath and seated myself in the witness's chair.

Fortunately the questions that followed imposed no moral dilemmas. He was asked if he had ever belonged to any of the United Irish Societies in the university; if he had ever known of any of the proceedings that took place in them; if he had ever heard of any proposals at their meetings for the purchase of arms and ammunition; if he had ever heard of any suggestions as to the expediency of assassination. To all these he could truthfully give the answer no. The Lord Chancellor consulted briefly with his assessor, then turned to him again: 'When such are the answers you are able to give, pray what was the cause of your great repugnance to taking the oath?' 'I have already told you, my lord, my chief reasons; in addition to which it was the first oath I ever took, and it was, I think, a very natural hesitation.'

He was dismissed without further questioning, tolerably certain in his own mind that he had acted as he should, but not fully reassured till he saw what the verdict of his friends would be when he returned to the body of the hall. Their reaction left him in no doubt: they crowded round congratulating him, while one senior fellow was heard to say that his last answer was the best that had yet been given. 'Of my reception at home, after the fears entertained of so very different a result,' he wrote, 'I will not attempt any description; it was all that *such* a home could furnish.'[2]

Events in Ireland were now hurrying to their climax. On 30 March martial law had been declared, and the policy of disarmament, with all its attendant horrors already applied in the north, put into practice on a far wider scale. As the toll of floggings, burnings and half hangings rose, goading the population into fury, the chief concern of the United Irish leadership was to hold back the uprising till the French forces arrived. But on 19 May Lord Edward was arrested in Dublin after a violent struggle with his captors; he died of his wounds in prison shortly after. His arrest threw the revolutionaries into confusion, hurrying on their plans for a rising despite the lack of French support.

Four days later the rebellion began, at first with scattered outbreaks around Dublin, then far more seriously in Wexford, where a force of largely Catholic insurgents captured the town. From then on the revolution gathered momentum; for a few days the fate of Ireland hung in the balance as the rebels advanced towards Dublin. Meanwhile, news had come from France that Napoleon, with a huge armada, had set sail from Toulon for an unknown destination. His goal in fact was Egypt, from whence he hoped to strike at Britain's possessions in India. Had it been Ireland, as was feared at the time, the rebellion would have had a very different ending. As it was it was too ill co-ordinated and disunited to succeed. In the north, where most of their leaders had been arrested, the Ulster Presbyterians dragged their feet at co-operating with the Catholics; the draconian searches of the previous year had done much to break the rural population's spirit, and the rising was late and ineffectual. In the south, the struggle was far longer and more bloody as the Catholic insurgents of Wexford, led by their priests, fought what became a largely religious and class war against their Protestant landlords and the local yeomanry. But the desperate courage of the rebels, armed only with pikes and pitchforks, was no match in the end for the better arms and discipline of the government forces. By the end of the summer, though the fighting simmered on in pockets, most of the countryside had been subdued. The only reinforcements from France, an expedition of some six thousand men which landed in County Mayo in August, were forced to surrender three weeks later. A second invading expedition in October was intercepted and defeated at sea.

There is a break in Moore's memoirs, marked by a space with three asterisks, over this period. Was there a missing section, perhaps destroyed by his editor Lord John Russell, or was it simply that its events were too traumatic to recount? When he picks up the story again he refers to having been ill; perhaps the shock and emotional tension of the tribunal and its aftermath led to some kind of nervous collapse. But though he does not discuss the course of the rising and the battles raging in Wexford only fifty miles away, he gives a brief description of its opening stages.

'It was while I was confined with this illness,' he wrote,

> that the long and awfully expected explosion of the United Irish conspiracy took place; and I remember well the night when the rebels were to have attacked Dublin [May 23, 1798], the feelings of awe produced through the city, by the going out of the lamps one after another, towards midnight. The authorities had, in the course of the day, received information of this part of the plan, to which the lamplighters must of course been parties; and I saw from my window, a small body of the yeomanry accompanying a lamplighter through the street to see that he performed his duty properly. Not withstanding this, however, through a great part of the city where there had not been time to take this precaution, the lights towards midnight all went out.[3]

Wolfe Tone, who had been captured with the French fleet in October, cut his throat in prison before sentence of execution could be carried out, and died of his wounds. Other leaders of the rising, more fortunate than their rank and file, great numbers of whom were hanged or transported, remained as state prisoners in Dublin and were eventually allowed to emigrate to France. Edward Hudson was among them. Moore showed courage in going to visit him, in Kilmainham Gaol, 'where he had lain immured for four or five months, hearing of friend after friend being led to death, and expecting every week his own turn to come'.[4] A good painter as well as a musician, Hudson had whiled away his time making a large charcoal drawing of the mythical origins of the Irish harp on the wall of his cell. Moore used the subject – a sea-nymph who falls vainly in love with a mortal, and is transformed into a harp – for one of his *Irish Melodies*.

'Tis believ'd that this Harp, which I wake now for thee,
Was a Syren of old, who sung under the sea…

In the wake of the '98 rebellion the arguments for abolishing Ireland's semi-political autonomy and bringing her into full union with England became almost irresistible. Ireland had narrowly escaped three attempts at invasion; the disastrous insurrection had shown how little the Irish Parliament could be relied on to keep order. By bringing its members into

'The Origin of the Harp' by the Irish painter Daniel Maclise, 1842. The painting illustrates Moore's Irish Melody of that name, inspired by his visits to Edward Hudson in prison.

the larger context of the British Parliament, Pitt hoped to restrict their power. At the same time the proportion of Protestants to Catholics in the united kingdoms would have shifted. With the Protestants in a huge overall majority, the question of Catholic emancipation would, he hoped, become more acceptable to its opponents, and the worst grievances of the Irish Catholics could be removed. He wished at first to make Catholic emancipation one of the keystones of the new act of union, but seeing difficulties ahead preferred to take the two questions one at a time.

In the short term, Pitt's solution had all the virtues of expediency. There were few protests when in the spring of 1800, encouraged by a massive distribution of patronage and places, and with the implicit promise of Catholic emancipation, the Irish Parliament voted for union with the British Parliament. The decision was ratified by the Act of Union in 1801, but the unyielding opposition of the King, who regarded any further concessions to Catholics as a violation of his coronation oath, and the reluctance of the Commons to challenge him, made it impossible to push through the sequel of Catholic emancipation. Unable to fulfil his promise, Pitt felt morally obliged to resign. It was an honourable gesture but little consolation to the Catholics or their supporters, who felt they had been tricked into the Union.

With the demise of the Irish Parliament, and the shift of power to London, Dublin gradually lost its importance as a capital city; economic and cultural activity dwindled; the magnificent Parliament building was transformed into a bank. Sean O'Faolain in his history of Ireland describes the years immediately following the Union as a period of spiritual starvation for the country: 'There was not, in any city, then, a street called after an Irishman – those commemorated were, instead, a Harcourt, a Sackville, an Essex, a Dorset, the instruments of official rule; whatever literature existed revelled chiefly in jokes about stage-Irishmen; no school book on Irish history was used in any school; there was, in short, nothing visible in which any common Irishman could take pride.'[5]

In all that spiritual desert, he writes, the only oases, apart from the speeches of O'Connell (whose campaign for Catholic emancipation began in the early 1800s), were the songs of Tom Moore – 'how precious they must have been!' He was referring of course to the *Irish Melodies*, those heartfelt lyrics set to Irish airs for which Moore will always be remembered. There were still seven years to wait for their appearance – the first edition was published in 1808. But the ground had been laid in the tragic happenings of the uprising. Its effects on Moore were long lasting, leaving him on the one hand with a horror of violence and bloodshed, on the other with a profound commitment to the seemingly hopeless cause of Irish liberty. The themes of loss and yearning, of heroism and past glories, which give his songs their bitter-sweet quality, would also give Ireland a voice at a time when it had been all but silenced. Whatever the sneers of later and more militant nationalists, it was Moore who first expressed the hopes and longings of the betrayed generation of 1798.

The *Irish Melodies* belong to another chapter. In the immediate aftermath of the uprising, Moore seems to have deliberately swept his feelings aside as being too painful to dwell upon; for the next few years he makes no mention of politics or Ireland's sorrows, at least in his letters that survive. For the moment the cause he had supported was dead. But he was young, and life was full of promise and excitement. His singing had won him a host of fine acquaintances, Marsh's Library was a studious refuge. Above all, his translations of Anacreon were taking shape and he was beginning to become conscious of his poetic destiny:

> The new stirrings of literary ambition, accompanied by the sense of pride and pleasure which the first exercise of power of any kind is sure to afford; the delight with which my early attempts at composition were welcomed by her whom it was my delight to please, – my dear and excellent mother; the bursting out of my latent passion for music, which was in reality the source of my poetic talent, since it was merely the effort to translate into words the different feelings and passions which melody seemed to me to express; – all this formed such a combination of mental stimulant as few, I think, of the same period of life have ever been surrounded by.[6]

In the spring of 1799 Moore took his degree of bachelor of the arts and left the university. There had been some anxiety at home that owing to the fact he had been questioned during the Lord Chancellor's enquiry there might be trouble about receiving his degree. However, the matter went off smoothly, perhaps thanks to the friendship of the Provost, Dr Kearney, who had always been kindly disposed to him. It was to Kearney that Moore submitted some twenty of his translations of Anacreon, in the hopes that they might be found worthy of entering for a classical award from the Board of the University. Kearney read them, and thought highly of them, but doubted that works 'so amatory and convivial' would be accepted by that solemn body. But he advised him strongly to complete his translation of the odes and publish it, saying that he had little doubt of its success. 'The young people,' he added, 'will like it.'[7]

Armed with this advice, Moore was now ready for the next stage of his career. His old friend Beresford Burston's father had entered both their names at the Middle Temple in London, and with much penny-pinching at home his parents had scraped together the money to send him there. Burston, who had not yet graduated, would follow at a later date. A friend of the family called Masterton had promised to help him find lodgings when he arrived. Other friends in Dublin, among them Dr Kearney and the King's printer, Mr Grierson, had given him letters of introduction. His mother prepared his packing, carefully sewing some of the guineas they had saved up for him into the waistband of his pantaloons. In another part of his clothing, unknown to him, she also concealed a scapular, or small piece of cloth blessed by a priest, which a fond superstition made her believe would keep the bearer from harm. 'And thus,' wrote Moore, 'with this charm about me, of which I was wholly unconscious, and my little packet of guineas, of which I felt deeply the responsibility, did I for the first time, start from home for the great world of London.'[8]

4

London Successes

Moore has often been accused of enjoying himself in London drawing rooms while his country languished. He left Dublin at a time when the Union with England was about to be imposed and all hopes of Irish independence had been destroyed. There was very little he could do about it. In a song from the *Irish Melodies* he would set out his dilemma:

'Oh! blame not the bard, if he fly to the bowers
Where Pleasure lies, carelessly smiling at Fame
He was born for much more, and in happier hours
His soul might have burn'd with a holier flame...
But alas for his country! – her pride is gone by,
And that spirit is broken, which never would bend;
O'er the ruins her children in secret must sigh,
For 'tis treason to love her, and death to defend...

Then blame not the bard, if in pleasure's soft dream,
He should try to forget, what he never can heal:
Oh! give but a hope – let a vista but gleam
Through the gloom of his country, and mark how he'll feel!
That instant, his heart at her shrine would lay down
Every passion it nurs'd, every bliss it ador'd;

While the myrtle, now idly entwined with his crown,
Like the wreath of Harmodius, should cover his sword.

The temptations of fame and pleasure were not immediately obvious
when Moore first arrived in London. He reached Holyhead after a 'most
tedious and sickening crossing', and after various adventures on the way,
including an encounter with a swindler who claimed he had lost his
luggage and suggested sharing his, had found his way to the house of his
parents' friends the Mastertons. They had taken lodgings for him in their
washerwoman's house nearby, a second-floor room in George Street, off
Portman Square, for which he paid six shillings a week. The area at the
time was the chief resort for the impoverished French émigrés then
abounding in London, and in the back room of his floor was an old
French curé, whose bed was on the other side of the wall from his; since
the partition between them was very thin not a snore of his escaped him.
He found a great convenience, however, in the numerous French eating-
houses, which abounded in the vicinity, 'of which their cheapness was
their sole attraction', and contrived to get his dinner – usually soup, some
kind of stew, rice pudding and a glass of porter – for as little as eightpence
or ninepence a day.

He was lonely and homesick at first, too discouraged to go to the theatre
since he had no-one to go with, and knowing none of his fellow students
at the Middle Temple. 'One of the forms of my initiation,' he wrote,

> …was a dinner, which, according to custom, I had to give to a small
> party of my brother Templars. But not being acquainted with a single
> creature round me, I was much puzzled how to proceed. I was soon
> relieved, however, from this difficulty by a young fellow who had,
> from the first, I saw, observed my proceedings (most probably with a
> view to this ceremony) and who, addressing me very politely, offered
> to collect for me the number of diners generally used on such
> occasions. I was much pleased, of course, to be relieved of this
> difficulty, and between this new friend of mine to provide the guests,
> and my poor self to pay the reckoning, we got through the ceremony
> very lawfully; and I never again saw a single one of the company.[1]

Gradually, however, things began to improve. The Mastertons lent him
a piano, on which he could practise and work on his songs; the
Mastertons' daughter Sally had a harp and there were musical evenings

to enjoy. His letters of introduction began to bear fruit, his new acquaintances ranging from the Irish painter (and future President of the Royal Academy) Martin Archer Shee to a Dublin apothecary named Macmahon, who 'had transported himself and his gallipots to London', and whose wife, on hearing he was having trouble in meeting his fees at the Middle Temple, took him aside one evening and offered to lend him a secret sum of money she had saved up for emergencies. 'I got through my difficulty however,' he wrote, 'without encroaching upon her small means; but such generous offers come too rarely in this world to allow themselves to be forgotten.'[2]

Other new acquaintances included the Secretary of the Irish Ordnance Board, Joe Atkinson, a brilliant and convivial figure who had written a successful comedy and a three-act opera for the London stage, and who showed a flattering interest in his Anacreon translations. Like almost everyone who met him, Atkinson was charmed by the young poet, whose sparkling personality and varied talents were assets in any company. Dublin society had always been more fluid than in London, and none of his fine friends there had held his humble beginnings against him. In London, where an English grocer's son might have found it impossible to break through the class barrier, his Irish origins, as Sheridan, another well-known charmer, had found before him, helped to by-pass the system. Nonetheless, it was an amazing step upwards when less than two months after his arrival he was introduced by Atkinson to one of the closest associates of the Prince of Wales, the Earl of Moira, a great Whig magnate, whose large estates in northern Ireland gave him a special interest in Irish affairs. 'I sat near an hour with Lord Moira,' he wrote to his father on 29 April, 'and am to dine with him on Saturday.'[3] It would prove to be one of the most influential relationships of his life.

A cultivated, well-read man, possessor of a famous library, Lord Moira had begun his career as a soldier, serving with distinction in the American War of Independence (where Atkinson had served under him) and later in the war with France. He had since turned his energies to opposition politics, and had spoken out strongly against the government's oppressive policies in Ireland in the run-up to the '98 uprising. But although he opposed the Act of Union in the Irish House of Lords, he would later withdraw his opposition to it in the English upper house; 'consistency,' remarks the *Dictionary of National Biography*, 'was not one of his political virtues'. It was something that Moore would discover to his cost, but for the moment he basked in the sunshine of Moira's friendship and approval. Thanks to the good offices of a fellow Trinity graduate, Thomas Hume, he had found a publisher for his Anacreon translations and Moira had promised to help him get subscribers for the forthcoming volume, perhaps even the Prince of Wales himself. Buoyed up with these exciting prospects, and with an invitation to stay at Donington Park, Moira's great country house near Derby, on his way back to London, Moore set off to spend the summer with his family in Dublin and to complete the translations for his publisher.

He returned to London in October, having made the promised visit to Donington on the way. One of the most vivid of his early English recollections, he wrote, was of his first night there, 'when Lord Moira, with that high courtesy for which he was remarkable, lighted me, himself, to my bedroom; and there was this stately personage stalking on before me through the long lighted gallery, bearing in his hand my bed-candle, which he delivered to me at the door of my apartment'.[4] He thought it all exceedingly grand and uncomfortable, little realising how soon he would become domesticated there.

Back in London, he was relieved to find that subscriptions for his forthcoming poems were beginning to come in. His publisher, Stockdale's of Piccadilly, was unwilling to risk an advance on an unknown author and he had to do the work of selling them himself. 'I am getting a good number of names here,' he wrote to his mother in December, 'and have received *two hard guineas* already ... They are the only guineas I ever kissed; and I have locked them up religiously.'[5] By early February the list had reached some fifty names, among them that of Mrs Fitzherbert: the Prince of Wales was almost in his sights. Meanwhile his social life was snowballing. His letters home, as affectionate as ever, were full of the parties and dinners he had attended, sometimes as many as three in one night. He had returned with a number of songs from Dublin, some of them set to music by Billy Warren, others by a new friend, John Stevenson, and was soon in great demand as an after-dinner singer. Recalling his first appearance in a London drawing room years later Mary Berry (the elder of Horace Wapole's beloved Berry sisters) described 'the sort of contemptuous titter with which the fine gentlemen and amateurs saw a little Irish lad led forth to exhibit after all the fine singing that had been going on', and their astonishment and pleasure once he began to sing. 'And he's going to the Bar – what a pity,'[6] a lady remarked as he got up from the piano to a storm of applause.

It was not only among amateurs that he was beginning to make his name. 'Johnson of Covent Garden, I hear,' he told his mother, 'sings some of my songs in company',[7] and the celebrated tenor Michael Kelly (brother of his Irish friend Joe Kelly) had approached him to collaborate on an operatic afterpiece, *The Gipsy Prince*, for the Haymarket Theatre. Meanwhile he was studying music more seriously and was taking lessons in 'thorough bass'. But the promotion of his poems remained his chief concern and in April or May (the date of the letter announcing it is uncertain) the greatest prize of all was in his hands. 'I have got the Prince [of Wales]'s name,' he wrote in high excitement to his mother, 'and his permission that I should *dedicate* Anacreon to him. Hurra, hurra!'[8]

No matter that his critics would regard this note as a betrayal of his nationalist principles – though it should be remembered that at this stage the Prince of Wales was still a supporter of Catholic emancipation – the fact that only a year after his arrival in London, he had received such an extraordinary mark of favour was an amazing tribute to his charm and talents. It must have been Lord Moira who had sung his praises, for he would not meet the Prince in person till after the book had appeared.

The *Odes of Anacreon* were published in July 1800 and created an immediate sensation. Even in an age when the appetite for poetry was far greater than it is to day, their success, in the words of an earlier biographer, was 'one of the minor wonders of literature'[9] only comparable to that of *Childe Harold* twelve years later. Like Byron, Moore awoke to find himself famous. The critics sang his praises, the *Morning Post* dubbed him 'Anacreon Moore', a nickname that survived till later triumphs made it out of date. The list of subscribers, beginning with the Prince, and including two dukes, sixteen earls, nine viscounts and a descending array of lesser nobility, ensured the poems' welcome in fashionable drawing rooms, but they quickly made their way in wider circles too and ran into nine editions in the next few years. 'The young people will like it,' Dr Kearney had told him, and it was among the younger generation that it found its most enthusiastic readers. (Only two of the senior members of Trinity, to Moore's disgust, had been subscribers.)

The romantic movement itself was still young. The previous year had seen the publication of the *Lyrical Ballads*, a far more important landmark, but in a lighter, more accessible way, the *Odes* too sounded a new note. Comparisons were made with the cavalier poets of the seventeenth century, though the mood was lusher, too lush perhaps for modern ears. But in a world just emerging from the elegant formality of eighteenth-century verse, their freshness and lyricism had an immediate appeal, while their vision of an idealised Grecian past set the scene for the romantic Hellenism of later poets, Byron and Keats above all.

Only fragments of the original poems of Anacreon remain; most of those gathered under his name are now known to be later imitations, dating from various periods in the last centuries BC. Moore could not have realised this at the time, but he worked from a facsimile of the Vatican MS from which the poems were printed in the sixteenth century, supporting his translations with an erudite, not to say pedantic, array of footnotes. There is nothing pedantic about the poems themselves; sensuous and evocative, they celebrate love and wine and song in a series of brief and joyous lyrics. Sometimes the theme is purely amorous,

> Would I were perfume for thy hair,
> To breathe my soul in fragrance there;
> Or better still, the zone, that lies
> Close to thy breast and feels its sighs!
> Or ev'n those envious pearls that show
> So faintly round that neck of snow –
> Yes, I would be that happy gem,
> Like them to hang, to fade like them.
> What more would thy Anacreon be?
> Oh, anything that touches thee;
> Nay sandals for those airy feet –
> Ev'n to be trod by them were sweet.

Sometimes there is a note of melancholy,

> I know that Heaven hath sent me here
> To run this mortal life's career;
> The scenes which I have journeyed o'er,
> Return no more – alas! no more...

But even here the poet refuses to repine,

> And oh! before the vital thrill,
> Which trembles at my heart, is still,
> I'll gather Joy's luxuriant flowers,
> And gild with bliss my fading hours;
> Bacchus shall bid my winter bloom,
> And Venus dance me to the tomb.

Light verses, perhaps slight verses, but already with that melodious quality that he would make his own. One is reminded of Verlaine's definition of poetry: '*De la musique avant toute chose...Et tout le reste est littérature.*'[10]

Amidst the chorus of congratulations on *Anacreon*, one eagerly awaited meeting gave Moore especial pleasure. 'I was yesterday introduced to his Royal Highness, George, Prince of Wales,' he wrote to his mother on 4 August.

> He is beyond doubt a man of very fascinating manners. When I was presented to him he said he was happy to know a *man of my abilities*; and when I thanked him for the honour he did me in permitting the dedication of Anacreon, he stopped me and said the honour was *entirely* his, in being allowed to put his name to a work of such merit. He then said that he hoped when he returned to town in the winter, we should have many possibilities of *enjoying each other's society*; that he was passionately fond of music and had heard of my talents in this way.

It is a delightful glimpse of the First Gentleman of Europe, whose passion for the arts would always be his most attractive characteristic. 'But my dearest mother,' added Moore, 'it has cost me a *new coat*; for the introduction was unfortunately deferred till my former one was grown confoundedly shabby, and I got a coat made up in six hours: however it cannot be helped; I got it on a very economical plan, by giving two guineas and an *old coat*, whereas the usual price of a coat here is near four pounds. By the bye, I am still in my other tailor's debt.'

Such niggling financial worries would be a recurring theme in Moore's letters. He hated to be a burden on his family and lived as economically as he could, but the price of going out in society in terms of clothes and laundry bills was high, and it was a constant struggle to make ends meet. But he had a new volume of poems under way and high hopes that his operatic afterpiece might make money; 'if a hundred or two hundred pounds be the result of it,' he told his mother, 'why then we shall have no reason to regret it.' We hear little more of his legal studies, which he seems to have let lapse in favour of his literary projects. The chances of advancement for Catholics in the law, in any case, were severely limited. Although they had been admitted to the profession in 1793, the most important offices, including those of King's Counsel, Judge and Attorney General were still closed to them, and the list of lesser exclusions ran to nearly two hundred. Even in the places left open by law, there was a wall of prejudice to surmount. The Catholic, wrote Moore years later, 'may raise his voice to ask for justice to his fellow slaves, but from the inner shrine, where it is dispensed, he is utterly excluded'.[11]

These were bitter words, not safe to be uttered in 1800, though at the time he probably left his studies with few regrets. Secure in the success of *Anacreon*, he spent the summer and autumn in Dublin, working on his new poems and collaborating with his friend John Stevenson in setting some of his earlier ones to music. Moore, as an amateur, could and sometimes did provide the airs, but it was Stevenson, Director of Music at St Patrick's Cathedral, and a popular composer for the theatre, who had the technical skills to arrange them. A genial, absent-minded man, ten years Moore's senior, he was an inspiring musical partner, as fertile in melodies as Moore was in poetry. Three years later his setting of one of Moore's songs from *Anacreon*, 'Give me a harp of epic song', so impressed the Viceroy at a concert of the Irish Harmonic Society that he knighted him for his services to Irish music.

Moore returned to London at the end of December, travelling through 'snows mountains deep'[12] to stay at Donington en route. He was beginning to feel at home there: 'There cannot be anything more delightful than this house – an inimitable library, where I have the honour of being *bound up* myself, a charming piano and very pleasant company.'[13] But he was in a hurry to be back in London, to arrange for the publication of his new volume, and to put the finishing touches to *The Gipsy Prince*. He was immediately caught up in a round of parties. There were routs and after-opera suppers; a 'most splendid' ball at the Duchess of Devonshire's; an affable encounter with the Prince of Wales – 'How do you do, Moore; I am very glad to see you'. There were convivial evenings too with Michael Kelly discussing the forthcoming production of *The Gipsy Prince*; the words for the songs, and at least one melody, were Moore's, the rest of the music being selected and arranged by Kelly. 'Poor *Mick*,' Moore confided, 'is rather an imposer than a composer. He cannot mark the time in writing three bars of music; his understrappers however do all that for him, and he has the knack of pleasing the many.'[14]

By May, despite sending 'showers of apologies'[15] he was worn out by the pace in London, and was glad to accept an invitation from Lord Moira to spend a few quiet weeks at Donington in the family's absence, where he browsed in the library, shot rooks, and gathered up his energies once more.

He returned to London in time for the opening of *The Gipsy Prince* on 21 July. Kelly sang the leading role, but although the airs were 'universally encored', the opera did not catch the public fancy and was withdrawn after only ten performances. Luckily Moore had no time to repine. His second volume of poems was due to appear that same month – only a year after the publication of the *Odes of Anacreon* – and his hopes were now pinned on repeating their success.

His first poems had been paraphrases, if not always strict translations, of another poet's work. In his second volume, *The Poetical Works of the late Thomas Little Esq* (the name perhaps was a reference to his own small stature) he distanced himself once more by appearing as the editor, not the author, of the poems. Little was supposedly a poet, a Chatterton-like figure, who had died in obscurity in his twenty-first year. 'His life,' wrote Moore, in his preface, 'was one of those humble streams which have scarcely a name in the map of life, and the traveller may pass by it without enquiring its source or direction', and he used Little's youth and untimely fate as an excuse to claim indulgence for his work.

It was a thin device. The second edition of the poems would be dedicated to Joseph Atkinson, the dedication signed with the letters T.M., so that the public could be in little doubt as to the identity of the author. But it gave him a freedom that he would otherwise have lacked, a freedom which, in the opinion of some censorious critics, he carried much too far. The poems of Anacreon, according to Moore, had been 'sportive without being wanton, and ardent without being licentious'. Those of Little, 'written at an age when the passions often give a colouring too warm to the imagination', were only slightly more outspoken. But the wave of middle-class prudery, so often associated with the reign of Queen Victoria, was already gathering momentum in the first years of the century; five years later, with a devastating article in the *Edinburgh Review*, condemning him for indecency and immorality, it would break over his head. The poems would do more harm to Moore's reputation – though not to his sales – than anything he ever wrote.

At the time when they first appeared, however, he had no inkling of what lay in store. The first reviewers welcomed the new volume, and the public flocked to buy it, without any criticism of its moral tone. But the private reaction of Coleridge, when he was asked to contribute to an anthology in which a poem by Moore was to be included, was a foretaste of the wrath to come. 'I have a wife, I have sons, I have an infant Daughter – what excuse could I offer to my conscience if by suffering my own name to be connected with those of Mr Lewis or Mr Moore, I was the *occasion* of their reading the Monk or the wanton poems of Thomas Little Esqre?...My head turns giddy, my heart sickens, at the very thought of seeing such books in the hands of a child of mine.'[16] (Moore, incidentally, was a good friend of Lewis, whose gothic novel *The Monk* had been a sensation six years before.)

Today it is hard to see what the fuss was about. The idea of Moore as a desperate seducer, flitting from flower to flower, and proclaiming his faithlessness in verse, is faintly ludicrous. In any case, his poems are not confessional: it is Little, not Moore, who strikes a pose. Light hearted, amorous, but never passionately involved, he plays with the idea of love just as he plays with rhymes and metres in his verses:

> Oh! Phillis, that kiss may be sweeter
> Than ever by mortal was given;
> But your lip, love, is only St Peter,
> And keeps but the key to your heaven.

Sometimes the tone is slyly titillating:

> Give me my love, that billing kiss
> I taught you one delicious night,
> When, turning epicures in bliss,
> We tried inventions of delight.
>
> Come gently steal my lips along,
> And let your lips in murmurs move, –
> Ah, no! – again – that kiss was wrong –
> How can you be so dull my love?
>
> 'Cease, cease!' the blushing girl replied –
> And in her milky arms she caught me –
> 'How can you thus your pupil chide;
> You know '*twas in the dark you taught me!*'

At others it is elegaic:

> When Time, who seals our years away
> Shall steal our pleasures too,
> The memory of the past will stay,

And half our joys renew.
Then Chloe, when thy beauty's flower
Shall feel the wintry air,
Remembrance will recall the hour
When thou alone wert fair!
Then talk no more of future gloom;
Our joys shall always last;
For hope shall brighten days to come,
And memory gild the past.

Time and its passing were always favourite themes with Moore and the song, which was later set to music by Sir John Stevenson, was one of his happiest ventures in this vein.

Read all at once, Little's poems can seem over-sweet and cloying, at times almost embarrassing. But there are individual treasures, like the lines above, among them and their grace and virtuosity make up for much. Above all they are redeemed by Moore's ability to laugh at the romantic conventions he is using and by the sense of fun that dances through them. Let one of them, 'Nonsense', make the point:

Good reader! if you've ever seen,
When Phoebus hastens to his pillow,
The mermaids with their tresses green,
Dancing upon the Western billow:
If you have seen, at twilight dim,
When the lone spirit's vesper hymn
Floats wild along the winding shore.
If you have seen, through mist of eve,
The fairy train their ringlets weave,
Glancing along the spangled green: –
If you have seen all this, and more,
God bless me, what a deal you've seen!

5

Bermuda Bound

Unconscious of the trouble brewing over Little's poems, Moore spent the next eighteen months enjoying the celebrity they had brought him. The list of grand engagements in his letters to his parents becomes almost breathless; inverted snobs may look askance at his pleasure in them, but who can blame him for enjoying himself? Now and for ever after, he was always more sought after than seeking.

What was the secret of Moore's charm – that Irish charm, which he shared with his great precursor Sheridan? His manners were easy and unassuming, his dark eyes sparkled with intelligence and wit, above all he radiated an infectious *joie de vivre*. 'Nothing could be more genial and delightful, frank, playful and exhilarating…' wrote a contemporary. 'He seemed so keenly and vividly to enjoy existence – making so light of its cares and burdens – on the other hand so heightening and intensifying the pleasures, that his society exercised over you a species of happy spell, which you grieved to be divorced from.'[1] Although he revelled in his social successes he never gave himself airs, or made a secret of his humble origins. There is a story, possibly apocryphal, of his being quizzed by the Prince of Wales, as to which grand branch of the Moore family he belonged, and replying simply that his father was a Dublin tradesman. Even his diminutive size caused him no complexes: when a tall friend asked him if he found the weather cold, he answered cheerfully, 'Why rather so. How is it up there with you?'[2]

Music, always the breath of life to him, added an extra dimension to his attractions. Just as his finest lyrics could never really be appreciated without the music that accompanied them, so his presence at a party only attained its maximum value when he began to sing. By now he had a number of his own songs set to music by Stevenson, though when he came to perform them it seemed as though they were newly minted every time. 'He seemed to improvise as he ran his fingers over the notes,' wrote one listener 'and as the tide of thought came over him, it was poured forth in harmonious cadences of exquisite variety.'[3] It was this apparent spontaneity that was the secret of his art, the gradations of emotion, now gay, now melancholy and yearning, reflected in the changing expressions of his face. Essentially intimate, his were very much drawing room performances, attuned to the fashionable audiences who crowded round the piano; though in later years, for instance at an official banquet, he could hold a large assembly spellbound.

Amidst a host of new acquaintances and admirers, Moore had made a number of real friends, usually those with a shared love of literature or music. 'Monk' Lewis, already mentioned, was one; the young Viscount Strangford, who was preparing a translation of the Portuguese epic poet Camoens, and looked to Moore, one year his senior, as his poetic mentor, was another. So too were William Spencer, son of Lord Charles Spencer, officially a commissioner of stamps, but also a poet and translator, and the Rev. John Dalby, the tutor to Lord Moira's family, and his wife, Moore's closest friends at Donington. Most important of all were two sisters, the Dowager Marchioness of Donegal, and Mary Godfrey, the clever daughters of an Irish rector, both passionately interested in the arts and safely enough his elders to take a semi-maternal interest in his welfare. We catch the tone of their friendship in one of Mary Godfrey's letters, written in December 1801, when Moore, who had retired to Donington to work, showed signs of chafing at his exile: 'Your talents might fit you for everything, but your idleness unfits you for anything. You want to come to town, I know you do, to get away from those country-bred, sentimental ladies, the Muses, and I pray that you may have no other ladies in view to supply their place ... You know my sermons make you laugh – *tant mieux*. I never despair of you when you laugh; if you yawned I should give up the whole thing as hopeless.'[4]

We hear very little of these 'other ladies' in Moore's letters of this period, and the gossip of the day has nothing to add. It seems strange that the author of such outspokenly amorous verses as Thomas Little's should be so discreet about his own affairs. But perhaps he practised the philosophy he preached, with all the worldly wisdom of his twenty-three years, to his friend Lord Strangford:

> Between ourselves, my dear Percy, and in the beaten way of friendship, I *must* condemn your levity about Mrs Walpole – it was unworthy of you – you make a discovery almost inevitable, and you *must* know too that this is not Diplomatique, for whatever a man may think of a woman, he should *seem* to respect her for indulging him, or he will hardly be indulged by any other – no, no, I agree with my friend Tom Brown that

> Of all the crimes on this side Hell
> The blackest sure's to – and tell.[5]

Despite the distractions of his social life Moore was continuing to work hard. There were new editions of *Anacreon* (with a portrait engraving of the translator) and Little's poems to prepare for the press; a suggestion from Colman, the manager of the Haymarket, that he should write another operatic afterpiece; a third volume of poetry under way; a string of sheet songs in collaboration with Stevenson to be published. But his projects, though full of promise, never brought in enough money. The Haymarket project turned out to be 'too expensive for Colman's theatre', his first two volumes of poetry, though selling fast, were of more benefit to his publishers than himself.

From the first he seems to have been a hopeless businessman. He had sold the copyright of *Anacreon* in order to repay a debt of £70 to his friend Hume for the expenses involved in launching it; since the poems, as we have seen, ran into nine editions, he was certainly the loser by the bargain. He had transferred to a new publisher, Carpenter, for the poems of Thomas Little, and having been encouraged to draw on him for expenses was dismayed to find himself in debt for £60. The publisher obligingly suggested that he should clear it by selling him the copyright of Little's poems, which Moore, in his innocence, was happy to do. Carpenter admitted some years later that he was still making £200 a year on the poems.

Beset by financial worries – which did not prevent him from sending a piano to Dublin as a present for his sister – Moore pinned his hopes on patronage, the almost universal system by which jobs were distributed at the time. The resignation of Pitt over his failure to secure Catholic emancipation in February 1801, and his replacement by Addington as First Lord of the Treasury, had raised his hopes that Lord Moira might become part of the new administration. But Moira was too much the Prince of Wales's man to be acceptable for high office under George III, and he was given the comparatively minor post of commander of the armed forces in Scotland. Obviously, there was nothing he could do for Moore in a military way, but both he and Atkinson lobbied the Secretary of State for Ireland to create an Irish Poet Laureateship, along English lines, for Moore. It was a superficially tempting offer, which, after consulting with his father, Moore refused. To accept the 'paltry and degrading stipend'[6] attached to it so soon after the suppression of Irish independence went against his Irish pride; he would only have taken it had his parents been in need. Fortunately, neither Atkinson nor Moira took offence at his refusal, Lord Moira continuing to be a generous host at Donington, and promising to see what else he could do.

Meanwhile, in Ireland, events were taking a dramatic turn. In October 1802 Robert Emmet arrived in Dublin from Paris, where he had been trying unsuccessfully to interest the French government in a further rising in Ireland. The Peace of Amiens, signed with Britain in March that year, had put paid to such hopes, and on his first return to Dublin (to which the authorities turned a blind eye) he made it clear that he was there in a private capacity only. But the lure of a conspiracy already hatching in Ireland soon drew him in, and by May 1803, when war with France broke out again, he was already one of the leading figures in a plot to overthrow the government in Dublin. On 23 July, acting on the assumption that the rest of the country would rise in sympathy if he seized Dublin, he donned the green uniform of a rebel general and advanced with a hundred followers towards Dublin Castle. They were joined by a mob, armed with pikes and blunderbusses, who surrounded the coach of the Lord Chief Justice and his son-in-law, and savagely piked them to death. Emmet, who was striding on ahead, knew nothing of this outrage at the time, but it soon became clear that his attempt was doomed to failure. After only a few hours fighting, the mob was dispersed by government troops and Emmet, unwilling to risk further bloodshed in what he realised was a hopeless cause, fled to the hills. He was arrested a month later, the fiasco of the failed uprising redeemed by his unforgettable words from the dock: 'I have but one request to ask at my departure from the world. It is the charity of its silence. Let no man write my epitaph; for as no man who knows my motives dare now vindicate them, let not prejudice or ignorance asperse them... When my country takes her place among the nations of the earth, then and not till then, let my epitaph be written.'[7]

Five years later, in a song that echoed his last words, Moore would set the seal on Emmet's legend:

Oh! breathe not his name – let it sleep in the shade,
Where cold and unhonour'd his relics are laid!
Sad, silent and dark, be the tears that we shed,
As the night-dew that falls on the grass o'er his head.

But the night-dew that falls, though in silence it weeps,
Shall brighten with verdure the grave where he sleeps;
And the tear that we shed, though in secret it rolls,
Shall long keep his memory green in our souls.

Emmet was hanged in Dublin on 20 September 1803. On 25 September Moore set sail from Spithead for the United States; he may not yet have heard the news of his friend's death, but he must have known what his fate would be. Not a word of his feelings escapes in his letters. A few weeks before, Lord Moira, calling in an obligation from the Treasurer of the Navy, George Tierney, had obtained the offer of a government post as registrar to the Naval Prize Court in Bermuda, for Moore; and Moore, after anxious discussions with his family and friends, had decided to accept it. It is hard to see what possible qualifications he had for the position, but the patronage system was notoriously capricious, and with Britain once again at war with France, there was a chance of earning substantial commissions on the prize money coming through the court. It was an opportunity too, to see the world and a step up on the ladder of preferment. Even if he did not make a shilling by it, Moore told his mother, 'the new character it gives to my pursuits, the claims it affords me upon government, the absence I shall have from all frippery follies ... all these are objects invaluable in themselves'.[8]

The greatest trial of course would be the distance from his family; the Irish Channel was a small enough divide, but crossing the Atlantic in those days of war and uncertainty was a very different matter. His parents, however, gave him their blessing, his mother consoling herself with thoughts of the good air and balmy climate of the Bermuda Islands, his father pleased that he had found 'so honourable a situation at this very critical time', an indirect reference perhaps to the troubles in Ireland. 'I am sure no one living can possibly feel more sensible than your poor mother and me do at losing the comfort we have so long enjoyed, of at least hearing from you once every week of your life that you are absent from us,' he told him, 'for surely no parents ever had such happiness in a child... [but] much as we regret the wide separation which this situation of yours will cause between us, we give you our full concurrence, and may the Almighty God spare and prosper as you deserve.'[9] It was a touching farewell, the only letter from Moore's father that survives.

The decision once made, there was much to be done before departure. In the first place, there were the expenses of the journey to be met. His publisher agreed to advance £100 against the publication of future songs and poems; his maternal uncle Joyce Codd gave him a loan. There was his piano to be sold – 'I shall be painfully at a loss without that favourite resource,' he wrote – a batch of songs to send to Stevenson, and a passage across the Atlantic to be found. Fortunately, thanks to an introduction to a Mr and Mrs Robert Merry, who were travelling to Washington, where Merry was to take up the post of British Minister, Moore was able to join them and their numerous retinue on board the *Phaeton*, a fifty-gun frigate under the command of Captain George Cockburn, bound for Norfolk, Virginia; from there he could pick up the next available ship to Bermuda. 'Hope sings in the shrouds of the ship that is to carry me,' he wrote to his mother as he went aboard; 'Goodby, God bless you all, dears of my heart.'[10]

Moore quickly became a favourite with the ship's officers, despite their initial prejudice against him as a poet and a dandy: 'I thought you the first day you came aboard the most conceited little fellow I ever saw, with your glass cocked to your eye,'[11] confessed the first lieutenant later. He was soon won over. Another officer, Captain Sir James Scott, then a midshipman on his first voyage, recalled in his memoirs thirty years later how Moore had been 'life and soul' of the company, and how 'the loss of his fascinating society was frequently and loudly lamented' when he left them.

A chance encounter with a ship bound for Lisbon in mid-Atlantic gave Moore an opportunity to send a letter to his mother. 'Our voyage hitherto has been remarkably favourable,' he wrote.

In the first week we reached the Azores, or the Western Islands, and though our second week has not advanced us much, from the almost continuous calms we have had, yet the weather has been so delicious that there is but little to complain of, and in another fortnight we hope to be landed in America... I have had but one day's sickness, which I feel has been of service to me; and though we are in as warm a climate as I shall have to encounter, I find not the least inconvenience from the heat.[12]

Perhaps by the same ship Moore sent back his lines to Lord Strangford, 'Written aboard the Phaeton frigate, off the Azores, by moonlight', a romantic evocation of the scene around him:

The sea is like a silvery lake,
And o'er its calm a vessel glides,
Gently, as if it feared to wake
The slumber of the silent tides…

The poem ends with the changing of the watch:

But hark! – the boatswain's pipings tell
'Tis time to bid my dream farewell;
Eight bells: – the middle watch is set;
Good night, my Strangford! – ne'er forget
That far beyond the western sea
Is one, whose heart remembers thee.

On 3 November, after a six-week voyage, the *Phaeton* harboured in Norfolk, the capital of Virginia. 'Mr and Mrs Merry left the Phaeton under the usual salute,' wrote Scott, 'accompanied by Mr Moore, to the great regret of all those who had largely shared in the pleasure to be derived from the brilliancy of his wit and humour. The gunroom mess hailed the day of his departure with genuine sorrow.'[13] So too did the captain (later famous when as Admiral Cockburn he captured and burnt Washington in the war of 1812); on the day of their landing, wrote Moore, 'he took a seal from his watch, which he begged I would wear in remembrance of him'.[14]

The Merrys took Moore under their wing when he first arrived in Norfolk. They presented him to Colonel Hamilton, the British consul, an old friend of Lord Moira's from the American campaign, who invited them all to stay till their onward journeys could be arranged. Moore was delighted to find a harpsichord in the Colonel's drawing room, and some of his own songs among the music books, 'but music here is like whistling to the wilderness' he told his mother ruefully, and Norfolk itself, destroyed by the British in the War of Independence, and more recently ravaged by fire and yellow fever, was depressingly ramshackle and run down. Mrs Merry was bitten into a fever by mosquitoes, and even Moore, with his propensity to cast a romantic veil over reality, was hard put to find poetic inspiration. The only poem he wrote there, a ballad based on a visit to the Dismal Swamp, a dreary wilderness some ten miles from Norfolk, tells the story of a young man who is driven mad by the death of the girl he loves and disappears while searching for her in the swamp. Their ghosts survive:

> But oft from the Indian hunter's camp,
> This lover and maid so true
> Are seen at the hour of midnight damp,
> To cross the Lake by a fire-fly lamp,
> And paddle their white canoe.

It was an appropriately dismal theme.

It was over a month before Moore found a passage on a naval ship, the *Driver*, which was travelling to join the British squadron wintering in Bermuda. Mrs Hamilton shed tears at his departure; the Colonel gave him letters of introduction to all the leading dignitaries in Bermuda. The week-long voyage was exceptionally rough, Moore noting proudly that he had eaten a hearty dinner of beefsteak and onions, and amused himself with writing 'ridiculous verses', when the gale was at its height. On 7 January 1804, with the storm left behind, the *Driver* sailed into St George's Bay, Bermuda. It was only natural that Moore should celebrate the scene that greeted him in verse:

> Bright rose the morning, every wave was still,
> When the first perfume of a cedar hill
> Sweetly awak'd us, and with smiling charms,
> The fairy harbour woo'd us to its arms.
> Gently we stole, before the whisp'ring wind,
> Through plantain shades that round, like awnings, twin'd
> And kissed on either side the wanton sails,
> Breathing our welcome to these vernal vales;
> While, far reflected o'er the wave serene,
> Each wooded island shed so soft a green
> That the enamoured keel, with whisp'ring play
> Through liquid herbage seem'd to steal its way...

It was an idyllic vision, but the realities of his situation were less enchanting. He soon discovered that his hopes of making money as a registrar were wildly optimistic. In the past the number of captured enemy vessels whose case had come through the prize courts was enough to generate a considerable profit, but by 1804 French commerce in the area had almost been swept from the seas, and the pickings were thin. The place of registrar had no fixed salary; it depended entirely on commission on the prizes coming through. Moore writes in one of his letters home of two American ships (presumably thought to be trading with France) coming up for trial; elsewhere he describes examining 'all the skippers, mates and seamen, who are produced as witnesses in the causes of captured vessels'.[15] But the cases were few and far between, and he soon despaired of earning anything worthwhile.

It was not in his nature, however, to be downhearted, and for the few months he was there he lived in a constant round of gaieties. His expenses were few. Admiral Mitchell, commanding the British squadron, insisted that he should make his house his home; the local families vied in getting up picnics and dances for him. 'The women in general dance extremely well,' he noted, 'though like Dogberry's "reading and writing" it "comes by nature to them" for they never have any instruction, except when some flying dancing master, by the kindness of fortune, happens to be wrecked or driven ashore on the island.'[16] This did not prevent him from seeking romance, at least if his poems are to be believed. A series of thirteen odes, written with far more warmth than any of his previous love songs, are dedicated to Nea, a name that he later claimed was inspired by two different women, but that legend has always attributed firmly to a certain Hester Tucker.

Hester Tucker, belonging to one of the grand families of the islands, had married her cousin William Tucker at the age of sixteen the previous June. When Moore first met her she was six months pregnant, so the affair was probably more a case of wishful thinking than fulfilment. Nonetheless it is not surprising that her husband William Tucker, who afterwards refused to have any of Moore's books in his house, should object to lines like these:

I saw you blush, you felt me tremble,
In vain would formal art dissemble
All that we wish'd and thought;
'Twas more than tongue would dare reveal
'Twas more than virtue ought to feel
But all that passion ought!

When Hester's baby was born Moore hailed the occasion with an ode, whose opening line, 'The first ambrosial child of bliss', caused lifelong embarrassment to the unfortunate child, who later became Rector of St George's. The story goes that when he was a young priest, he was presented to the Archbishop of Canterbury, who being a little hard of hearing did not catch his name, and was prompted by a mutual friend, 'The first ambrosial child of bliss, my Lord.' 'Oh how d'ye do, Mr Tucker,' exclaimed the prelate without a moment's hesitation.[17]

Moore left happy memories in Bermuda. 'Tom Moore is as much poet laureate of the Bermuda Islands today,' wrote one inhabitant long afterwards, 'as if he were living and such an appointment existed, with an annual perquisite of Bermuda milk punch.'[18] But by March 1804, he had resolved to leave. Having appointed a deputy to handle his almost non-existent duties, he secured a place on the frigate *Boston*, under the command of Captain John Douglas. It left for New York on 25 April. 'I shall endeavour, if my purse will compass it, to see a little more of America than before I had the opportunity of doing,' he wrote to his parents; 'so that, about the end of summer, darling mother, you may *look to the signal post* for your Tom, who will bring you back a sunburnt face, a heart not the worse for wear, and a purse, like that of most honest fellows, as empty as – richer fellows' heads!'[19]

6

American Travels

Moore spent a week in New York, while the *Boston* lay at harbour, before going on to Norfolk. His plan was to leave the ship at Norfolk, and travel across country, seeing all he could, before rejoining it at Halifax; from thence he would sail direct to England. The greatest novelties he encountered in New York were a glimpse of Jerome Bonaparte, who much to his brother's displeasure had recently married an American bride, and the 'slight shock of an earthquake', which, as he told his mother, 'are two things I could not often meet with upon Usher's quay'.[1] Like other celebrated travellers of the time, Mrs Trollope in the 1830s, Dickens in the 1840s, Moore took a poor view of the young American republic. 'Such a place! Such people!' he wrote from New York; 'barren and secluded as poor Bermuda is, I think it a paradise to any spot in America that I have seen.'[2]

It was not a view that did him credit, and one that he would later regret, but it coloured his whole attitude while he was there. There were pleasant interludes, of course, beginning with a brief stay with the Hamiltons in Norfolk, where Mrs Hamilton gave him some earrings for his sister Kate, and 'won her way to my heart', he wrote, 'by calling herself my *mother*'.[3] Moore responded with some gallant verses, not altogether filial in their sentiments, on the occasion of her letting down her fashionably rolled up hair:

But oh! 'twould ruin saints to see
Those tresses thus, unbound and free,
Adown your shoulders sweeping;

They put *such thoughts* into one's head,
Of dishabille, and night, and bed,
And – anything but sleeping!

From Norfolk Moore made his way to Washington where he found the Merrys installed in their ministerial quarters, and thoroughly discontented with their lot. 'They have been treated with the most pointed incivility by the present democratic president, Mr Jefferson,' Moore told his mother; 'and it is only the precarious situation of Great Britain which could possibly induce it to overlook such indecent, though at the same time petty, hostility.' What had happened, apparently, was that at a state dinner at the White House in December, the President had affronted their dignity as British envoys by not intervening when a member of the House of Representatives pressed ahead of Merry to sit by the wife of the Spanish Minister. Since the President had abolished diplomatic precedence for what he called the '*péle mèle*' system, it was not clear that any insult was intended, but the Merrys took it very much to heart, and were still complaining of it when Moore arrived to stay in June. Plainly influenced by their attitude, Moore gave an unflattering picture of the raw new capital – it had only become the seat of government four years earlier – in a verse epistle to Thomas Hume,

In fancy now, beneath the twilight gloom,
Come, let me lead thee o'er this modern Rome...
This famed metropolis, where fancy sees
Squares in morasses, obelisks in trees;
Which travelling fools and gazeteers adorn
With shrines unbuilt and heroes yet unborn,
Though naught but woods and J*******n they see,
Where streets should run and sages *ought* to be,

and in lines that he later he cut out from his *Poetical Works* described the President, who was said to have a black mistress, as dreaming of freedom 'in his slave's embrace'.

When Merry presented Moore to the President as a literary celebrity, Jefferson looked down at him coolly, with only a brief word of greeting, and though Moore wrote later that 'to have seen and spoken to the man who drew up the Declaration of American Independence was an event not to be forgotten',[4] he was annoyed enough at the time to add a snide footnote to the poem. 'The President's house, a very noble one,' he wrote, 'is by no means suited to the philosophical humility of its present possessor, who inhabits but a corner of the mansion itself, and abandons the rest to a state of uncleanly desolation, which those who are not philosophers cannot look at without regret.'[5]

Some years after the poem was published Jefferson picked up a copy of an early number of Moore's *Irish Melodies*. 'Why this is the little man who satirised me so!' he exclaimed, and then, after perusing the work for a while, 'Why he is a poet after all!'[6] Thereafter Moore was only rivalled by Burns as Jefferson's favourite poet. He particularly loved such songs as 'Oh! Blame not the Bard' and 'Oh! Breathe not his name', and in his last letter to his daughter, written when he was dying, he quoted several lines from one of Moore's first melodies, 'It is not the Tear at this Moment shed'.

Such a literary apotheosis seemed unimaginable during Moore's visit to the United States. He wrote fluently while he was there, but most of his verses are of only moderate interest, mellifluous but too conventional and generalised to make much impact. The most striking perhaps are those in which he denounces the American version of democracy,

> Where every ill the ancient world can brew
> Is mix'd with every grossness of the new,

reserving his greatest scorn for the anomaly of slavery, in a land professing freedom and equality:

> Who can, with patience, for a moment see
> The medley mass of pride and misery,
> Of whips and charters, manacles and rights,
> Of slaving blacks and democratic whites,
> And all the piebald polity that reigns
> In free confusion o'er Columbia's plains?

Disenchanted by Washington, he spent only a week there before travelling via Baltimore to Philadelphia, complaining bitterly of 'break neck roads' and 'wretched rumbling vehicles' en route. 'Oh dear! I am almost tired of thus jogging and struggling into experience.'[7] In Philadelphia, however, things took a turn for the better. It was America's most cosmopolitan city, with a thriving social and intellectual life. Moore's fame as a poet had gone before him, and he was feted by society there, in particular the circle surrounding Joseph Dennie, the editor of the *Port Folio*, the leading literary magazine in the republic. It had already published a number of his *Anacreon* odes with flattering comments; to judge by some lines in its pages after his departure, his visit left an equally favourable impression:

> Ye, who saw Genius like a meteor's gleam,
> On glowing fancy's sportive pinion soar,
> When wak'd by rapture from the pleasing dream
> Will find the fleeting prodigy was Moore.[8]

He also caught up with his old friend Edward Hudson, who had been released from prison into exile at the time of the Peace of Amiens, and had married the daughter of a rich Philadelphia bookseller. Moore felt awkward with him now: he had become convinced of the futility of violence; Hudson remained an unrepentant rebel. 'He has perhaps had reason to confirm him in his politics,' he told his mother ruefully, 'and God knows I see every reason to change mine.'[9]

From Philadelphia he travelled to New York, where he arranged to meet the *Boston* in Halifax in early August, then set off up the Hudson to Saratoga. 'The country around here seems the very haunt of savages,' he wrote.

> Nothing but tall forests of pine, through which the narrow, rocky road with difficulty finds its way; and yet this neighbourhood is the fashionable resort, the watering-place for ladies and gentlemen from all parts of the United States. At Bell Town Springs, eight miles from this, there are about thirty or forty people at present (and, in the season triple that number), all stowed together in a miserable boarding house, drinking the waters, and performing every necessary evolution in concert.[10]

After pausing briefly to try the waters, he set off towards the Canadian border, travelling by wagon and sleeping in whatever primitive lodgings he could find. 'Nothing was ever so dirty or miserable,' he told his mother, 'but powerful curiosity sweetens all difficulties.' He was impressed by the wildness and magnificence of the scenery and moved by an encounter with a chief of the Oneida Indians, whose gentle and intelligent manners, he wrote, 'almost inclined me to be of the Frenchman's opinion, that the savages are the only well-bred gentlemen in America'. Already, in 1804, it was clear what their eventual fate would be: 'The government of America are continually deceiving them into a surrender of the lands they occupy, and are driving them back into the woods farther and farther, till at length they will have no retreat but the ocean.'[11]

On 21 July, having crossed the Canadian border, he found himself at Chippewa, within a mile and half of the Niagara Falls, whose tremendous roar already resounded in his ears. He visited them the next day, overwhelmed like every other traveller by the stupendous sight.

> Never shall I forget the impression I felt at the first glimpse of them which I got as the carriage passed over the hill that overlooks them. We were not near enough to be agitated by the terrific effects of the scene, but saw through the trees this mighty flow of waters descending with calm magnificence, and received enough of its grandeur to set imagination on the wing...I felt as if approaching the very residence of the Deity; the tears started into my eyes; and I remained, for moments after we had lost sight of the scene, in that delicious absorption which pious enthusiasm alone could produce.[12]

Held up by contrary winds, he stayed for a fortnight at the local fort, well entertained by the Colonel and his officers, before setting sail down the St Lawrence to Montreal. The winds were so unfavourable that the boatmen were forced to row all the way, singing in unison as they rowed. One of their songs was the haunting French air which later became the inspiration for one of Moore's best loved compositions – still sung by Canadian school children today – 'A Canadian Boat Song':

> Faintly as tolls the evening chime,
> Our voices keep tune and our oars keep time.
> Soon as the woods on the shore look dim,
> We'll sing at St Ann's our parting hymn.
> Row, brother, row, the stream runs fast,
> The rapids are near and the day-light's past.

'I remember,' he wrote, 'when we have entered at sunset, upon one of those beautiful lakes into which the St Lawrence so grandly and unexpectedly opens, I have heard this simple air with a pleasure which the finest compositions of the first masters have never given me, and now there is not a note of it which does not recall to my memory the dip of our oars in the St Lawrence, the flight of our boat down the rapids, and all those new and fanciful impressions to which my heart was alive during the whole of this very interesting voyage.'[13]

After a brief stay in Montreal, with just time to compose some sentimental verses to a 'Mrs -------', he arrived in Quebec towards the end of August. 'After seventeen hundred miles of rattling and tossing through woods, lakes, rivers & c., I am at length upon the ground which made Wolfe immortal, and which looks more like the elysium of heroes than their death place,'[14] he told his mother. The scenery was sublime, but there was no time to explore it further. He was now in a fever of anxiety lest the *Boston* should already have left for England; he was already a fortnight late for his rendezvous. On 6 September, after a further voyage of thirteen days, he finally arrived in Halifax where luckily the *Boston* was still refitting, with a comfortable margin of three weeks before she sailed. There was time for a visit to Windsor, fifty miles away, where the Governor of Nova Scotia had asked him to attend the first examinations of a new university founded there. 'This attention is, as you may suppose, very singular and flattering; indeed where have I failed to meet cordiality and kindness? They have smoothed every step of my way, and sweetened every novelty I met.'[15]

It was a happy note on which to end his stay, a tribute too to his gift for making friends and fitting in with every kind of company. But he was glad to be leaving, his sense of relief undisguised as the *Boston* prepared to set sail:

With triumph this morning, O Boston! I hail
The stir of thy deck and the spread of thy sail,
For they tell me I soon shall be wafted, in thee,
To the flourishing isle of the brave and the free,
And that chill Nova Scotia's unpromising strand
Is the last I shall tread of American land.

After a convivial voyage, his evenings spent chatting with Captain Douglas over a bottle of good wine, Moore landed in Plymouth on 12 November 1804. 'I almost cry with joy, my darling mother, to be able to write to you on English ground,' he wrote. 'After a passage of eight-and-twenty days, here I am ... within a few hundred miles (instead of *thousands*) of those that are dearest to me.'[16]

His year away, often in rough and arduous circumstances, had immensely increased his sense of self-reliance and made him one of the best-travelled literary figures of his time. But though it had left him rich in experiences, it had given him very little else. Lord Moira had offered him the post in Bermuda in good faith; the fact that it had turned out to be a fiasco was no-one's fault. In Halifax, Moore had met a nephew of Lord St Vincent's sent out on 'the same wild goose chase' as himself; it was beyond a doubt, he wrote, that their posts had been considered to be good appointments. Now he could only hope to make the best of his experiences in literary terms. He could not afford to go home till his new volume of poems was ready for the press, and for

Breakfast with Samuel Rogers: detail from a mezzotint by Charles Mottram, 1815. Seated from left to right are Sheridan, Moore, Wordsworth, Southey, Coleridge, Washington Irving, Byron and Rogers.

the first few months after his return he shut himself up in strict seclusion to finish them.

Moore's idea of strict seclusion, of course, was only relative. There were some invitations that it was impossible to resist, for instance a supper party at Lord Harrington's at which the Prince of Wales was present. 'Every one noticed the cordiality with which he spoke to me,' he told his mother joyfully. 'His words were these: "I am very glad to see you here again, Moore. From the reports I heard, I was afraid we had lost you. I assure you (laying his hand on my shoulder at the same time) it was a subject of general concern." Can anything be more flattering?.'[17] For the most part, however, he foreswore temptation, dining occasionally with Lady Donegal and Mary Godfrey, and seeing old friends like Thomas Hume, Lord Strangford and William Spencer.

In the autumn of 1805, a new friend, the most important he had yet met in literary terms, came into his life, the poet Samuel Rogers. With Wordsworth and Coleridge still relatively unknown, and Moore a rising rather than an established star, Samuel Rogers was probably the best-known poet of his time. Moore had been only fourteen when he read his most famous poem 'The Pleasures of Memory' in the pages of the *Anthologica Hibernica*, an experience so vivid, wrote Moore, 'that the particular type in which it is there printed, and the very colour of the paper, are associated with every line of it in my memory'.[18] They met with Lady Donegal at her house in Tunbridge Wells and despite the difference in their ages – Rogers was sixteen years older than Moore – were soon on intimate terms. A wealthy banker, with an income of £5,000 a year, Rogers lived in considerable splendour in St James's Street, just round the corner from the rooms in Bury Street where Moore had taken lodgings on his return. His literary breakfasts, at which he gathered most of the leading writers, painters and politicians of the day, were famous; his drawing room, with its Flaxman mantelpiece, red silk hangings and Renaissance paintings, was almost a temple to the fine arts. Pale and cadaverous in appearance – his friends used to call him the 'departed poet' – he concealed a generous heart behind a biting and sarcastic manner; his greatest quarrels with Moore were when Moore, always proud, refused to accept his help when he was in financial difficulties.

Financial worries were the only fly in the ointment during Moore's first months in London. Although he resisted engagements, he was still much in demand. 'Every one I ever knew in this big city seems delighted to see me back in it,' he told his mother; 'this is comfortable, and if the flowers strewed before me had a little *gold leaf* on them, I should be the happiest dog in the world. All in good time; but it is strange that people who value the *silk* so much, should not feed the *poor worm* who wastes himself in spinning it out to them.'[19]

Moore never found writing easy – his manuscripts are hatched and cross-hatched with corrections – and it was not until the spring of 1806 that his *Epistles, Odes and Other Poems*, preceded by an engraving of the *Phaeton* under sail, and dedicated to Lord Moira, first appeared. ('Your dedication,' wrote Lord Moira, 'will be a memorial of me which will keep me from total oblivion.')[20] It had been five years since the publication of Little's poems. In his new volume there was no pseudonym to hide behind; the love poems, supposedly to women encountered on his travels, could be taken as personal confessions, revealing him – at least on paper – to be as amorous and faithless as Little himself. The rest of the collection included poems on classical and mythological subjects, descriptions of natural scenery, and a series of verse epistles to friends in England and Ireland, written at various stages of his journey, and giving full rein to his distaste for the American version of democracy. It was a mixed bag and his introduction, setting the poems in the context of his American experiences, closed on an unexpectedly apologetic note: 'The glare of publication is too strong for such imperfect productions; they should be shown but to the eye of friendship in that dim light of privacy which is as favourable to poetical as female beauty...Few now have the leisure to read such trifles, and I sincerely regret that I have had the leisure to write them.' It seems as though he was already preparing himself for an unfavourable reception.

In the meantime the political situation in England had been transformed by the death of Pitt (who had replaced Addington in 1804) in January 1806. Worn out by the anxieties of the war, he had lived to hear the news of Nelson's victory at Trafalgar, before succumbing under the crushing blows of Ulm and Austerlitz, which left Napoleon as invincible on land as Britain was at sea. In this embattled situation, George III had been forced to accept a widely based administration – the Ministry of All the Talents – bringing Fox and the Whigs back into office. Lord Moira, as Master General of the Ordnance, and a Privy Counsellor, was now a senior member of the government. Moore's hopes rose high. 'Lord Moira has everything in his power,' he wrote in great excitement to his mother, 'and my fate now depends on his sincerity which I think it profanation to doubt.'[21]

Alas, Lord Moira had heavy demands on his patronage – principally from the Prince of Wales's friends – and his promises were vague and inconclusive. Moore was still in a 'bewilderment of hope and fear and anxiety' when he fell dangerously ill, from an abscess or tumour (probably caused by an ulceration of the large intestine), which formed in his right side. If the tumour had discharged inwardly it would almost certainly have caused his death by peritonitis; the surgeon's decision to apply caustic to the abscess, causing it to break outwardly, may well have saved his life. But the operation and its aftermath were painful and debilitating, leaving him bedridden for the best part of two months. It was mid-May before he was able to take a brief walk outside the house, still weak but rejoicing at his return to health. 'I have been basking about the streets in great happiness,' he wrote to his uncle Joyce Codd; 'everything looked so new and bright to me – the coaches all made of gold and the women of silver; besides, every one was so glad to see me, and I saw one poor man who had been as ill as myself, and we met like two newly raised bodies on the day of resurrection...If my side keeps well and the sun keeps shining, I have some very, very happy weeks before me.'[22]

There seemed every reason to be cheerful. Although Lord Moira had not yet found him a suitable appointment, he had used his position as Master General of the Ordnance to find a post for Moore's father as Barrack Master of Island Bridge in Dublin. It was a welcome consolation prize, for the grocery business in Aungier Street had suffered badly in the economic recession following the Act of Union; and there were still hopes of better things – an Irish Commissionership perhaps – for Moore himself. Meanwhile, his poems, with their dedication to Moira, were selling well and the Prince of Wales had complimented him on them personally. But the main reviews, in particular that in the formidable and recently founded *Edinburgh Review*, were yet to come. By the beginning of July, Moore was ready to make his long-deferred trip to Ireland, spending a few days with Lady Donegal and her sister in Worthing beforehand. The notice of his poems would appear in the *Edinburgh Review* that month; he planned to stay in London till he had seen it. 'I await but the arrival of the *Edinburgh Review*,' he wrote forebodingly to Mary Godfrey, 'and then "a long farewell to all my greatness".'[23]

7

The Interrupted Duel

The *Edinburgh Review* had been founded in Scotland by three brilliant young men, Sydney Smith, Henry Brougham and Francis Jeffrey, two of whom – Smith and Jeffrey – would become close friends of Moore's in later years. Its politics were broadly Whig, reflected in the buff and blue (Fox's colours) of its cover; its literary opinions, for which Jeffrey was chiefly responsible, tended to be conservative and conventional. First published in October 1802, and appearing quarterly thereafter, it rapidly acquired an enormous influence, both as a force for political reform and a forum for serious literary discussion. Most literary criticism till then had been little more than hackwork; the *Edinburgh Review*'s opinions, however one might disagree with them, were always vigorous, lively and well argued. Moore had already received some glancing blows in the third issue of the *Edinburgh Review* in 1803, with a review of a new edition of *Anacreon*: 'A style so wantonly voluptuous is at once effiminate and childish; and it is as unlike the original, as it is unmanly in itself.' But the paper was too newly founded, *Anacreon*'s success too well established, and he himself too busy preparing his voyage to Bermuda to pay attention to it. By 1806 the *Edinburgh Review* was a power in the land, while his new volume, the first in which he showed himself without disguises, was still untried.

In the event, he had left London before seeing the July number, and was staying with Lady Donegal in Worthing when it arrived. War was declared from the first paragraph:

A singular sweetness and melody of versification... with some brilliancy of fancy, and some show of classical erudition, might have raised Mr Moore to an innocent distinction among the song-writers and occasional poets of his day. But he is indebted, we fear, for the celebrity he actually enjoys to accomplishments of a different description; and may boast, if the boast can please him, of being the most licentious of modern versifiers, and the most poetical of those who, in our times, have devoted their talents to the propagation of immorality.

Moore's main intention, the reviewer claimed, was to corrupt the purity of innocent – especially female – hearts:

We can scarcely conceive of any being more truly despicable than he who, without the apology of unruly passion or tumultuous desires, sits down to ransack the impure places of his memory for inflammatory images and expressions, and commits them laboriously to writing, for the purpose of insinuating pollution into the minds of unknown and unsuspecting readers... He takes care to intimate to us, in every page, that the raptures which he celebrates do not spring from the excesses of a innocent love, or the extravagance of a romantic attachment; but are the unhallowed fruits of cheap and vulgar prostitution, the inspiration of casual amours, and the chorus of habitual debauchery.

It was not only unsuspecting females but the middle classes who were at risk. Moore's poems had been dedicated to persons of the highest rank and influence in the country, whom he seemed to consider his intimate friends: 'If the head be once affected, the corruption will spread irresistibly through the whole body.' Since the morals of the early nineteenth-century aristocracy, particularly in the circles surrounding the Prince of Wales, were already notoriously free and easy, it seems hard that Moore should be held responsible for them; but the reviewer had the bit between his teeth: 'We have been induced to enter this strong protest,' he wrote,

and to express ourselves thus warmly against this and former publications of this author...from our conviction that they are calculated, if not strongly denounced to the public, to produce at this moment, peculiar and irredeemable mischief. The style of composition, as we have already hinted, is almost new in this country; it is less offensive than the old fashion of obscenity; and for these reasons, is perhaps less likely to excite the suspicion of the modest, or to become the object of precaution to those who watch over the morals of the young and inexperienced.

It was for the sins of Little, as much as for his current volume, that Moore was really paying. The love poems, in any case, were only one element in the collection; the political epistles and poems relating to his travels were equally important. The reviewer dealt with these more mildly, even finding 'occasional point and vivacity' in the political epistles. But it did not prevent him from returning to the attack in his last paragraph. 'Whatever may be thought of the poetry or the politics of these passages, they are at least innocent in point of morality. But they bear but a small proportion to the objectionable contents of the volume, and cannot be allowed to atone for the demerits of a publication which we would wish to see consigned to universal reprobation.'

Moore's first reaction to the article was to make light of it, though its contemptuous tone, he admitted 'a good deal roused my Irish blood'.[1] The review had been unsigned, but it was no secret that the author was Francis Jeffrey; even had he wished to challenge him to a duel, however, he had not the money to travel to Edinburgh to do so. There the matter might have rested, had he not returned to London (having postponed his journey to Ireland for a few weeks) to learn from Samuel Rogers that Jeffrey was in London for a brief visit. Rogers had met him the day before, he told Moore, at dinner with a friend, Lord Fincastle; in the course of the evening the conversation had turned to Moore, whom Lord Fincastle described as 'possessing great amenity of manners'. 'I am afraid he would not show much amenity to *me*,'[2] said Jeffrey laughingly.

By now it was probably clear to Moore how damaging and much discussed the *Edinburgh Review*'s attack had been. The chance to challenge Jeffrey was too good to miss, his motives as he later confessed being not unmixed with vanity and a 'certain *Irish* predilection for such encounters'.[3] He wrote first to his friend Stephen Woolriche, his doctor during his illness, to ask him to act as his second in the duel; as a surgeon he would be well fitted for the role. But Woolriche was too cautious to do so at short notice, and Moore, whose blood was now up, wrote to Thomas Hume (also a medical man) to ask him to act for him instead.

Hume readily agreed to do so, and Moore, having secured his second, lost no time in drawing up his challenge. Jeffrey, as a reviewer, was entitled if he wished to cover Moore's poems with scorn, but he had no right to accuse him, as he had done, of a deliberate intention to corrupt his readers' minds. It was on this ground that Moore sent his challenge. 'You are a liar; yes, sir, a liar; and I choose to adopt this harsh and vulgar mode of defiance, in order to prevent at once all equivocation between us, and to compel you to adopt for your own satisfaction, that alternative you might otherwise have hesitated in affording to mine.'[4]

Jeffrey, as Moore had intended, could only give one answer to his challenge. Appointing his fellow reviewer Francis Horner as his second he arranged to meet Moore the next morning at Chalk Farm, 'a place as famous for duels as Parnassus is for poets,' according to the London *Star*. Moore spent the night with Thomas Hume, in order to arouse no suspicion, but could not resist a farewell letter to his friend Lord Strangford.

> The cloth has been but just taken from the table, and though tomorrow may be my last view of the bright sun, I shall (as soon as I have finished this letter) drink to the health of my Strangford with as unaffected a warmth as ever I felt in the wildest days of our fellowship. My dear friend, if they want a biographer when I am gone, I think in your hands I should meet with a most kind embalment, so pray say something for me, and remember me as one who has felt your good and social qualities...and who hopes that his good genius tomorrow will allow him to renew them hereafter. So goodbye and God bless you.[5]

As neither Moore nor Jeffrey had pistols, Moore had borrowed a pair from William Spencer – apart from shooting rooks at Donington he had never used a firearm in his life. The next morning he and Hume set out in a chaise for Chalk Farm. Jeffrey and his second were already there when they arrived, Horner 'looking anxiously around him', Jeffrey, a diminutive figure, scarcely taller than Moore, carrying the case of pistols in his hand. Having agreed that the spot was as good a place as any for their purposes, Horner and Hume retired behind some trees to load the pistols, leaving Jeffrey and Moore alone together. The two men, of course, had bowed on seeing one another, and now fell into conversation. 'What a beautiful morning it is!' were Jeffrey's first words; 'Yes', replied Moore, with a slight smile, 'a morning made for better purposes', to which Jeffrey responded with an assenting sigh. As they strolled up and down, they caught sight of the two seconds who were making rather heavy weather of the loading. This prompted Moore to tell the story of an Irish barrister on a similar occasion, who was sauntering about while the pistols were being loaded, and was angrily told by his opponent to hold his ground. 'Don't make yourself unaisy, my dear fellow,' said the barrister, 'sure isn't it bad enough to take the dose, without being by at the mixing of it?'[6]

Jeffrey had barely time to smile at this story, when their two friends, issuing from behind the trees, placed them at their respective posts – having previously measured the distance between them – and put their pistols into their hands. They then retired to a little distance; the pistols were raised; and the two men were only waiting for the signal, when some police officers, whom nobody had seen approach, rushed out from behind the hedge behind Jeffrey. One of them, striking Jeffrey's pistol with his stick, knocked it some distance into the field, while another ran over to Moore to take his from him. The would-be duellists were then bundled into their respective carriages, and taken off to Bow Street.

What had happened was that Moore's friend William Spencer, though sworn to secrecy, had talked freely of the duel at dinner with Lord Fincastle, the previous day. Fincastle, without Spencer's knowledge, had immediately informed Bow Street what was intended; too many duels had ended tragically for him to turn a blind eye to the matter. Moore, not unnaturally, was furious at this humiliating check – 'I had rather have lost a limb,'[7] he told Lady Donegal – but Fincastle's intervention may well have saved his or Jeffrey's life. Fortunately, any later talk of transferring the affair abroad was scotched by the peace-making Samuel Rogers, who consulted General Fitzpatrick, a expert on such affairs. Fitzpatrick pronounced the opinion that Jeffrey was not honour bound to accept a second challenge, and the matter went no further.

Meanwhile, however, the protagonists were shut up in Bow Street till their bail could be secured, and having expressed no objection to being put in the same room, soon fell into conversation. Jeffrey, lying on his back on a bench, which stood beside the wall, discoursed fluently and in a strong Scots accent on various literary topics, Moore, less given to such discussions, joining in more tentatively. Jeffrey later confessed that he had taken an instant fancy to Moore, when they first met at Chalk Farm. 'I can truly say,' wrote Moore, 'that my liking for him is of the same early date.'[8] They were already on the best of terms when Hume, Samuel Rogers, and a friend of Jeffrey's arrived to arrange their bail, and Samuel Rogers completed the process a few days later by bringing them together at one of his breakfasts in St James's Street. Here Jeffrey apologised for the intemperance of his review, which both he and his colleagues on the *Edinburgh Review* acknowledged contained 'too much that was exceptionable'. He followed it up with a written apology, which concluded, 'I shall always hold myself bound to bear testimony to the fairness and spirit with which you have conducted yourself throughout this transaction.'[9]

On a personal level all was satisfactory; Moore and Jeffrey became lifelong friends. But on a public level the episode did Moore lasting damage. Unluckily for him the police, on examining the pistols, had found that only Moore's was loaded, perhaps because the bullet in Jeffrey's had somehow been dislodged when the policeman knocked it out of his hand. Horner came to his rescue by insisting that he himself had been present when Hume loaded Jeffrey's pistol. The police suspicions of Moore were removed, but in their report, given to one of the evening papers, they stated correctly that 'in the pistol of one of the parties a bullet was found, and nothing at all in the pistol of the other'. A wag on the paper changed the word 'bullet' to 'pellet', and the report was passed on to all the other papers in its altered state. The press had a field day with the story, turning the affair to ridicule in a variety of ways. The *Times*, for instance, reported: 'The pistol of Mr Jeffries [sic] was not loaded with ball, and that of Mr Moore had nothing more than a pellet of paper. So that if the police had not appeared, this alarming duel would have turned out to be a game at pop-guns.' The *Star* made fun of the seconds, and their difficulties in measuring the right distance between the antagonists, 'whether it should be a *hexameter* or a *pentameter*, of dactyls or spondees'. The *Morning Post* devoted eighty-eight lines to a doggerel poem entitled 'The Paper Pellet Duel', which ended with the quatrain,

> And God preserve all writing blades,
> Who fain would cut a caper;
> Yet nothing at each other's heads,
> But pellets shoot of paper.

It was in vain that the *Times* issued a retraction the next day, admitting that the pistols had been properly loaded. The harm was done, and Moore's mortification was increased when Hume, taking fright at the publicity surrounding the affair, refused to sign a public statement in which Moore gave the true facts. The statement was published in the *Morning Post* the following week, but its impact was weakened by the fact that it lacked corroboration from his second. Moore very seldom lost a friend, but the coolness between himself and Hume after this act of betrayal lasted over twenty years.

Still worse than the ridicule attached to the duel was the knock-on effect of the hostile notice in the *Edinburgh Review*. Other papers followed suit, and Moore, till then so feted and admired, was subjected to a stream of hostile criticism. He was generally agreed to be licentious, a corrupter of public morals; the *Beau Monde* accused him of prostituting his genius; the *Critical Review* hinted darkly that he was trying to initiate youth into 'most impure mysteries'; the *British Critic* announced sanctimoniously that it would not add to the evil it engendered by deigning to review his volume. Poor Moore was crushed by the weight of so much disapproval; he could not challenge every editor who attacked him, and though his friends like Lady Donegal and Lord Moira did their best to console him, his cheerful spirits were at their lowest ebb.

The poems in the long term sold extremely well; by 1817 they had reached their fifteenth edition, and the 'Canadian Boat Song', set to music, had become one of his most popular pieces. In the autumn of 1806, however, there was nothing to be done but to flee to Ireland till the hue and cry died down.

'Well,' wrote Mary Godfrey on 2 October,

and how are you after your seasickness, and how do you feel yourself in Dublin after your brilliant career among the learned and the dissipated? If it were not for the extreme joy which I know you feel at being with your family again, I should grieve for the change; but you have contrived, God knows how! amidst the pleasures of the world, to preserve all your home, fireside, affections true and genuine as you brought them out with you and this is a trait in your character that I think beyond all praise.[10]

It was a sympathetic comment and Moore's delight at being re-united with his family was genuine. But there was little else to cheer him. His father's business was in a parlous state, and he was soon writing to Lord Moira to see if a house could be provided to go with his post as Barrack Master, as he could no longer afford to stay on in Aungier Street. (It seems that Lord Moira obliged over this, Moore's parents moving to a house in Abbey Street soon after.) Meanwhile, Moore himself was struck down with a threatened recurrence of his old illness – a week in bed and an army of leeches to draw the blood from the suspected abscess were needed to deal with the problem. Dublin, once so lively, had lost much of its sparkle, or perhaps his years in London in the cream of Whig society had spoiled him for its slower pace. 'You cannot imagine how desperately dull and vulgar this place has become,' he complained rather pettishly to Mary Godfrey, adding that if it were not for his family, and hours spent in St Patrick's Library, he would 'die the death of the desperate here'. In fact he was made much of by local grandees, among them the new Provost of Trinity College, 'who as being the depository of the morals of the country…gave me more pleasure by his visit than any of them'.[11] But the parties he attended were 'all winter *sunshine, dazzling* but cold';[12] Lord Moira's promise of an Irish commissionership had not materialised; and his literary confidence, after his recent setbacks and humiliations, was at rock bottom.

In this mood of dejection his thoughts turned naturally to the wrongs and troubles of his country, his nationalist feelings revived by tragic memories of Robert Emmet, and the indignation aroused by the 'pride, self interest and…fatal insufficiency'[13] of those in charge of Ireland's destiny. His poem in memory of Emmet – 'Oh! Breathe not his name' – was written during this period, and it was at this time too that the idea of his *Irish Melodies* began to take shape. We hear the first mention of them in a letter to Sir John Stevenson, obviously the result of discussions in Dublin, written shortly after his return to England in February 1807:

I feel very anxious that a work of this kind should be undertaken. We have for too long neglected the only talent for which our English neighbour ever deigned to give us any credit. Our National Music has never been properly collected; and while the composers of the Continent have enriched their operas and sonatas with melodies borrowed from Ireland – very often without the honesty of acknowledgement – we have left these treasures to a great degree unclaimed and fugitive…

The task which you propose to me, of adapting words to these airs is by no means simple. The poet, who would follow the various sentiments which they express, must feel and understand that rapid fluctuation of spirits, that unaccountable mixture of gloom and levity, which composes the character of my countrymen, and has deeply tinged their music… Another difficulty (which is, however, purely mechanical) arises from the irregular structure of many of these airs, and the lawless kind of metre which it will in consequence be necessary to adapt to them. In

these instances the poet must write not to the eye but to the ear...
However, notwithstanding all these difficulties, and the very little talent
which I can bring to them, the design appears to me so truly national,
that I shall have pleasure in giving it all the assistance in my power.[14]

It was to this task that Moore would now devote himself.

8

The *Irish Melodies*

Although Moore had been disappointed by Lord Moira, it was to Donington that he betook himself on his return to England. His host was very willing to give him the run of the house and the library, though as Moore complained rather ungratefully, '*Il me donne les manchettes et je n ai point de chemise.*'[1] But he was determined to stay away from the temptations and expenses of London social life, and to work on his *Irish Melodies* undisturbed.

The collaboration with Sir John Stevenson had been suggested while he was in Dublin by two young music publishers, James and William Power, who had been inspired by the success of recent collections of traditional Scottish songs, many of them adapted by Robert Burns, to try to do the same for Ireland. Much of the work of collecting Irish airs had already been done by John Bunting and these, arranged by Stevenson, would be the basis of many of the *Irish Melodies*. There is no place here to deal with the criticisms of those who claimed that Stevenson's arrangements were too elaborate for their simple themes; or that Moore sometimes altered the mood or tempo of Bunting's tunes. The *Irish Melodies* made their own rules, and would go round the world undeterred by the objections of specialists and scholars.

For most of 1807 the *Irish Melodies* were Moore's chief occupation, at first in Donington and later back in Dublin. His hopes of advancement under Lord Moira had been given a decisive blow when in March that year the Ministry of All the Talents fell. To their credit the issue had been that of Catholic relief, a minor measure, which would have enabled Catholics to hold higher ranks in the armed forces, but which was blocked by the irrational opposition of the King. Grenville, the Prime Minister, was replaced by the Duke of Portland, and Moira, who had refused to serve under Portland because of his support for the Act of Union, retired from office. Spurred by these events, Moore told Lady Donegal, he had given up writing love verses: 'I begin to find out that *politics* is the only thing minded in this country, and that it is better even to *rebel* against government, than have nothing at all to do with it; so I am writing politics.'[2]

The result of his resolution were two political satires, *Corruption* and *Intolerance*, in which, anticipating the possibility of further unrest in Ireland, he deplored the religious bigotry that bedevilled Irish politics and sounded the call for reform before it was too late. It was all very well, he wrote in *Corruption*, for the English to boast of the freedoms conferred by the Glorious Revolution of 1688. In Ireland,

> ... the bright light of England's fame is known
> But by the baleful shadow she has thrown
> On all our fate – where doom'd to wrongs and slights,
> We hear you talk of Britain's glorious rights
> As wretched slaves, that under hatches lie,
> Hear those on deck extol the sun and sky.

It seems as though, having given up hope of patronage under the English system, he felt he had nothing to lose by attacking it. The two poems, which were published anonymously by Carpenter the following year, made little stir, perhaps because the author was anonymous. *Intolerance* had only one edition, *Corruption* two. But by the time they came out the first two numbers of the *Irish Melodies* – each containing twelve songs – had appeared simultaneously in London and Dublin, putting Ireland's case more eloquently, and more movingly, than any satires could have done.

From the moment they first appeared the *Irish Melodies* were a huge success. To examine the first volume, writes Moore's 1930s biographer Howard Mumford Jones, is to catch a glimpse of the reasons: a tall thin folio almost fifteen inches high, bound so as to open for the pianofortes of the day, a border of shamrocks and willows running around the grey green cover, a woodcut of the Muse of Ireland, her right hand negligently resting on a Celtic harp – 'what a world of artifice and sincerity, of rococo grace and innocent simplicity arises as one picks up the book!'[3] Inside it was dedicated, amidst a flourish of decorative scrollwork, to 'the Nobility and

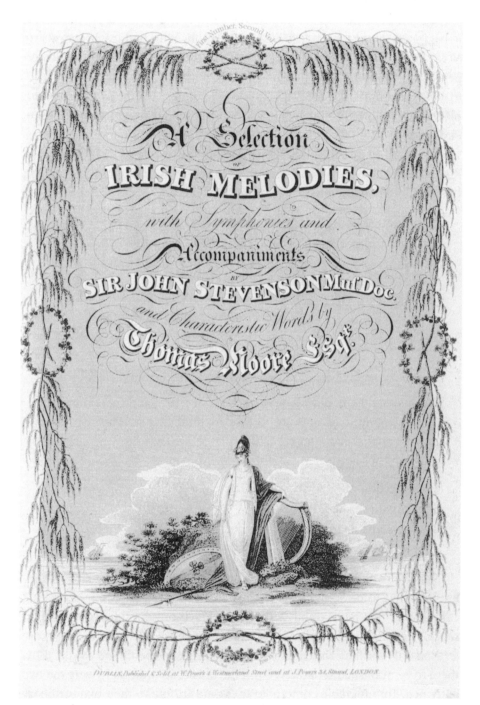

First Number of Moore's *Irish Melodies*, 1808.

Gentry of Ireland': though the *Irish Melodies* would penetrate the humblest cottages in both the old world and the new, composer and poet believed in beginning at the top. Indeed, as Moore wrote in his preface, his hope was to reach the 'pianofortes of the rich and educated', whose influence would be the most helpful in furthering Ireland's cause.

The first number of the *Melodies* gave the pattern for the rest; four piano pieces first, followed by twelve songs, their traditional airs chosen by Moore, and arranged for the piano by Stevenson. Already the nationalistic note was sounded with songs like 'Oh! Breathe not his name' and 'The Harp that once through Tara's Halls', setting the mood of nostalgia and yearning that would be characteristic of so many of them:

> The harp that once through Tara's halls
> The soul of music shed,
> Now hangs as mute on Tara's walls
> As if that soul were fled.
> So sleeps the pride of former days,
> So glory's thrill is o'er
> And hearts, that once beat high for praise,
> Now feel that pulse no more.
>
> No more to chiefs and ladies bright
> The harp of Tara swells;
> The chord alone, that breaks at night,
> Its tale of ruin tells.
> Thus Freedom now so seldom wakes,
> The only throb she gives
> Is when some heart indignant breaks,
> To show that she still lives.

Music had always been the inspiration for the *Irish Melodies*, and 'as they are intended to be sung rather than read,' wrote Moore in his preface, 'I can answer for their sound with somewhat more confidence than their sense.'[4] Inevitably his lyrics are simpler and more immediate than those written only for the printed page; it was a long time before he would allow them to be published separately from the music, so intimately were the two entwined. Innumerable contemporaries paid tribute to their extraordinary effect when sung, above all by the poet himself. Sydney Smith, the clerical wit, expressed his enthusiasm in characteristically boisterous terms. 'By the Beard of the prelate of Canterbury, by the Cassock of the prelate of York, by the breakfasts of Rogers...I swear I would rather hear you sing than any other person, male or female. For what is your singing but beautiful poetry floating in fine music, and guided by exquisite feeling?'[5]

Beautiful poetry indeed. At their best the lyrics to Moore's songs are his finest achievement, their verbal music arising naturally – but with what subtlety and art – from the melodies to which he matched them. Belonging to the first stage of the romantic movement, their mood of smiling melancholy and their haunting evocation of a mythic past were his most important contributions to it. And at a time when Ireland's national pride was at its lowest ebb, they revived the vision of lost glories and the possibility of a nobler future – later when nationalism became a sterner, more hard-edged force, they would be dismissed as too conciliatory and too sweet. But not until Yeats, almost a century later, would Irish poetry find a world wide audience again.

For composers across Europe Moore's special blend of poetry and music was a source of inspiration. Berlioz's settings of Moore's songs in translation, '*Neuf Melodies*', gave a new word '*mélodie*' (as opposed to '*chanson*' for lighter or cabaret songs) to French musical terminology. Other composers of the romantic movement who arranged, or re-set, the *Melodies* included Beethoven, Weber, Mendelssohn and Schumann, who also based his choral composition, *Das Paradies und die Peri*, on *Lalla Rookh*. In the twentieth century, Benjamin Britten's arrangements of ten *Melodies* by Moore gave a fresh dimension to some of his most familiar tunes. To take only one example, in Britten's hands 'The Minstrel Boy', martial and bracing in the original, becomes a mini requiem, a reminder of the many children who died in the wars of the past. 'The melodic line,' writes the accompanist Graham Johnson, 'has decisive manly chords throughout, but the piano writing, with its chords on the weaker beats of the bar suggests uncertainty, youth, vulnerable tenderness.'[6]

The second volume of Moore's *Melodies* appeared six months after the first. It included the haunting song of Fionnuala, the swan princess of Irish legend, its liquid vowel sounds and murmuring alliterations matched perfectly to its melancholy tune,

Silent, oh Moyle! be the roar of thy water,
Break not, ye breezes! your chain of repose,

While, murmuring mournfully, Lir's lonely daughter
Tells to the night-star her tale of woes.
When shall the Swan, her death-note singing,
Sleep with wings in darkness furl'd?
When will Heaven, its sweet bell ringing,
Call my spirit from the weary world...

Ending the volume was one of the best loved of all the *Melodies*, sentimental perhaps but as irresistible now as then.

Believe me, if all those endearing young charms
Which I gaze on so fondly today,
Were to change by tomorrow, and fleet in my arms,
Like fairy-gifts fading away, –
Thou wouldst still be ador'd as this moment thou art,
Let thy loveliness fade as it will;
And around the dear ruin each wish of my heart
Would entwine itself verdantly still.

It is not while beauty and youth are thine own,
And thy cheeks unprofan'd by a tear,
That the fervour and faith of a soul can be known,
To which time will but make thee more dear;
No the heart that has truly lov'd never forgets,
But as truly loves on to the close,
As the sun-flower turns on her god, when he sets,
The same look which she turn'd when he rose.

To Berlioz, a passionate admirer of Moore's poetry, this tribute to love's enduring power expressed a truth of which 'Balzac, nay even Shakespeare, the great painter of the passions', never dreamed. 'Only one poet, Thomas Moore, believed that it was possible,' he wrote, 'and described that rare feeling in these exquisite lines.'[7] On a less exalted level, we read of a supper party in *Bleak House* where Inspector Bucket gives a rendering of the song. This ballad, he tells his hostess, Mrs Bagnet, 'he considers to have been his most powerful ally in moving the heart of Mrs Bucket when a maiden, and inducing her to approach the altar – Mr Bucket's own words are, to come up to the scratch'. Dickens loved Moore, whose works are quoted more often than any other poet's in his novels.

From 1808 to 1834 the *Irish Melodies* punctuate Moore's career, their fame and popularity spreading with each successive edition; they will find their place in the narrative as each new volume appears. Meanwhile, there is something of a mystery about Moore's movements between 1807 and 1809. In June 1807, he writes to his mother from Donington Park where he insists that he is thriving in his solitude. Thereafter there are no more letters till April 1808 when in a letter to Lady Donegal, presumably also from Donington Park, he writes that he is too poor to come to London that summer. As usual he seems to have been short-changed by his publishers: Carpenter, despite having published *Corruption* and *Intolerance*, refused to finance a trip to London to publicise them; he had only received £50 from the Power brothers for the first volume of the *Irish Melodies*. 'I quite threw away the Melodies,' he told his mother ruefully, 'they will make that little smooth fellow's fortune.'[8] Later the situation would be righted; from 1811 onward he would receive £500 a year as a retainer – an arrangement based on the understanding that he would do his best to popularise them in society.

There was no question of society that summer. By early October 1808 he was back in Ireland and apart from a letter to Dalby asking for help about some lost luggage – Moore was always hopelessly disorganised about practical arrangements – and another to his old friend Captain Douglas, recently returned to London – we hear no more from him till December 1809. This time the occasion is a sad one. His mother's brother, Joyce Codd, little older than Moore himself, had died and he was writing to console her. Moore had always loved his uncle, with whom he had shared a room as a child, and it had been thanks to a loan from him that he had been able to set out for Bermuda. In a letter to Lady Donegal soon after, he described the effect – a kind of slow release of sorrow – that the loss had had upon him:

> I am so hourly prepared for these inroads on our social happiness that the death of even the healthiest friend about me could scarcely, I think, take my heart by surprise; and the effect which such calamities are likely to have upon me will be seen more in the whole tenor of my life afterwards, than in any violent or deep-felt grief of the moment: every succeeding loss will insensibly sink the level of my spirits, and give a darker and darker tinge to all my future hopes and feelings.

'I am not doing much', he wrote in the same letter, 'indeed the downright necessity I feel of doing something is one of the great reasons why I do nothing. These things come of their own accord, and I hate to make a *conscript* of my Muse.'[9]

It would be a mistake, however, to take Moore's saddened or discouraged tone as typical of his state of mind. Though the *Melodies*, comprising only twenty-four songs, had not received much coverage in the press they had made their way by word of mouth and were already enormously popular. Moore would certainly have sung them at Dublin gatherings, and when there was company at Donington – for most of this period he divided his time between the two places. But he would also have given them an airing while acting in a series of amateur theatricals taking place in the Kilkenny Theatre in 1808 and 1809, and it is through press reports of these occasions that we get some further clues to his activities.

Amateur theatricals had long been a passion among the Irish upper classes – it was at Lady Borrowes' private theatre in Dublin, we will remember, that the fourteen-year-old Moore had given his first performance. The Kilkenny Theatre had first been opened on a professional basis by Robert Owenson, the actor-manager father of Sydney Owenson (later Lady Morgan), whose novel *The Wild Irish Girl*, published in 1807, had made her a celebrity. Owenson senior had soon gone bankrupt and the theatre had fallen into disuse till it was revived in 1802 by a local landowner, Richard Power, who assembled his own private company for a yearly festival each autumn. The actors were drawn from the neighbouring gentry, the leading actresses usually coming from the professional Dublin stage. Moore's introduction to the company in 1808 was probably through his old friend Joseph Atkinson, who had written the prologue for the festival. He arrived there in early October, making his début as David in *The Rivals* on 21 October, when according to the *Leinster Journal*, he 'kept the audience in a roar by his Yorkshire dialect and comic simplicity'.[10] He soon moved on to other comic parts; there is little doubt that, had he wished it, he could have had a successful career on the stage.

A partial silence falls once more after the Kilkenny season. A trio of letters from Lady Donegal and her sister, reproaching him for failing to write, and another two from Rogers, are all we learn of him till October 1809 when he is once more at Kilkenny. But the intervening year had not been idle. He had published another satirical poem, *The Sceptic*, that summer, once more pointing out the hypocrisy of English attitudes to Ireland.

Whole nations, fooled by falsehood, fear or pride,

Their ostrich-heads in self illusion hide;

Thus England, hot from Denmark's smoking meads,

Turns up her eyes at Gallia's guilty deeds;

Thus selfish still, the same dishonouring chain

She binds in Ireland, she would break in Spain;

While praised at distance, but at home forbid,

Rebels in Cork are patriots in Madrid!

To set the lines in context, it is worth remembering that Nelson had destroyed the neutral Danish fleet in Copenhagen eight years earlier, and that the Spanish freedom fighters, or guerrillas, were honoured allies of the British in the war against the French in Spain.

But Moore, the serious political commentator, was never without his lighter side, and we glimpse him in more frivolous mode in his second theatrical season where, according to the *Leinster Journal* once more, 'the delight and darling of the Kilkenny audience appears to be *Anacreon Moore*... He speaks and moves, in a way that indicates genius at every turn.' The *Irish Melodies* were already familiar to the audience, the actor playing Lorenzo in *The Merchant of Venice* going so far as to insert one in his role; 'he sang,' wrote the *Leinster Journal*, 'in a sweet and unaffected manner and was rapturously encored'.[11]

Moore opened the season in the role of Peeping Tom in Dibdin's comedy of that name; his Lady Godiva was a Miss Bessy Dyke, one of the youngest and prettiest of the actresses brought down from Dublin. It was the first occasion on which his name was linked with that of the girl, barely fifteen at the time, who eighteen months later would become his wife. Once again there is a tantalising lack of information on the intervening period, though years later, on a visit to Kilkenny in 1823, he recalled the first days of their courtship there, snug dinners with Bessy and her mother and sister in their lodgings, evening strolls along the river walk below the castle. 'Happy times! but not more happy than those which I owe to the same dear girl still.'[12]

9

A Married Man

As has already been stated we know very little of Moore's private life prior to his marriage, despite the racy reputation his supposedly licentious poems had brought him. Given the social system of the time, it is unlikely that he would have aspired to any of those aristocratic ladies in whose drawing rooms he had sung in happier times. How much did he look elsewhere? Were the Caras and Fannys of his poems real personages, perhaps drawn from the theatre or the demi-monde? According to an unnamed friend of Thomas Hume, Moore's habits were 'the most loose and disreputable' imaginable. The comment comes in an unfinished letter, now in the National Library in Dublin, to the Irish writer and antiquarian Thomas Crofton Croker. But by the time it was written both Moore and Hume were dead and Moore's account of his aborted duel – revealing, among other things, that he had brought his own sheets when he stayed with Hume the night before, knowing Hume would have no clean ones – had just been published in his memoirs. The accusation about the sheets, the writer declared indignantly, was 'ungentlemanly and false'; moreover, Hume had not even spent the night in the house, as he had been afraid to bring his beautiful young wife – 'naturally a coquette' – into proximity with Moore.

Such long past hearsay, especially in view of Moore's falling out with Hume, is little enough to go on. Crofton Croker, with whom Moore had been on good terms in his lifetime, would attack him in print after his death, and was willing enough to listen to disobliging gossip, and to pass it on as well. It is from Croker too that we get our only picture – not a very flattering one – of Bessy's family background.

'[The] father, old Dyke,' he wrote to his namesake, the Tory politician John Wilson Croker,

> gave me a few lessons in a Street off Patrick Street in Cork…He (Dyke) wandered about to teach dancing at the Schools in Fermoy…and Middleton, and became a great favourite by making puppet Shows for the boys…But I well remember he was a drunken fellow, who generally brought home with him a black eye or two from the weekly visits to Fermoy and Middleton, and I think my lessons in that or any piece of tuition under his instruction did not exceed half a dozen in consequence of some desperate affray in which a poker was used to the disadvantage of a very dirty wife.[1]

There were three Dyke sisters, of whom Bessy was the middle one, all of them trained up as dancers before transferring to the stage. Despite their unpromising beginnings all three did very well in life. The eldest, Mary Anne, married the Dublin actor John R. Duff, and found fame as an actress in America; the youngest, Anne, married the manager of the Theatre Royal, Edinburgh; Bessy, of course, became the wife of one of the best-known poets of the age. Although neither she nor her sisters can have had much formal education, the Theatre Royal, Dublin, to which all three belonged, provided an education in itself. As actresses, working in a fast changing repertory, they would have been exposed not only to Shakespeare but to a wide variety of distinguished playwrights, from Congreve to Sheridan, as well as to the more ephemeral writers of the day. Both Mary Anne and Anne became well known as Shakespearean actresses, though Bessy, only sixteen when she married, never progressed beyond minor roles.

We do not know what Moore's first intentions were. According to another, not very charitable witness, who apparently knew Bessy before Moore was acquainted with her, Moore 'wished to have her on other than conjugal terms – which however her sharp English mother prevented by forbidding his further visits until a formal proposal was made'.[2] We hear nothing more of her before their wedding, in March 1811, beyond a mention with her sisters, in a short-lived Irish journal, *The Satirist*: the Miss Dykes, it pronounced, were certainly pretty, but had 'an unconquerable propensity to coquetry'.

For Moore, 1810 was an eventful year, marked above all by two episodes, whose consequences, both bad and good, would enormously affect his future life. The first, seemingly trivial at the time, was the appointment of a new deputy, John William Goodrich, to the post of registrar to the Naval Court in Bermuda. His earlier deputies had been unsatisfactory. 'I gave them *half* the profits of the office & they took care not to send me the *other* half, so that I could hardly get into worse hands,'[3] he told John Wilson Croker, then Secretary to the Admiralty. After trying vainly to get rid of the position altogether, Moore signed the deed for his new deputy on 17 January 1810. By the terms of the deed Moore, as Principal Registrar, was liable for any misdemeanour by his agent, but the sums involved had always been so trifling that no security was given or demanded. The deed would prove to be a time bomb, which exploded 'like a thunderclap'[4] nine years later.

The other episode, this time entirely happy in its consequences, began on 1 January 1810, with a letter to Lord Byron challenging him to a duel. It had its origins in 1807, when Byron's third collection of poems, *Hours of Idleness*, had been savaged by Brougham in the *Edinburgh Review*. Stung and humiliated, he had taken his revenge in his long satirical poem, *English Bards and Scotch Reviewers*, published in March 1809. Few, whether poets or critics, were spared in his sweeping attack on the literary figures of the time, though compared to other victims of his satire, Moore got off relatively lightly: Byron describes him as

> ...Little! young Catullus of his day,
> As sweet but as immoral as his lay!

concluding somewhat disingenuously,

> Griev'd to condemn, the Muse must still be just
> Nor spare melodious advocates of lust...
> Yet, kind to youth, this expiation o'er
> She bids thee 'mend thy line and sin no more'.

For Moore, hypersensitive about accusations of immorality, these condescending lines were bad enough. What drove him to fury, however, were Byron's sneers about his duel with Jeffrey, in which (despite Moore's printed denial in the papers) the old story of the unloaded pistol was revived.

> Can none remember that eventful day,
> That ever glorious, almost fatal fray,

When Little's leadless pistol met his eye,
And Bow-street myrmidons stood laughing by?

The first edition of the poem had been published anonymously, giving Moore no chance to seek redress. The second, which appeared that summer, had Byron's name attached to it. In his Irish semi-exile, away from literary society, it was several months before Moore became aware of it. He reacted immediately with his challenge:

Having just seen the name of "Lord Byron" prefixed to a work entitled "English Bards and Scotch Reviewers", in which as it appears to me, the *lie is given* to a public statement of mine, respecting an affair with Mr Jeffrey some years since, I beg you will have the goodness to inform me whether I may consider your Lordship as the author of this publication.

I shall not, I fear, be able to return to London for a week or two; but in the mean time, I trust your Lordship will not deny me the satisfaction of knowing whether you avow the insult intended in the passages alluded to ...[5]

He transmitted this letter to a friend in London, asking him to have it delivered into Byron's hands. A week later he heard from his friend that Byron had left the country some months earlier; however, he had given Moore's letter to a friend of Byron's, Francis Hodgson, who had promised to forward it to him. This was not exactly what Moore had wished, but he decided, on the whole, that it would be best to let the letter take its chance, and postponed all further thoughts of the matter.

He soon had other things to think about. Catholic concerns, left in abeyance since the fall of the Ministry of All the Talents, had recently been revived with a proposal by the Whigs in opposition, that the customary practice whereby Irish Catholic bishops were appointed by the Pope should be modified to allow a veto of appointments by the Crown. The hope was that, by removing Tory fears of foreign influence, the way to Catholic emancipation could once more be opened; the King, of course, stood in the way, but since he was over seventy and in fragile health, he was unlikely to be an obstacle for long. It was a suggestion that had been accepted by the Irish bishops when the question of Catholic emancipation was first raised by Pitt before the Act of Union. In the interval, however, a new class of activists had arisen, drawn from the increasingly powerful and articulate

Catholic middle classes, who found their spokesman in Daniel O'Connell. Unshakeably opposed to the Union, he argued that any form of veto was a betrayal of Irish interests; his protests found a ready echo in Irish public opinion, and in 1808 the synod of Irish bishops voted overwhelmingly against it.

For Moore this decision, re-affirmed in March, 1810, seemed the height of sectarian folly. In a powerful pamphlet, entitled 'A Letter to the Roman Catholics of Dublin', he pointed out the inconsistency of the Irish hierarchy who, having accepted the idea of a veto in 1800, now rejected it. Almost every other European country accepted the separation of Church and state; Ireland itself had done so up till the Reformation. To lose the chance of Catholic emancipation by insisting on the right of the Pope to override the British government – thus confirming Protestant suspicions of Papal interference – was perverse and self-defeating: 'The bigots of both sects are equally detestable; but if I were compelled to choose between them, I should certainly prefer those who have the Constitution on their side.'

Moore's arguments reflected the conciliatory views of Grattan and the Whigs in opposition, who hoped to take the liberal Tories with them by the promise of the veto; for O'Connell the issue was one of Irish independence from British domination, and therefore not negotiable. Both men were alike in their total abhorrence of political violence – no constitutional change, O'Connell once declared, was worth the shedding of a single drop of blood – and in their long-term hopes for Ireland. But even at this early stage they differed on the means, Moore aligning himself with the Whigs in Parliament, O'Connell, a supreme political organiser, drawing his strength from popular support and gradually taking the lead in the campaign for Catholic emancipation.

It is not clear how much effect Moore's pamphlet had on public opinion, but it was warmly praised by Grattan, and other leading Whigs, among them Lord Lansdowne and Lord Holland, to whom it would serve as a recommendation when he returned to London the following year. For the rest of 1810, however, music and poetry were his chief concerns, first in a third volume of the *Irish Melodies*, where the songs included 'Oh! Blame not the Bard', and second in his so-called *Melalogue on National Music*, a combination of music and spoken declamation, performed at the Kilkenny Festival that autumn. 'We hardly ever heard a more beautiful composition, and never, perhaps, a more delightful piece of recitation,' enthused the *Leinster Journal*. 'Mr Moore's voice is to a degree musical, his accent pure,

his elocution articulate, and his manner simple, spirited and feeling.'
(Though the two other Dyke sisters were performing at the festival, Bessy's
name is not recorded in the playbills – perhaps she was there nonetheless
and the evening walks beside the river were resumed.)

Except for a visit to Donington Hall in the summer, Moore spent most
of 1810 in Dublin, his lodgings 'most romantically situated at the end of
Dirty Lane' and swept by the 'odiferous breezes of a tanyard'. But he was
eager to get back to London, where he had been commissioned to write an
operetta, and where the changing political situation – the King had been
declared insane in December 1810 – had once more raised his hopes of
patronage from a Whig administration. He must have been seeing Bessy all
this time, for in February 1811, when he returned to London, she followed
him there. On 25 March, with James Power and Anne Dyke as witnesses,
they were married at the church of St Martin's in the Fields.

No marriage could have been more impractical on paper. Moore was
thirty-one, Bessy was only sixteen. He was a Roman Catholic, she was a
Protestant; he was accustomed to move in the great world, she was
penniless and obscure. Perhaps not surprisingly, Moore did not tell his
parents of his marriage till two months later, afraid that they might resent
his choice of an actress with no fortune or connections. But no union could
have been happier, or a greater tribute to Moore's good judgement, and
Bessy's gifts of character and heart. 'From 1811, the year of his marriage,
to 1852, that of his death,' writes Lord John Russell in his introduction to
Moore's memoirs,

> this excellent and beautiful person received from him the homage of a
> lover, enhanced by all the gratitude, all the confidence, which the daily
> and hourly happiness he enjoyed were sure to inspire. Thus whatever
> amusement he might find in society, whatever sights he might behold,
> whatever literary resources he might seek elsewhere, he always returned
> to his home with a fresh feeling of delight. The time he had been absent
> had always been a time of exertion and exile; his return restored him to
> tranquillity and peace.

It was a pattern that Moore followed almost from the first. Bessy was
lovely enough to shine at any gathering – graceful, dark eyed, with delicate,
almost Grecian features and a profusion of soft brown curls. But she was
too timid and retiring to enjoy grand occasions, and had neither the

worldly background nor the wardrobe to do so. (Even Moore, with far simpler masculine requirements, was often hard put to afford the right clothes.) In private, and at smaller gatherings, Moore's friends were quick to appreciate her qualities. Samuel Rogers, who could never resist a pretty face, christened her Psyche; Lord Moira was full of kind attentions; Lady

Bessy Moore: drawing (date unknown) by Gilbert Stuart Newton from a notebook at Bowood.

Donegal and her sister became steadfast friends. But when it came to going out in the great world Moore sallied forth alone.

In part, of course, it was professionally necessary for him to circulate, to sing his songs, and to remain in touch with the Whig grandees, whose spokesman he was beginning to become. But parties were the breath of life to him, and after four years of exile and semi-disgrace, it was a joy to be in the swim once more. His *Irish Melodies* had eclipsed the memory of Little's indiscretions; in Leigh Hunt's poem 'The Feast of the Poets', published in his journal, *The Reflector*, he was welcomed back into the literary fold.

> There are very few poets, whose cap or whose curls,
>
> Have obtain'd such a laurel by hunting the girls.
>
> So it gives me, dear Tom, a delight beyond measure
>
> To find how you've mended your notions of pleasure.[6]

Appropriate sentiments to greet a newly married man, and Moore, delighted, wrote to thank him. It was the start of a friendship in which their shared Whig sympathies were an important element. Less than two years later Hunt would be sent to prison for a libel on the Prince Regent, and Moore, so recently a fervent admirer of the Prince, would add his own share of satire in a series of sarcastic verses.

What happened to cause this dramatic shift of attitude? Once again, Irish politics were at the back of Moore's thinking. In December 1810, when the King was officially declared insane, all the hopes of the Whigs had been focused on the Prince of Wales. But on becoming Regent he had changed his tune. During the first year of his Regency, when his powers were restricted by Parliament, and the King's recovery still a possibility, there had been good reasons not to change the existing government. The opposition, though disappointed, still expected to return to power when the year-long period of restriction ended. But in February 1812, to their surprise and fury, he confirmed the Tory government in office: they would remain in power for nearly twenty years. To some extent this had been due to the Prince's dislike of Grey and Grenville, the Whig leaders, but it was also because, when the moment came, he was not prepared to accept the Whigs' demand for Catholic emancipation. For Moore, who had been so flattered by his favour, it was the great betrayal, and with Lord Moira's exclusion from office, the end of his hopes of political preferment. From then on, he would align himself definitively with the Whig opposition, using his gifts as a political satirist to further their cause.

Even without the Prince Regent as its leader, Whig society, in the early decades of the nineteenth century, was a byword for its brilliance and self-confidence. It was the golden age of those great Whig families – 'they are all cousins,' someone once complained – who looked to the aristocratic liberalism of Charles James Fox as their ideal. Since Fox's death, in 1806, his mantle had fallen on his nephew, Lord Holland, and Holland House in Kensington had become the chief focus of Whig social and intellectual life. Lady Holland, clever, acerbic and demanding, was not received in the strictest circles because she had been divorced. Together with her husband, as benevolent as she was sharp tongued, she presided over a salon that was almost entirely masculine in character, but included some of the most enlightened spirits of the age. Introduced by Samuel Rogers and Lord Moira, Moore soon became a welcome visitor there, renewing his acquaintance with figures such as Sheridan (first met with the convivial Michael Kelly), Grey, Lord Lansdowne and the young William Lamb, and making new friends among the writers of the *Edinburgh Review*, Brougham, Sydney Smith and later Macaulay, who treated Holland House as their unofficial London headquarters.

The summer of 1811 found Moore putting the finishing touches to an operetta, *M.P. or the Blue Stocking*, which was to be performed at the Lyceum Theatre that September. He was nervous about its reception, having little confidence in his dramatic powers, and his thoughts were more cheerfully engaged with a new poetic project: a long narrative poem on an Eastern subject (the suggestion was that of Samuel Rogers) to be entitled *Lalla Rookh*. Supported by a wealth of oriental scholarship, the poem would take him six, often wearisome, years to write, though he began it eagerly, delighted to exchange the 'vile joke making' of his comedy for 'the maids of Cashmere, the sparkling springs of Rochabad, and the fragrant bouquets of the Peris.'[7]

The Blue Stocking was only a partial success; Moore himself had been in such a fever of worry about it that he did not attend its opening night. A routine story of mistaken identities and long-lost heirs, it ran for nineteen performances, and was well reviewed in the *Times* and *Morning Post*. But Leigh Hunt, writing in the *Examiner*, expressed his disappointment: to say that a play by Moore was 'more amusing that our farces in general' was to damn it; Moore ought to be far ahead of the general run. Moore privately agreed. 'I knew all along I was writing down to the mob,' he told Mary Godfrey, 'but that was what they told me I must do ... I have therefore made a final resolution never to let another line of mine be spoken upon the stage, as neither my talents nor my nerves are at all suited to it.'

In the midst of the agitation running up to his first night, Moore had received news that Byron had returned to England. His letter of challenge, written a year and a half before, was still outstanding, though now, in his newly married state – and with Bessy expecting a baby – he was no longer in a position to risk a duel. He must extricate himself as honourably as he could. Since Byron's mother had died at the beginning of August, he had to wait a decent interval before broaching the subject once again. It was not until 22 October that he wrote the difficult letter explaining his new situation: his continuing sense of injury at having been given 'the lie direct' over the duel, but the impossibility, in his present circumstances, of seeking the satisfaction he had previously demanded. He ended on a more conciliatory note, saying he would be happy to make Byron's acquaintance if a suitable explanation could be given, and suggesting Samuel Rogers as a go-between. It was an awkward composition – 'one hand presenting a pistol, and another held out to shake'[8] in Byron's words – but it was the start of the most important friendship in Moore's life.

I O

Meeting Byron

In October 1811, Byron was twenty-three, recently returned from two years of travel in Greece and the Levant. Although he had satirised Moore in his *English Bards and Scotch Reviewers*, he had been greatly influenced by his poetry, above all Little's erotic verses, which he had first read as a schoolboy. 'I have just been turning over Little, which I knew by heart in 1803, being then in my fifteenth summer,' he wrote to Moore years later. 'Heigho! I believe all the mischief I ever done, or sung, has been owing to that confounded book of yours.'[1] In 1809 he had sprung to Moore's defence in the second edition of his *Hours of Idleness*, soon after Moore's denunciation by Jeffrey in the *Edinburgh Review*:

> Poor LITTLE! sweet, melodious bard!
> Of late esteem'd it monstrous hard,
> That he, who sang before all;
> He who the lore of love expanded,
> By dire Reviewers should be branded,
> As void of wit and moral.
>
>
> And yet, while Beauty's praise is thine,
> Harmonious favourite of the nine!
> Repine not at thy lot;
> Thy soothing lays may still be read,

When Persecution's arm is dead,

And Critics are forgot.[2]

Now back in England, he was taken by surprise by Moore's letter. He had never received the original demand for satisfaction, since his friend Hodgson, suspecting a challenge, had deliberately withheld Moore's letter from him. He answered courteously but cautiously. He had known nothing, he wrote, of Moore's public statement about the duel, and had written his verses with no thought of giving him the lie. He could not retract or apologise for something he had never done, but was happy to extend an olive branch: 'Your friend Mr Rogers or any other gentleman delegated by you will find me most ready to adopt any conciliatory position which shall not compromise my own honour, – or failing in that, to make the atonement you deem it necessary to require.'[3]

'This,' wrote Moore in his *Life of Byron*, 'was all the explanation I had a right to expect and I was, of course, satisfied with it.'[4] Expansive perhaps from relief, he ended his answering letter with another tentative suggestion that they should meet: 'We Irishmen, in businesses of this kind, seldom know any medium between decided hostility and decided friendship; – but as any approaches towards the latter alternative must now depend entirely on your Lordship, I have only to repeat that I am satisfied with your letter, and that I have the honour to be, in perfect goodwill and sincere respect for your talents &c. &c.'[5]

Byron did not immediately take up the offer. 'Was I to anticipate friendship from one who conceived me to have charged him with falsehood?...' he asked rather sharply. 'I should have felt proud of your acquaintance, had it commenced under other circumstances; but it must rest with you to determine how far it may proceed after so *auspicious* a beginning.'[6]

Piqued by his answer, and angry at having put himself in an inferior position, Moore replied briefly and conclusively. 'You have made me feel the imprudence I was guilty of in wandering from the point immediately in discussion between us – I shall now, therefore, only say that, if in my last letter, I have correctly stated the substance of your Lordship's explanation, our correspondence may, from this moment, cease for ever.'[7]

It is worth looking twice at this reply, since so many of Byron's biographers have accused Moore of 'tuft hunting' in these exchanges. This was far from the case; Moore had aristocratic friends enough and to spare, and although Byron's *English Bards and Scots Reviewers* had achieved a certain notoriety, he was far less well known as a poet than Moore. If Byron had chosen to leave things there, Moore would not have given the matter a second thought. But Byron genuinely admired Moore and it was he who now stretched out a friendly hand. 'I felt, and still feel, very much flattered by those parts of your correspondence, which held out the prospect of our becoming acquainted', he wrote in reply. 'If I did not meet them, in the first instance, as perhaps I ought, let the situation in which I was placed be my defence. You have now declared yourself *satisfied*, and on that point we are no longer at issue. If, therefore, you still retain any wish to do me the honour you hinted at, I shall be most happy to meet you, when, where and how you please...'[8]

The way was now open to a meeting, with Samuel Rogers as the host. 'Mr Rogers (whom I never saw) has sent me an invitation to meet the Irish Melodist,'[9] wrote Byron to his friend John Cam Hobhouse, to whom he had described the whole imbroglio. The appointment was fixed for the evening of 3 November; the poet Thomas Campbell, who happened to call on Rogers that morning, made a fourth. It was Byron's first sortie into literary society, in which his three companions were already famous figures. Byron had long idolised Rogers; he and Campbell were almost the only poets who had escaped his satire in *English Bards and Scots Reviewers*. As for Moore, he admitted later, he had only fixed on the 'trite charge of immorality' because he could think of nothing else to say against him. 'I was angry – & determined to be witty – & fighting in a crowd dealt my blows against all alike without distinction or discernment.'[10]

By pre-arrangement with the others, Rogers met Byron alone in the drawing room when he arrived; the other two guests then returned and were introduced. Byron was still in mourning for his mother at that time and the colour, 'as well of his dress, as of his glossy, curling and picturesque hair,' wrote Moore, 'gave more effect to the pure, spiritual paleness of his features, in the expression of which when he spoke, there was a perpetual play of lively thought, though melancholy was their habitual character when in repose.'[11]

There was an initial awkwardness at dinner when Byron refused all the dishes he was offered, and asked for biscuits and soda water instead. (His pallor owed something to rigid dieting.) Unfortunately there were none available, but Byron professed himself equally happy with potatoes and vinegar, and 'of these meagre materials,' wrote Moore, 'contrived to make rather a hearty dinner'. But the rest of the evening was a great success, lasting late into the night, and with no further mention of the duel. As Rogers remarked to Byron later, Moore's challenge had been 'rather Irish'.

From the time of their first meeting, wrote Moore in his biography of Byron, 'there seldom elapsed a day that Lord Byron and I did not see each other; and our acquaintance ripened into an intimacy and friendship with a rapidity of which I have seldom known an example'.[12] It was an instant rapport on both sides. By 16 November Byron could write to Hobhouse: 'Moore and I are on the best of terms...Rogers is a most excellent and unassuming soul, and Moore an epitome of all that's delightful.'[13]

Eight years older than Byron, Moore would be something of a father confessor (the words are Byron's) to his friend. He was a good listener, as well as a sparkling talker, and, though a far less complex character than Byron, was gifted with great psychological insight. Byron never had to attitudinise to him. Their friendship, beginning when Moore was the more successful of the two, was never marred by jealousy. Moore was sincerely delighted by Byron's literary successes – 'I am...superstitiously fond of every line of his,'[14] he wrote – and Byron, in his turn, was always quick to encourage Moore, whose diffidence about his work was unexpected in one so successful and well known. Above all they enjoyed one another's company. Byron's air of melancholy and hauteur, as Moore was quick to realise, was partly temperamental, but also due to shyness. What the public did not see was Byron's love of gossip, conviviality and witty intellectual conversation. With Moore, and congenial spirits such as Rogers, he was at his best. The contrast to his proud reserve in general company was striking. 'It was like the bursting gaiety of a boy let loose from school, and seemed as if there was no end of fun or tricks of which he was not capable.'[15]

At the time they first met Byron was lonely and relatively friendless in London. His *English Bards and Scots Reviewers* had done him no good in fashionable Whig circles; Lord Holland, whom he had mistakenly regarded as the power behind the *Edinburgh Review*, was among those he had attacked. But great things were expected of a long new poem, *Childe Harold*, which was already going through the press with his publisher John Murray. Moore and Rogers were among the few who were allowed to see its pages in proof. 'It was in the hands of Mr Rogers I first saw the sheets of the poem,' wrote Moore, 'and glanced hastily over a few of the stanzas which he pointed out to me as beautiful. Having occasion, the same morning, to write a note to Lord Byron, I expressed strongly the admiration which this foretaste of his work had excited in me.'[16]

His letter found Byron in 'a state of ludicrous tribulation', caused by his discovery that one of his maid servants, Susan, of whom he had been 'foolishly fond', was carrying on behind his back. 'I feel very, very much obliged by your approbation,' he told Moore ruefully; 'but, *at this moment*, praise, even *your* praise, passes me by like "the idle wind". I meant and mean to send you a copy the moment of publication, but now I can think of nothing but damned deceitful – delightful woman, as Mr Liston says in the Knight of Snowdon.'[17]

All the same, as the moment of publication drew near, he was increasingly apprehensive about its reception, his nervousness augmented by a comment, kindly meant, that 'it was too good for the age'. 'Whoever may have pronounced this opinion – and I have some suspicion I am myself the guilty person,' wrote Moore, 'the age has, it must be owned, most triumphantly refuted it.'[18]

Childe Harold was published on 8 March 1812, and instantly took the world by storm. Its effect, wrote Moore, was electric: Byron's fame 'had not to wait for any of the ordinary gradations, but seemed to spring up, like the palace of a fairy tale, in the night. As he himself briefly described it in his memoranda, – I awoke one morning and found myself famous.'[19] Society flung open its doors to him, and for Moore, already accustomed to move in the same fashionable circles, it increased their opportunities of meeting. 'In that society where his birth entitled him to move, circumstances had already placed me notwithstanding mine,' he wrote; 'and when, after the appearance of "Childe Harold", he began to mingle with the world, the same persons who had long been my intimates and friends, became his; our visits were mostly to the same places, and, in the gay and giddy round of a London spring, we were generally (as in one of his own letters he expresses it) "embarked in the same Ship of Fools" together.'[20]

In the meantime, the fourth edition of Moore's *Irish Melodies* had appeared, published in London in November 1811, and in Dublin early the following year. They included such well-known songs as 'Love's Young Dream' and in a return to Irish sorrows, a lament for Sarah Curran, who had been engaged to Robert Emmet,

She is far from the land where her young hero sleeps,
And lovers around her are sighing;

But coldly she turns from their gaze, and weeps,
For her heart in his grave is lying...

He had lived for his love, for his country he died,
They were all that to life had entwined him;
Nor soon shall the tears of his country be dried,
Nor long will his love stay behind him...

Sarah Curran, who had married a British officer, and gone to live in Italy, died there, supposedly of a broken heart, the year after the song was published. More outspoken than Moore's earlier lament – Emmet had, after all, been executed for treason – it was a further contribution to the Irish martyr's legend. Moore followed it soon after with a stinging attack on the Prince Regent, who on abandoning the Whigs, had written an open letter to his brother, the Duke of York, explaining that his sense of duty to 'our Royal father' had prompted him to keep the Tories in power. In his 'Parody of a Celebrated Letter', privately printed but widely circulated in Whig circles, Moore made fun of his excuses:

I need not remind you how cursedly bad
Our affairs were all looking when Father went mad;
A strait waistcoat on him and restrictions on me,
A more *limited* Monarchy could not well be...
I thought the best way as a dutiful son,
Was to do as Old Royalty's self would have done.
So I sent word to say, I would keep the whole batch in,
The same set of tools, without cleansing or patching...

The parody was the first of a series of political satires, whose light and sparkling style did not conceal Moore's real indignation at the Regent's volte face, and the government's policy towards Ireland. It is hard to re-capture the political atmosphere of the time, or the long-vanished figures of whom he made fun. But they were hugely popular in their day. Even the Regent was sometimes amused by his attacks. 'Don't you remember Tom Moore's description of me at breakfast?' he once asked Walter Scott:

The table spread with tea and toast,
Death warrants and the MORNING POST.[21]

A few weeks before this opening salvo in his war against the Tories, Moore had become a father. On 4 February 1812, Bessy gave birth to a daughter, Jane Anne Barbara, or Barbara, as she was usually known. Bessy had been ill during the pregnancy, and took a long time to recover. Alarmed by her weak and emaciated state, Moore was now eager to leave London for the healthier air of the country. It was also a chance to economise. 'If we had staid much longer in town, the curiosity to see "Moore's wife", combining with the kindness of my friends, would have ruined us,'[22] he wrote to his friend James Corry, when they moved to a cottage in Kegworth that May.

Kegworth, in Leicestershire, was only six miles from Donington, an important consideration for Moore, who relied on the library there for his researches for *Lalla Rookh*. Lord Moira was friendly as ever, but Moore's hopes for advancement through his influence had finally evaporated. Having been the Prince's right-hand man for over twenty years, Moira had broken with him over his decision to keep the Tories in power, and was contemplating going to live abroad. In a letter to Miss Godfrey, Moore gives a vivid description of the scene:

> When he told the P[rince] that in a very short time he should make his bow and quit the country, this precious gentleman began to blubber (as he did once when he was told that Brummell did not like the cut of his coat) and said, "You'll desert me then Moira?" "No, sir" says he; "when the friends and counsels you have chosen have brought your throne to totter beneath you, you will then see me by your side to sink, if it please God under its ruins with you!"[23]

Noble sentiments, and for Moore, if he had needed it, a further incentive for the anonymous satires with which he assailed the Regent and his circle in the pages of the *Morning Chronicle*. Some of his poems were so personally insulting to the Prince – for instance one in which his overweight mistress Lady Hertford is weighed in the balance against a starving Britannia – that it was only his anonymity that saved him from being prosecuted for libel. Byron too joined in the fray. His 'Sympathetic Address to a Young Lady', written after a banquet at Carlton House at which Princess Charlotte had burst into tears at her father's abuse of his erstwhile Whig friends, was published anonymously in the *Morning Chronicle* a few days later.

Weep, daughter of a royal line,
A Sire's disgrace, a realm's decay;

Ah! happy if each tear of thine
Could wash a father's fault away...

Throughout the early months of 1812, till he moved to the country in May, Moore saw Byron constantly, sometimes for supper tête-à-tête, sometimes with friends such as Rogers and Sheridan, the latter very frequently the worse for drink. 'It occasionally fell to my lot to convey him home –' wrote Byron, 'no sinecure – for he was so tipsy I was obliged to put on his cocked hat for him – to be sure it tumbled off again, and I was not myself so sober as to be able to pick it up again.'[24]

It was – ironically – to Moore that Byron turned as a mediator in a potential duel with another victim of the *English Bards and Scotch Reviewers*, a certain Colonel Greville, manager of the Argyle Rooms, who had been offended by some lines about the gaming there, and had angrily demanded satisfaction. Byron, incensed by Colonel Greville's tone, had been ready to reply in equally intemperate terms. He was persuaded, however, to leave the matter to Moore's discretion, and thanks to Moore's tactful negotiations, the matter was peacefully resolved.

If not as an intermediary, Moore was certainly present when Byron first came to call on Lady Caroline Lamb at Melbourne House. 'Rogers and Moore were standing by me', she told Lady Morgan later, 'I was on the sofa. I had just come in from riding. I was filthy and heated. I flew out of the room to wash myself. When I returned, Rogers said, "Lord Byron, you are a happy man. Lady Caroline is sitting here in all her dirt with us, but when you were announced she flew to beautify herself." Lord Byron wished to come and see me at eight o'clock, when I was alone...I said he might.'[25]

From then onwards, the romance took fire, Lady Caroline dazzled by Byron's fame and air of moodily romantic mystery, Byron fascinated by her boyish looks, her Devonshire House drawl, her wildness and originality. A few days after their first meeting he was writing almost proprietorially to Moore: 'Know all men by these presents, that you, Thomas Moore, stand indicted – no – invited, by special and particular solicitation to Lady C L* * *'s tomorrow even, at half-past nine o'clock...Pray come – I was so examined after you this morning I entreat you to answer in person.'[26]

As time went on Moore became worried about the scandal their affair was causing. 'M[oore] is in great distress about us,' Byron told Lady Caroline in May, '& indeed people talk as if there were no other pair of absurdities.' But by this time Moore was leaving London. Byron went to see him to say goodbye, reporting to Lady Caroline: 'I have seen Moore's wife; she is beautiful, with the darkest eyes.'[27] He repeated the compliment in a letter to Moore: 'My best wishes and respects to Mrs * *[Moore]; – she is beautiful. I may say so even to you, for I never was more struck with a countenance.'[28]

For the rest of year the Moores stayed in the country, Moore working quietly at *Lalla Rookh* and launching the occasional shaft of satire in the *Morning Chronicle*. There were visits to neighbours, mostly 'methodists and manufacturers', from time to time, and a long summer stay with Lord Moira at Donington. (Bessy, less overawed by its grandeur than Moore had expected, remarked that she liked Samuel Rogers' house far better.) Since the collapse of the Whig party's hopes, Lord Moira's political future had been in limbo. There was a suggestion that he should go to Ireland as Lord Lieutenant, withdrawn when he made it clear that he would only do so if Catholic emancipation was introduced. Then, in November, perhaps as a consolation prize, he was appointed Commander in Chief in India and Governor of Bengal. For a brief moment Moore's hopes of patronage revived. Would there be a place for him in Moira's retinue? The newspapers confidently announced his appointment as Moira's private secretary, with a salary of four or five thousand pounds a year. But Moira himself was strangely silent. When he came to Donington in late November, he did not send for Moore for several days. Moore saw him once by chance when he was shooting in the fields, but he only called out, 'You see a schoolboy taking his holiday',[29] as if avoiding further conversation.

When at last they met at Donington, Moira's manner was distant and embarrassed. He had not been oblivious of Moore, he told him – 'not been *oblivious* of me!' wrote Moore bitterly – but had already exhausted all his patronage for India; however, if anything suitable occurred when he arrived he would certainly let him know. In the meantime he was owed various favours by the Ministry, and would try to use his influence to find him something in exchange. 'To this I replied', wrote Moore, recounting the scene to Lady Donegal, that, '*from his hands* I would always be most willing to accept anything … but that I begged he would not take the trouble of applying for me to the patronage of the Ministry, as I would rather struggle on as I was, than take anything that would have the effect of tying up my tongue under such a system as the present.'[30]

It was an dignified response, which he repeated in a letter to Lord Moira the next day, though as he admitted frankly to James Power, 'I have not so much merit in these refusals as I appear to have, for I could see very plainly, through Lord Moira's manner, that there was very little chance of his making any proper exertion for me whatever, and, putting conscience out of the question, policy itself suggested to me that I might as well have the merit of declining what it was quite improbable would ever have been done for me.'[31]

So ended Moore's long relationship with Lord Moira, to whom, despite everything, he owed much for his kindness over the years, above all in finding a post for his father in Dublin. But he had been led on to expect far more, and now felt miserably let down. 'I cannot trust myself in speaking of the way he has treated me,' he wrote to Power. 'Gratitude for the past ties up my tongue.' But he was consoled for his disappointment by the approval of his friends. 'Rogers tells me he hears nothing but praises of my conduct,' he wrote to his mother; 'which is very pleasant to be told, though I want nothing but my own heart and conscience to tell me I have acted rightly.'[32] If the episode had dashed his hopes, at least it had left him in possession of the moral high ground.

I I

Mayfield Cottage

In January 1813, Lord Moira sailed for India. The awkward interview with Moore once over, he had been full of kind attentions to the last, presenting him with fifteen dozen bottles of wine on his departure. Moore's dreams of patronage had ended; perhaps they had always been illusory. Younger sons and cousins of the aristocracy could expect to be found sinecures; but Moore had not been born into that charmed circle. From now on he had only his own exertions to rely on. Since 1811 he had had a guaranteed retainer of £500 a year from the Power brothers, but his parents needed his support, and, as usual, he was very short of money. At one point when he and Bessy were staying at Langley Priory, a grand house in the neighbourhood, they were unable to leave because they had not a shilling with which to tip the servants. They were rescued from their predicament by James Power: Moore's letters to Power over the years are full of requests for advances on his retainer.

He was still in debt to his other publisher, James Carpenter, and it was partly to repay this that in January 1813 he gathered up and added to his recent political satires, and offered them to him under the title *Intercepted Letters; or, the Twopenny Post-Bag* by 'Thomas Brown, the Younger'. The bag containing the verses had supposedly been dropped by a two-penny postman, and picked up by an 'emissary for the Society for the Suppression of Vice' who, on perceiving that their 'discoveries of profligacy' lay too high up for him to handle, had left it under a bookshop counter. They had been bought for a trifle by Thomas Brown – in other words, Tom Moore – who now put them before the public.

Carpenter, who was the Prince Regent's official bookseller, was too cautious to publish the poems under his own imprint, and arranged for them to be printed by a lesser figure in the trade. He had every reason to be nervous. That very month Leigh Hunt and his brother John had been sentenced to two years' imprisonment for a libel on the Prince Regent – 'a violator of his word, a libertine over head and ears in debt and disgrace' – in their paper, the *Examiner*. The two brothers had been offered a remission of their sentence if they promised to refrain from further criticism, but had indignantly refused.

For Moore, their sentence was the occasion for two last-minute additions to his *Twopenny Post-Bag*: a serious poem praising the Hunts for

the fresh spirit that can warble free,
Through prison bars, its hymn of liberty,

and a verse letter, supposedly written by the Regent, to describe a dinner given to celebrate the judgement:

The dinner, you know, was in gay celebration
Of my brilliant triumph and H – nt's condemnation:
A compliment too, to his Lordship the Judge
For his speech to the Jury – and zounds! who would grudge
Turtle soup though it came to five guineas a bowl,
To reward such a loyal and complaisant soul?

The Hunts' imprisonment had been a gift to liberal opinion, and Moore's *Twopenny Post-Bag*, pouring ridicule on the Regent and his coterie, was hugely successful, reaching its fourteenth edition in just over a year. 'Whether it be from any talent shown in it, or its courage, or the general dislike towards the Prince,' he wrote, 'nothing I ever wrote has gained me so much pleasant fame.'[1] The Tory press accused him of ingratitude, flinging the dedication of *Anacreon* in his face; but it was the Prince's politics, not his, that had changed, and he saw no reason to excuse himself.

Meanwhile Bessy had been going through a difficult pregnancy. It was a relief when on 16 March, 'after staying up all night', he was able to scribble a quick note to Mrs Dalby: 'About six o'clock this morning my Bessy produced a little girl about the size of a twopenny wax doll. Nothing could be more favourable than the whole proceeding, and the mama is now eating buttered toast and drinking tea, as if nothing had happened.'[2]

The child was called Anastasia Mary, and like their first one, was christened in the Church of England. As a point of honour, Moore would never abandon his Catholic faith, but he saw no need to impose it on his family; he may well have been secretly relieved that his children would not have to suffer the disadvantages he had done. A firm believer in religious tolerance, he made his own position clear in one of his first *Irish Melodies*:

Shall I ask the brave soldier who fights by my side
In the cause of mankind, if our creeds agree?
Shall I give up the friend I have valued and tried,
If he kneel not before the same altar with me?
From the heretic girl of my soul shall I fly,
To seek somewhere else a more orthodox kiss?
No, perish the hearts, and the laws that try
Truth, valour, or love, by a standard like this!

Bessy recovered quickly from the birth; 'indeed', wrote Moore to his mother, 'she says she has not felt so well since her marriage'.[3] But the cottage at Kegworth was draughty and expensive; its propinquity to Donington had been its chief attraction, and with Lord Moira gone, he decided to look for something cheaper elsewhere. Luckily there was a temporary solution close at hand. A friend of Sir John Stevenson's, Mrs Ready, offered them rooms in her house, Oakhanger Hall in Cheshire, while they searched for something suitable. At the beginning of April, having sold most of their furniture and packed up their belongings, they set off for their new lodgings. Within four miles of their destination, however, they were met with bad news: their host, Mr Ready, had died two days before. 'You may imagine the perplexity this threw us into,' Moore wrote to Mrs Dalby, 'for I regarded our visit as completely frustrated, and I passed a miserable night at the miserable inn of Sandbach, turning over in my mind, with an anxiety I have seldom felt, the extreme awkwardness of our situation, and the difficulty I should find in disposing of myself and the dear little group along with me, after the abandonment of our house, furniture and everything like a home.'[4]

The next morning, luckily, dispelled his fears for, in answer to a note he sent to Mrs Ready, a barouche with two smiling servants drew up at the inn, and carried them off to Oakhanger Hall, where 'if there was not such a thing as a *corpse* still in the house, you would scarcely suppose that Death had ever showed his ugly face within the walls'. Mrs Ready made them welcome, and 'after the will reading and funeral are over,' he wrote, 'I think we shall be as if nothing had happened'.

It proved to be so. Mrs Ready took 'most violently' to Bessy, and the family was soon settled into a pleasant set of rooms, a bedroom, a study, and a room for Barbara and a maid. (The baby, according to the custom of the time, was boarded with a wet nurse.) By early May, Moore felt happy enough about leaving Bessy to set off to London, where there were last-minute details to arrange with James Power for the publication of a new volume of the *Irish Melodies*, and where, as agreed, he would air his music in society.

Having gone there more as a task than a pleasure, he was agreeably surprised by his reception. 'I have never met with so much kindness,' he told his friend James Corry, 'and certainly never with half so much deference, or half so many flattering tributes to me both as a man and an author.' As usual his singing was a star attraction at grand parties, but he had grown a little tired of 'bustle and dissolution',[5] and was at his happiest with a few congenial friends. Byron, of course, was among them. 'Among the many gay hours we passed together this spring,' wrote Moore in his biography of the poet, 'I remember particularly the wild flow of his spirits one evening, when we had accompanied Mr Rogers home from some evening assembly, and when Lord Byron, who, according to his frequent custom, had not dined for the last few days, found his hunger no longer governable, and called aloud for "something to eat". Our repast, – of his own choosing, – was simple bread and cheese; and seldom have I partaken of so joyous a supper.'[6]

It happened that Rogers had just received a presentation copy of Lord Thurlow's poems, and Byron and Moore began searching through the volume for absurdities – 'in turning over the pages,' wrote Moore, 'we found, it must be owned, abundant cause for mirth'. In vain Rogers pointed out the beauties of some passages: they continued to pounce on the ridiculous ones. At last Byron discovered some verses in praise of Rogers himself.

'We were, however, too far gone in our nonsense,' wrote Moore,

for even this eulogy, in which we both so heartily agreed, to stop us. The opening line of this poem was, as well as I can recollect, 'When Rogers o'er this labour bent'; and Lord Byron undertook to read it aloud – but he found it impossible to get beyond the first two words. Our laughter had now increased to such a pitch that nothing could restrain it. Two or three times he began; but no sooner had the words 'When Rogers' passed his lips, than our fit burst forth afresh, – till even

Mr Rogers himself, with all his feeling of injustice, found it impossible not to join us.

Soon after he arrived in London, Moore had been to visit Leigh Hunt in Horsemonger Lane Gaol (his brother was confined in Clerkenwell). Byron, who shared his admiration for Hunt's courageous stand, asked Moore to introduce him. It was arranged that they should dine with him in prison, Byron confirming the appointment in a rhyming epistle, flung off while he was dressing for dinner the night before:

Oh you, who in all names can tickle the town,
Anacreon, Tom Little, Tom Moore, or Tom Brown, –
For hang me if I know of which you may most brag,
Your quarto two-pounds, or your Two Penny Post Bag…
Tomorrow be with me, as soon as you can, sir,
All ready and dress'd for proceeding to spunge on
(According to compact) the wit in the dungeon –
Pray Phoebus at length our political malice
May not get us lodgings within the same palace![7]

They found 'the wit in the dungeon' in possession of two rooms, freshly wallpapered and painted, with books, busts, pictures and a pianoforte around him, and a trellised garden in the yard outside. Hunt had made the best of his imprisonment thanks to the leniency of the governor and contributions from his friends; he was allowed to see his family daily, and astonishingly, continued to edit the *Examiner* from gaol. The Prince Regent might have betrayed his allies by switching to the Tories, but even his harshest critics could not have described him as a tyrant.

Moore stayed only a few weeks in London. He was eager to get back to Bessy and to find a permanent home for his family. After calling briefly at Oakhanger Hall, he set off for Wales, which, he had been told, was 'the cheapest county in England'. Its cheapness, however, was a 'flim flam', and he finally settled for a cottage near Ashbourne in Derbyshire, with a rent of £20 a year. Mrs Ready sent them over in her barouche, the Moores secretly relieved to see the last of her: 'she is about the most trumpery person I ever met with,' he told Mary Godfrey, 'and the more tiresome and oppressive to us, for we were obliged to seem grateful to her for a vast deal of really very good-natured, but at the same time, very disagreable civilities.'[8]

Mayfield Cottage, their new home, was about a mile and a half from the village of Ashbourne. It was a small, stone-built, slate-roofed house, set among fields, and approached by a narrow, often muddy lane. A distant church spire, half hidden in the trees, was the only other building in sight. Here Moore and his family would remain for the next three years. We catch glimpses of their life there from his letters: Moore rolling in the hayfields outside their house with Barbara, or reading Maria Edgeworth's novels to Bessy in the evenings; Bessy, looking beautiful in a new turban, at a county ball; the two of them practising country dancing in a 'retired green lane' when they arrived half an hour too early for a party. There were sympathetic neighbours, among them the Arkwrights, of the famous industrial family, at Ashbourne Hall, and the Strutts, the enlightened owners of a cotton mill at Derby, progressive employers after Moore's own heart. But except for his yearly sorties up to London, to keep his singing before the public, it was a deliberately quiet existence. 'It was indeed,' he wrote in his preface to the eighth volume of his Poetical Works, 'to the secluded life I led during the years 1813–1816, in a lone cottage in the fields in Derbyshire, that I owed the inspiration, whatever may have been its value, of some of the best and most popular portions of *Lalla Rookh*.'

In May 1813 Byron had published his poem *The Giaour* (we remember Anne Elliott discussing how to pronounce the title in *Persuasion*). His choice of an Eastern theme, anticipating that of *Lalla Rookh*, was a major blow to Moore. It was not that there had not been earlier poems on oriental themes. Southey's oriental epics *Thalaba* and *The Curse of Kehama* – his 'unsaleables' as Byron called them – had appeared in 1801 and 1810 respectively. But Byron's *Giaour*, rapidly running into five editions, was a very different matter. 'Never was anything more unlucky for me than Byron's invasion of this region, which when I entered it, was as yet untrodden, and whose chief charm consisted in the gloss and novelty of its features...' Moore wrote to Mary Godfrey. 'I sometimes doubt whether I shall publish it at all.'[9] Byron, however, was quick to reassure his friend: 'You will have no competitor; and if you had, you ought to be glad of it. The little I have done in that way is merely a "voice in the wilderness" for you; and if it has had any success, that also will prove that the public are orientalizing, and pave the path for you.'[10]

Moore's was not a jealous nature, and though chagrined by the co-incidence of subject, he was full of praises for *The Giaour*. He even suggested a minor improvement. In the first edition of the poem, Byron had used the word 'Giamschid' as a trisyllable: 'Bright as the gem of Giamschid'. When

Moore remarked, on the authority of Richardson's *Persian Dictionary*, that the word should be a disyllable, he changed the line to 'Bright as the ruby of Giamschid'. On this Moore wrote to him that 'as the comparison of his heroine's eye to a "ruby" might unluckily call up the idea of its being bloodshot, he had better change the line to "Bright as the jewel of Giamschid"',[11] an amendment that Byron promptly made.

The exchange, recorded in a footnote in Moore's life of Byron, is significant, not only as an example of co-operation between poets, but also of the laborious, almost obsessive, scholarship that Moore was bringing to *Lalla Rookh*, and that eventually so weighed it down that today, despite some beautiful passages, it is almost unreadable as a whole. It is a relief to turn to the seemingly effortless lyricism of the *Irish Melodies*, the fifth volume of which appeared at the end of 1813.

Moore was now at the height of his powers, both as a poet and musician. Almost every song is memorable, whether the foretaste of Yeats's 'Innisfree' in 'Oh! had we some bright little isle of our own', or the lilting, light hearted rhythms of 'The Young May Moon':

The young May moon is beaming, love,
The glow-worm's lamp is gleaming, love,
How sweet to rove
Thro' Morna's grove
When all the world is dreaming, love.

The best-known songs in the volume, 'The Minstrel Boy' and ''Tis the Last Rose of Summer' are so familiar that one hesitates to repeat them, though the second at least repays quotation, if only for its sad foreshadowing of Moore's lonely final years:

'Tis the last rose of summer
Left blooming alone;
All her lovely companions
Are faded and gone;
No flower of her kindred,
No rose-bud is nigh,
To reflect back her blushes,
Or give sigh for sigh.

I'll not leave thee, thou lone one,
To pine on the stem;

Since the lovely are sleeping,
Go, sleep thou with them.
Thus kindly I scatter
Thy leaves o'er the bed,
Where thy mates of the garden
Lie scentless and dead.

So soon may *I* follow,
When friendships decay,
And from Love's shining circle
The gems drop away.
Where true hearts lie wither'd
And fond ones are flown,
Oh! who would inhabit
This bleak world alone.

''Tis the Last Rose of Summer' was perhaps the most popular of all Moore's songs. During the nineteenth century, a million and a half copies of the sheet music were sold in America alone, though it was in the latter half of the century, when almost every home had its cottage piano, that the majority of the sales were made. 'The Minstrel Boy', his 'wild harp' symbolic of Ireland's national identity, was almost equally well loved, stirring the souls of those millions of Irishmen who had been forced to emigrate by poverty or famine, with patriotic nostalgia.

There was no way that Moore, in 1813, could foresee the enduring popularity of the *Irish Melodies*, or the emotional link they would form with their homeland for generations of Irish emigrants. But he was pleased by their continuing success, though he warned in his introduction that his next and sixth volume would probably be his last. He felt that he had exhausted the best airs available, and that subsequent lyrics might reflect this lack of inspiration. Nevertheless, if people could find him other 'really sweet and expressive' Irish airs he might pursue the project further. In fact, a number of enthusiasts did so, and the *Melodies* continued to appear.

Byron was a passionate admirer of the *Irish Melodies*. 'I have them by rote and by heart...' he told Moore, 'they are my matins and my vespers.'[12] In his journal for November 1813, he drew a pyramid of poetic excellence with Scott at the top, Rogers below, then Moore and Campbell together, Southey, Coleridge and Wordsworth as a trio beneath them, and after that the many. 'I have ranked the names upon my triangle more upon what I believe to be popular opinion, than any decided opinion of my own,' he wrote. 'For to me some of M * * 's [Moore's] last Erin sparks...are worth all the Epics that ever were composed.'[13]

Byron had not seen Moore again since he left London at the end of June 1813. But although out of sight he was not out of his mind, and Moore's biography of Byron quotes numerous letters from him during the second half of this year. Moore's letters were less frequent; except to his parents, he was always a hopeless correspondent. For Byron, however, he was the ideal audience, someone who shared his amusement in society, and with whom he could talk of literary matters, and touch discreetly on his tangled love affairs. (The discretion may have been Moore's, not his, for when he came to use the letters in his life of Byron, he deleted any passages that might cause scandal or offence.)

Having extricated himself from the tempestuous Lady Caroline, Byron had passed into the arms of Lady Oxford, some twenty years his elder, an autumnal romance, which had ended when the Oxfords went abroad in June. Since then he had cast round in various directions. He had been 'amazingly inclined – remember I say but inclined,' he wrote to Moore on 13 July, 'to be seriously enamoured with Lady A[delaide] F[orbes] – but this * * has ruined all my prospects'.[14] The episode in asterisks was probably a hysterical – and scandal-provoking – scene by Lady Caroline, when she had attempted to stab herself at a dance where he had been present. In August there was further trouble: 'I am at the moment, in a far worse, serious and entirely new scrape than any of the last twelve months – and that is saying a good deal. * * *'[15] he told Moore. The new scrape may well have been his liaison with his half sister Augusta, who had recently become pregnant, though it is unlikely that Moore knew the full story at the time. He was not so much a sentimental confidant – a role fulfilled by Byron's old friend Lady Melbourne – as a delightful correspondent and companion, whose gifts Byron hugely admired.

'M * * e has a peculiarity of talent, or rather talents – poetry, music, voice, all his own,' he wrote in his journal for November, 'and an expression that never was, nor will be, possessed by another...In society, he is gentlemanly, gentle, and, altogether more pleasing than any individual with whom I am acquainted. For his honour, principle, and independence, his conduct to * * * * [Moira] speaks "trumpet tongued". He has but one fault – and that one I daily regret – he is not *here*.'[16]

12

A Record Contract

'I have got a devil of a long story in the press, entitled the "Corsair", in the regular heroic measure,' wrote Byron to Moore in January 1814. 'It is a pirate's isle, peopled with my own creatures, and you may easily suppose they do a lot of mischief through three cantos.'[1]

The Corsair appeared a few weeks later, another Eastern story, whose haughty, mysterious hero was widely supposed to be a portrait of the author. It also included Byron's 'Lines to a Lady Weeping' as an addition to the text, and was dedicated to Thomas Moore. Byron had difficulty pushing through the dedication, since his publisher, John Murray, was a Tory, and disliked his praising Moore as an Irish patriot, in whose projected oriental tale, 'the wrongs of your own country, the magnificent and fiery spirit of her sons, the beauty and feeling of her daughters', would be reflected. But Byron refused to change the dedication; its final description of Moore, 'the poet of all circles and the idol of his own', would be inscribed on the cross above Moore's grave.

Moore could only be delighted by the dedication. It was 'just such as might be expected from a profuse, magnificent-minded fellow who does not wait for scales to weigh what he says, but gives praise, as sailors lend money, "by handfuls",'[2] he told Rogers – to whom, incidentally, Byron had dedicated *The Giaour*. *The Corsair* was hugely successful, selling 25,000 copies in little over a month. But Byron's inclusion of his 'Lines to a Lady Weeping', its authorship till then unknown, aroused the fury of the Tory press. 'You can have no conception of the uproar the eight lines on the little Royalty's weeping in 1812 (now republished) have occasioned,' he wrote to Moore on 14 February, 'The R * *, who had always thought them *yours*, chose – God knows why – on discovering them to be mine, to be affected "in sorrow rather than anger". The Morning Post, Sun, Herald, Courier, have been in hysterics ever since.'[3]

Thanks to the dedication, Moore got his 'full share of the be-spatterment'[4] that Byron was suffering. The *Courier* led the attack with a series of articles entitled *Byroniana*, in the course of which Moore was ridiculed for his duel with Jeffrey, his licentiousness, his Irish politics and his cowardice in publishing the *Twopenny Post-Bag* under a fictitious name. Moore might be the idol of his own circle, it remarked, 'but he would find some little difficulty in obtaining admittance to any other'. Moore was more accustomed to abuse than Byron, and even when the papers suggested that Byron had given him the proceeds of *The Corsair* – in fact he had given them to a kinsman, R.C. Dallas – he refused to break 'the sacred silence of contempt with which such things should be heard'. But he sensed that Byron was uncomfortable and out of spirits, and wrote to him offering to come up to London immediately, if he could be of help in any way. 'If I am, after all, mistaken,' he concluded, 'and you are not suffering any unusual uneasiness of mind, pray lose no time in telling me, for I am very anxious about you.'[5]

> I have a great mind to tell you I am "uncomfortable",' replied Byron, if only to make you come to town; where no one has ever delighted more in seeing you, nor is there any one to whom I would sooner turn for consolation... The truth is, I have no 'lack of argument' to ponder upon of the most gloomy description, but this arises from *other* causes. Some day or other, when we are *veterans*, I may tell you a tale of present and past times; and it is not from want of confidence that I do not now, – but – but – always a but to the end of the chapter.[6]

What were the other causes? Perhaps his amorous entanglements, his love for his sister Augusta, now in her eighth month of pregnancy; his epistolary courtship of Annabella Milbanke, 'the princess of Parallelograms',[7] as he called her; and the importunities of Lady Caroline Lamb, still not entirely shaken off. But these were not subjects for Moore, whose discouragement at Byron's oriental successes had tempted him to put *Lalla Rookh* aside. It was Byron's turn to offer consolation: '*Think again* before you *shelf* your Poem … The best way to make the public "forget" me is to remind them of yourself. You cannot suppose that I would ask or advise you to publish, if I thought you would *fail*. I really have *no* literary envy; and I do not believe a friend's success ever sat nearer another than yours do to my good wishes.'[8]

Moore gathered up his courage; he could not write in a 'nervous fever' like Byron, who admitted to having written *The Corsair* in ten days, but he devoted himself once more to *Lalla Rookh*, which with a further volume of the *Irish Melodies*, was his chief occupation for the next few months. In April came the news that Paris had fallen to the Allied troops, and that Napoleon had abdicated. The war with France, which had been the background to Moore's life for almost twenty years, had come to an end. Following Whig opinion, Moore had deplored the Tory prosecution of the war, and thought the French 'shabby dogs' for taking back a Bourbon king. On 24 April, after a whirl of celebrations in London, Louis XVIII set sail for France. Peace seemed to be restored, Napoleon safely out of the way, at least, as Byron presciently remarked, 'till – Elba becomes a volcano and sends him out again. I can't think it is all over yet.'[9]

Moore arrived in London for his yearly visit a few days later. He saw Byron almost daily while he was there, sometimes at the theatre, where the electrifying acting of Edmund Kean was the latest sensation, sometimes at late night supper parties, where 'as usual on such occasions', it was daylight before they parted. Although he does not speak of it in his biography, he must soon have been aware, as Leslie Marchand puts it, 'that a secret love affair was gnawing at his friend's vitals'.[10] The object was amost certainly Augusta whose baby, born on 15 April, could have been either Byron's or her husband, Colonel Leigh's. When Moore in the course of conversation asked Byron to write the words for a song, the stanzas he sent him – never published in his lifetime – seemed to express the conflicts he was suffering:

I speak not, I trace not, I breathe not thy name,
There is grief in the sound, there is guilt in the fame;
But the tear which now burns on my cheek may impart
The deep thoughts that dwell in that silence of heart.

Too brief for our passion, too long for our peace
Were those hours – can their joy or their bitterness cease?

We repent, we abjure, we will break from our chain –
We will part, we will fly to – unite it again![11]

Moore left London at the end of May. 'I *could* be very sentimental now, but I won't', Byron wrote to him. 'The truth is, that I have been all my life trying to harden my heart, and have not yet quite succeeded – though there are great hopes – and you do not know how it sinks at your departure.' He had lent Moore his journal, written over the winter of 1813–14; 'Keep the Journal', he added in a PS; 'and if it has amused you, I am glad I have kept it.'[12] Moore did indeed keep it, a priceless record of Byron's thoughts and experiences, from which he would quote extensively when he came to write his life.

Moore returned home at the end of May. He found the summer weather 'very favourable to poetry',[13] and spent long hours writing out of doors. Bessy was expecting a baby; on 18 August, their third daughter was born. 'Another girl!' wrote Moore to Mary Dalby, 'but no matter; Bessy is safe over it, and that's all I care about.'[14] Byron was one of the godfathers, and the child was christened Olivia Byron Moore.

As soon as Bessy was sufficiently recovered, Moore set off on a visit to the Dalbys at Donington, where he needed to check some information for an article for the *Edinburgh Review*. He took in the Derby Races and Ball on the way, and was flattered to be asked to stay at Chatsworth by the Duke of Devonshire on his way home. 'I do not think I shall go,' he wrote to Rogers. 'I have no servant to take with me, and my hat is shabby, and the seams of my best suit are growing white...I can meet them on pretty fair terms at a dinner or a ball; but a whole week in the same house with them detects the poverty of a man's ammunition deplorably.'[15]

Moore's review was the second he was writing for the *Edinburgh Review*; the first, in the September issue, was a drolly ironical notice of Lord Thurlow's poems – over which he and Byron had laughed so much the previous year. He was now reviewing a translation from the Greek of the writings of St Chrysostom, St Gregory Nazianizen and St Basil, a learned subject with which his long hours of study in Bishop Marsh's Library had made him reasonably familiar; he was able to check on any details in the library at Donington. 'I have redde thee upon the Fathers,' wrote Byron when it appeared, 'and it is excellent well. Positively you must not leave off reviewing...you have all the airs of a veteran critic at the outset.'[16]

It was a honour to be asked to write for the *Edinburgh Review*, and Jeffrey had offered well above the usual fee. But Moore's heart was not really in reviewing. Critics, he wrote to Leigh Hunt,

> expose a great deal of absurdity to be sure ... but I am quite certain that the watchful rigor they exercise in these days is, among other things, fatal to the little genius that's left us. If Wordsworth's absurdities had not been so rudely handled, we should have had more of his greatnesses; and I am quite certain that if Shakespeare had critics standing sentinel over every pun and conceit that wanted to escape, we should have lost many a beauty that rushed out headlong with them... No man of sensibility or modesty (and these qualities generally accompany true genius) can write a line without having the dread of these persons before his eyes.[17]

One has only to think of the savage reviews of *Endymion* in *Blackwoods* and the *Quarterly Review* in 1818, and their destructive effect on even Keats's gallant spirit, to see the justice of Moore's observations. He himself always avoided writing about any of his poetic contemporaries, and despite the attractiveness of Jeffrey's offer, did no more reviewing for six years.

Meanwhile *Lalla Rookh* was making progress. Thanks to an intervention from Byron, he had already had an informal offer of two thousand guineas for the poem from John Murray, to which he had not yet replied. Now his friend James Perry, editor of the *Morning Chronicle*, suggested approaching Longmans – an old established publisher whose list of authors included such stars as Rogers, Walter Scott and Wordsworth – on his behalf. Moore was happy to accept this suggestion, and in December 1814, he came up to London to meet them, at the same time as seeing to the printing of the sixth volume of his *Irish Melodies*. He asked Perry to come as his adviser to the interview with Longmans; 'and what with the friendly zeal of my negotiatior on the one side, and the prompt and liberal spirit with which he was met on the other,' wrote Moore, 'there has seldom occurred any transaction in which Trade and Poesy have shone out so advantageously in one another's eyes.'

Perry began by asking 'the largest price that has been given, in our day' for a narrative poem of similar length. The publishers answered that this was three thousand guineas, the sum paid to Walter Scott for *Rokeby*. Perry demanded that Moore should be paid the same amount. The publishers objected, very reasonably, that they had not yet seen a line of the poem, but Perry, taking a lofty tone, insisted that Moore's existing reputation was a sufficient guarantee. 'This very generous view of the transaction' wrote Moore, 'was, without any difficulty acceded to, and the firm agreed, before we separated, that I was to receive three thousand guineas for my Poem.'[18]

It was a staggering sum (later modified to £3,000) news of which swept the publishing world: to give some comparable figures Byron was paid £600 for the first two cantos of *Childe Harold*, and £2,000 for the third. Moore now had to face the awkward task of breaking with his existing publishers, Carpenters. Fortunately, the sales of the *Twopenny Post-Bag* had cancelled out his debts, and since they had only offered him £2,000 for the poem – and that at the very last moment – he was able to leave them in good faith. In the past, they had often taken advantage of his unworldliness to drive a hard bargain; he would be far better treated by Longmans, both Longman and his partner, Owen Rees, becoming lifelong friends.

Moore saw Byron frequently during this visit, and though their friendship was as great as ever – Byron now writing to him as 'My dearest Moore' – he was full of foreboding about Byron's forthcoming marriage. Byron had informed him of his acceptance by Annabella Milbanke in September. He knew that Moore was uneasy about the match: 'My mother of the Gracchi (that *are* to be) you think too strait-laced for me,'[19] he wrote gaily, and in the postscript to another letter: 'By the way my wife elect is perfection, and I hear of nothing but her merits and her wonders.'[20]

It was this very perfection that Moore feared; someone more easy going and indulgent would have suited Byron far better. But he doubted that genius and the married state could ever exist comfortably together. While he, on the gentler slopes of poetry, could enjoy a happy family life, those called to its highest summits, he felt, were almost always doomed to a tempestuous destiny. 'However delightful, therefore,' he wrote in his life of Byron, 'may be the spectacle of a man of genius tamed and domesticated in society ... we must nevertheless, in the midst of our admiration, bear in mind that it is not thus smoothly or amiably immortality has ever been struggled for, or won.'[21]

Moore returned from London in good spirits. As well as the favourable negotiation with Longmans, he had received £500 from his Bermuda agent (the last he would ever receive) and had invested it in stock. 'I look forward most sanguinely to being a rich old fellow,'[22] he told his mother cheerfully. On January 1815 he heard from Byron that he had been married at Seaham, the Milbankes' home in Durham, the week before. In his biography of the poet he recalls Byron's description of the occasion:

> He described himself [in his burnt Memoirs] as waking on the morning of his wedding, with the most melancholy reflections...In the same mood, he wandered about the grounds alone, till he was summoned for the ceremony, and joined, for the first time that day, his bride and her family. He knelt down, he repeated the words after the clergyman; but a mist was before his eyes...and he was awakened by the congratulations of the bystanders, to find himself – married.[23]

At the end of January 1815, Moore let himself be persuaded to accept a second invitation to Chatsworth. Bessy was too shy to come with him, and Moore himself was still concerned about his clothes: a new coat which he had ordered in London did not fit, and he had to make do with a substitute from a local tailor. But as usual, he found himself the centre of attention when he arrived. 'I snatch a moment from the whirl of lords and ladies I am in here, to write a scrambling line to you,' he wrote delightedly to his mother; 'they are all chattering at this moment about me, dukes, countesses, & c. &c. It is to be sure a most princely establishment.'[24]

It was an opportunity to introduce the songs from his forthcoming volume of the *Irish Melodies*. They included such light-hearted numbers as 'The Time I've lost in Wooing', very much in the mood of his earlier verses in *Anacreon*:

> The time I've lost in wooing,
> In watching and pursuing
> The light, that lies
> In woman's eyes,
> Have been my heart's undoing.
> Though Wisdom oft has taught me,
> I scorn'd the lore she brought me,
> My only books
> Were woman's looks,
> And folly's all they've taught me.

Questionable sentiments perhaps for a father of three, but they delighted his listeners. Particularly successful too, was his song 'When first I met thee', supposedly addressed by a lover to his faithless mistress, but easily interpreted as a reproach to the Prince Regent, for having abandoned and deceived his loyal supporters.

> Go – go – 'tis vain to curse,
> 'Tis weakness to upbraid thee;
> Hate cannot wish thee worse
> Than guilt and shame have made thee.

'You cannot conceive what a sensation the Prince's song excited at Chatsworth,' Moore told James Power. 'It was in vain to guard your property; they had it sung and repeated over so often that they all had copies of it, and I dare say, in the course of the next week, there will not be a Whig lord or lady in England who is not in possession of it.'[25]

The songs were published the following month. Contrary to Moore's stated resolve in his fifth volume, they were not to be his last. In fact, thanks to a stream of contributions from the public, there would be four more volumes of the *Irish Melodies*. But he used this, the sixth, to make his adieux:

> Dear Harp of my Country! farewell to thy numbers,
> This sweet wreath of song is the last we shall twine!
> Go, sleep with the sunshine of Fame on they slumbers,
> Till touch'd by some hand less unworthy than mine;
> If the pulse of the patriot, soldier or lover,
> Have throbb'd at our lay, 'tis thy glory alone;
> I was but as the wind, passing heedlessly over;
> And all the wild sweetness I wak'd was thy own.

13

'A health to thee, Tom Moore'

Back from Chatsworth, Moore spent the early months of 1815 – a time when Napoleon's flight from Elba had made international politics almost unbearably exciting – working quietly at *Lalla Rookh* and a collection of melodies, *Sacred Songs*, which he had promised to Power by the end of the year. On 25 March this studious routine was shattered when his youngest daughter, Olivia, aged only eight months, was taken suddenly ill and died after twenty-four hours of convulsions. Poor Bessy was utterly distraught and, though she tried hard to hide her feelings, Moore grew so alarmed by the state of her health that he determined to set his work aside to take her to Ireland for a change of scene.

They arrived in Dublin at the end of May, where Moore's friend Richard Power (of the Kilkenny theatricals) put his fine house in Kildare Street at their disposal. 'The sight of us has been quite a renewal of life to my dear mother and father,' he told Samuel Rogers. 'They loved Bessy *upon trust* before they saw her, and the little children are never out of their arms.'[1] They were soon caught up in a flurry of visits and dinners, Moore noting with pleasure the attention that was paid to Bessy, but sickened by the political situation. Away from Ireland his patriotism could be idealised and romantic; in Dublin, where disputes about the veto were still raging, he came face to face with squabbling reality. 'Alas! alas! it must be confessed that my poor country is altogether a most wretched concern,' he wrote to Lady Donegal; 'and as for the Catholics (as I have just said in a letter written within these five minutes) one would heartily wish them all in their own Purgatory, if it were not for their adversaries whom one wishes *still further*.'[2]

A visit to his sister Kate, now married to a squireen in Tipperary, only deepened his disgust. 'A sick house [his sister had just had a miscarriage] and a dull ugly country render our visit here rather a melancholy proceeding...' he told his friend James Dalton. 'The only *stimulants* here are the Shanavests [local *banditti*] who enter the houses here at noonday for arms and start out, by twenties and thirties, upon the tithe-proctors in the fields, stark naked and smeared all over with paint like Catabaws...The rector of this place has just passed the windows on a tithe hunting expedition, with a large gun in his gig. This is one of the ministers of peace on earth!'[3]

Returning to Dublin, they were thrown into new alarm when their elder daughter Barbara, now four years old, became dangerously ill from a 'bilious fever', delaying their departure for more than a week. The arrival of Moore's publisher James Power, to discuss the publication of his *Sacred Songs*, was a further complication, and Moore spent his last days in Dublin, in 'one uninterrupted paroxysm of bustle, wrangling and anxiety'[4] before, with Barbara just recovered, they at last set sail for England.

They arrived home at the end of September, after a long and difficult journey, which left Bessy 'alarmingly indisposed' for several weeks. But it was a relief to be back in their own surroundings and to pick up the threads of work once more. The enforced idleness of their Irish visit had played havoc with Moore's schedule. His only production that summer had been a squib in the *Morning Chronicle*, 'Epistle from Tom Crib to Big Ben', written in the language of the boxing ring and attacking the Regent ('Big Ben') for his unsporting behaviour in banishing Napoleon to St Helena:

Having floor'd, by good luck, the first *swell* of the age,

Having conquered the *prime one*, that *milled* us around,

You kick'd him, old BEN, as he lay on the ground...

In fact Moore's rhyming war against the Tories was running out of steam. Napoleon's defeat at Waterloo in June had left the government temporarily triumphant, and apart from the ever present woes of Ireland, it was difficult to see from what angle to attack them. Like many of the opposition Moore was ambivalent in his attitude towards the allied victory; the liberal prospects first opened up by the French Revolution had finally been dashed by the restoration of the Bourbons. 'How do you like the way your friends the legitimates are disposing of the world?' he wrote to Mary Godfrey. 'At all events the ball is completely at their feet and we shall see whether old women priests, assisted by French renegades and drunken corporals, are after all the best agents of Providence for mankind.'[5]

For the time being politics were put aside. For the next few months he settled back to his quiet routine at Mayfield, working by day in his study or pacing round their little garden – he liked to compose outdoors – and reading to Bessy in the evening. Jane Austen's *Emma* was a particular discovery. 'It is the very perfection of novel writing...' he told Samuel Rogers. 'So much effect, with so little effort!'[6] December found Bessy ill once more, painfully thin and racked with violent coughing; the cottage, so pleasant in summer, was damp and freezing in the winter. 'Smoky, wet rooms, with a chorus of coughers and sneezers for inhabitants – our Cook at the point of death, and ourselves almost forgetting the use of her, from a long probation of water gruel and cathartics – such is the amiable state of our establishment,'[7] wrote Moore to his old friend Captain (now Rear-Admiral) Douglas, putting off a plan for him to come and stay.

Moore had seen very little of Douglas, whose naval duties kept him at sea for long periods, since they had travelled back from America together in 1804. They had met once, after an interval of five or six years, in 1811. On that occasion, Douglas, who had just inherited £10,000, had offered Moore the use of £700: 'Now my dear little fellow, you know I've grown rich... here is a blank cheque, which you may fill up while I am away, for as much of that as you may want.'[8] Although he had refused the offer, Moore had been deeply touched by this continuing evidence of friendship. Douglas had now been appointed Commander in Chief in Jamaica and had immediately written to Moore to offer him the post of his Secretary there, with a house and a certain salary of £500 a year. A few years before Moore would have jumped at the offer, but the risks of the climate and the journey, as well as his literary commitments, put it out of the question. 'I have of course declined it...' he told his mother, 'but the friendliness and *courage* of the offer (considering the interest by which Douglas must have got the appointment) can never be forgotten by me.'[9] In asking for Moore, well known for his attacks on the government, Douglas could well have jeopardised his own career. It was a revealing illustration of both men's qualities, the sturdy loyalty of Douglas, Moore's gift of inspiring the love of his friends.

Another friend was much in Moore's mind that winter. He had not seen Byron for a year, though they had been in intermittent correspondence during that time, Byron condoling with him on the loss of his daughter, and at first seeming happy in his marriage. 'I could not however but observe that these indications of a contented heart soon ceased,' wrote Moore in his biography of Byron. 'His mention of the partner of his home became more rare and formal, and there was observable, I thought, through some of his letters, a feeling of unquiet and weariness that brought back all those gloomy anticipations with which I had, from the first, regarded his fate.'[10]

On 6 January 1816, Byron wrote to him announcing the birth of his daughter, Ada, some three weeks before. Moore was struck by his melancholy tone. 'Do you know, my dear B.' he wrote, 'there was a something in your last letter – a sort of unquiet mystery, as well as a want of your usual elasticity of spirit – which has hung upon my mind unpleasantly ever since.'[11]

On 14 January, harassed by duns who were besieging his house in London, Byron sent Annabella and her baby to stay with her parents in Leicester, intending to follow her a few weeks later. On 2 February, however, after much to-ing and fro-ing as to whether his wild and erratic behaviour over the previous few months was due to insanity, Annabella's father wrote to Byron proposing an amicable separation. In view of Byron's enormous fame, it was hardly possible that such a separation could be quietly achieved, and London was soon buzzing with rumours, and scandalous speculations. It was Mary Godfrey who broke the news to Moore. 'The world are loud against him and vote him a worthless profligate ... Every one praises and pities her. He is completely lost in the opinion of the world ... I hope he will go abroad for your sake, as he will certainly cling to you. Give him good advice and tell him to go.'[12]

Whatever the rights and wrongs of the break-up of Byron's marriage, there was never any doubt where Moore's own loyalties lay – 'I could love the Devil himself if he were such a bon diable as you are ...'[13] he told him once – and on receiving Mary Godfrey's letter his chief reaction was one of affectionate concern. 'I am most anxious for you,' he wrote, 'though I doubt whether I ought to mention the subject on which I am so anxious. If however, what I heard last night, in a letter from town be true, you will know immediately what I allude to, and just communicate as much or as little upon the subject as you think proper – only *something* I should like to know, as soon as possible, from yourself in order to set my mind at rest.'[14]

'I have not answered your letter for a time,' wrote Byron on 29 February, 'and at present, the reply to a part of it might extend to such a length that

I shall delay it till it can be made in person…In the mean time, I am at war "with all the world and his wife"; or rather, "all the world and my wife" are at war with me, and have not yet crushed me – whatever they may do…By the way, however, you must not believe all you hear on the subject; and don't attempt to defend me.'[15]

Moore was sincerely grieved by what had happened. 'As for defending you,' he wrote, 'the only person with whom I have yet attempted this task is myself and considering the little I know upon this subject (or rather perhaps owing to it) I have hitherto done it with very tolerable success. After all your *choice* was your misfortune. I never liked – but I'm here wandering off…and so must change the subject for a far pleasanter one, your last new poems…'[16]

Byron's letter, by return of post, was quick to absolve his wife of any blame: 'The fault was *not* – no, nor even the misfortune – in my "choice" (unless in *choosing at all*) – for I do not believe – and I must say it…that there ever was a better, a brighter, a kinder, or a more amiable and agreable being than Lady B…Where there is blame it belongs to myself, and if I cannot redeem, I must bear it.'[17]

'I had certainly no right to say anything about the unluckiness of your choice…' replied Moore. 'What I meant in hinting a doubt with respect to the object of your selection did not imply the least impeachment of that perfect amiableness which the world, I find, by common consent, allows to her. I only feared that she might have been too perfect – too *precisely* excellent – too matter-of-fact a paragon for you to coalesce with comfortably…'[18]

Lady Byron, the 'paragon', remained silent as to the reasons for the separation, creating an atmosphere of mystery in which every kind of dark hint and insinuation flourished. 'In consequence of all this exaggeration,' wrote Moore, 'an outcry was now raised against Lord Byron as, in no case of private life, perhaps was ever before witnessed; nor had the whole amount of fame which he had gathered, in the course of the last four years, much exceeded in proportion the reproach and obloquy that were now, within the space of a few weeks showered upon him.'[19]

Moore did not see Byron before he left England, in a cloud of scandal, on 25 April. It was Hobhouse who had been Byron's closest confidant in the previous four months and who accompanied him to Dover to catch the packet to Ostend. But it was to Moore, his fellow poet and the cheerful companion of his bachelor days, that Byron addressed his last lines before leaving:

My boat is on the shore,
And my bark is on the sea;
But, before I go, Tom Moore,
Here's a double health to thee!

Here's a sigh to those who love me,
And a smile to those who hate;
And, whatever sky's above me,
Here's a heart for every fate.

 Sixteen months later he completed the poem, which he sent to Moore
from Venice:

Though the ocean roar around me,
Yet it still shall bear me on;
Though a desert should surround me,
It hath springs that may be won.

'Fare Thee Well': Byron's Departure from England, in a cartoon by Cruikshank, 1816.

Were't the last drop in the well
As I gasped upon the brink,
'Ere my fainting spirit fell,
'Tis to thee that I would drink.

With that water, as this wine,
The libation I would pour
Should be – peace with thine and mine,
And a health to thee, Tom Moore.

Moore arrived in London for his annual visit in early May, missing Byron by only one week. 'I see him now,' Rogers told him, 'as he looked when I was leaving him one day, and as he cried out after me, with a gay face and a melancholy accent, "Moore is coming, and you and he will be together, and I shall *not* be with you." It went to my heart, for he loves you dearly.'[20]

Moore spent only three weeks in London, 'in *terrible* request, never half so much as before',[21] but eager to return to Bessy and his work. Byron was no longer there. Sheridan left another gap. The dazzling orator, the playwright and the wit, who even in his drunken decline had been the star of many a convivial evening where Moore and Byron had been present, was now entering his final illness. Bedridden, with bailiffs camping in his house, he no longer had the immunity from arrest for debt which he had enjoyed as an MP and lived in terror of being carried off to prison. Moore returned home with Rogers late one evening, to find a note from Sheridan on the hall table. 'I find things settled so that £150 will remove all difficulties. I am absolutely undone and broken hearted. I shall negotiate for the Plays successfully in the course of a week when all shall be returned...

They are going to take the carpets out of the window and break into Mrs S.'s room and *take me* – for God's sake let me see you. R.B.S.'[22]

Although it was after midnight Moore and Rogers hurried round to Sheridan's house in Savile Row, where they learned from a servant that the arrest had not yet taken place, but that bills would be posted on the house the next day. Moore returned in the morning with a draft for £150 from Rogers, to find Sheridan talking with his usual optimism of publishing his dramatic works and settling all his affairs if he could only leave his bed.

It was not to be. Sheridan died less than two months later. He was buried in Westminster Abbey, the grandees who had neglected him in his last days

now gathering to give him a magnificent funeral procession. The pall
bearers included the Duke of Bedford and Earl Spencer; the mourners were
led by two royal dukes, the Dukes of York and Sussex, with the Duke of
Argyll and a phalanx of marquesses, earls, viscounts and barons behind
them. The contrast with the scenes that had gone before was striking and
Moore, in a generous burst of indignation, put his feelings into verse:

> O it sickens the heart to see bosoms so hollow,
> And friendships so false in the rich and high-born; –
> To think what a long line of titles may follow
> The relics of him who lay friendless and lorn!
>
> How proud they can press to the fun'ral array
> Of him whom they shunn'd in his sickness and sorrow –
> How bailiffs may seize his last blanket today,
> Whose pall may be held up by nobles tomorrow…

The poverty of writers, Byron pursued by duns, Sheridan dying in misery,
seemed to be a recurring theme that year. Coleridge was another case in
point. Writing to Francis Jeffrey in May, with the idea of doing something
for the *Edinburgh Review*, Moore told him: 'I had some idea of offering
myself to you to quiz Christabel… but I have lately been told that Coleridge
is poor – so poor as to be obliged to apply to the Literary Fund – and as
this is no laughing matter – why – I shall leave him alone.'[23] Despite this,
many of Moore's contemporaries, including Coleridge himself, believed
that Moore was responsible for the insulting anonymous review of *Christabel*
that appeared in the *Edinburgh Review* that autumn; Moore's letter, first
published over a century later, makes it clear that he was not. Moore's own
opinion of the article – making it doubly plain that he was not the author
– appears in a letter to John Murray (Coleridge's publisher) that December:
'The article upon Coleridge in the E.Rev. was altogether disgraceful both
from its dullness and illiberality – You know I had some idea of laughing
at Christabel myself – but when you told me that Coleridge was very poor
and had been to the Literary Fund, I thought this was no laughing matter
and gave up my intention.'[24]

Moore would have his own troubles with reviewers that autumn when
the first number of his *Sacred Songs* appeared. Consisting of sixteen airs,
including three by Haydn, two by Beethoven and one by Mozart, they
were arranged by Stevenson; more intricate than the *Irish Melodies*, eleven

of the sixteen were also set in a special arrangement for three voices. But it was the words, not the airs, which attracted criticism. Many of them were based on biblical passages, as for instance, 'Fall'n is thy throne' from Jeremiah:

> Fall'n is thy throne, oh Israel!
> Silence is o'er thy plains;
> Thy dwellings all lie desolate,
> Thy children weep in chains.
> Where are the dews that fed thee,
> On Etham's barren shore?
> The fire from Heaven which led thee,
> Now lights thy path no more.

But others had more general themes, vaguely religious without a scriptural basis, and in these, according to his critics, there was too much that was secular. They were not 'the effusions of a devout mind,' claimed the priggish *British Review*, 'nor has the Jordan in which he has immersed his Muse, so washed out the stains of her leprosy as to qualify her to sing the glories of him who is the God of purity.'[25] Moore was still being damned for the sins of Thomas Little.

The *Sacred Songs*, with their slightly dubious mix of sentiment and religion, would never match the popularity of Moore's *Irish Melodies*. He was already working on his next, and seventh, collection of these for Power. 'There are two or three of the Irish ones equal to any I have done,' he wrote to him in late September, 'and one in particular ("This Earth is the Planet") which will be very popular in my own singing of it.'[26] Let us join Power in a preview of this, its first lines already quoted, but so characteristic of Moore's cheerful philosophy that it is worth repeating.

> They may rail at this life – from the hour I began it,
> I found it a place full of kindness and bliss;
> And until they can show me some happier planet,
> More social and bright, I'll content me with this.
> As long as the world has such lips and such eyes,
> As before me this moment enraptur'd I see,
> They may say what they will of their orbs in the skies,
> But this earth is the planet for you, love and me...

As for those chilly orbs on the verge of creation,

Where sunshine and smiles must be equally rare,

Did they want a supply of cold hearts for that station,

Heav'n knows we have plenty on earth we could spare.

Oh! think what a world we should have of it here,

If the haters of peace, affection and glee,

Were to fly up to Saturn's comfortless sphere,

And leave earth to such spirits as you, love, and me.

Meanwhile *Lalla Rookh* was drawing to its weary close; by the end of 1816, in the teeth of persistent colds and headaches, Moore was able to tell Longmans that he would bring them the completed poem in February. Writing it had ceased to be a pleasure; he was weighed down by the burden of research and the heavy responsibility he felt at the risk his publishers were taking. To make matters worse, Britain was in the throes of a severe economic depression. The country was exhausted by long years of war; agricultural and commercial distress was widespread; and the chances of 'so light and costly' a venture as *Lalla Rookh* succeeding in such unpromising conditions seemed particularly bleak. With this in mind, Moore wrote to Longmans, offering to postpone or even cancel his contract altogether if they were in financial difficulties. Their reply was as generous as the impulse that inspired it: 'We shall be most happy in the pleasure of seeing you in February. We agree with you, indeed, that the times are most inauspicious for "poetry and thousands"; but we believe that your poetry would do more than that of any other living poet at the present moment.'[27]

Moore needed all the encouragement he could get. At the beginning of January 1817, he received the unwelcome news that, due to government retrenchments, his father had lost his post as Barrack Master. 'This is a heavy blow to me – as I shall have to support them [his parents] for the remainder of their lives,'[28] he told James Power. Embarrassing though it was, his only hope was to write to the Tory minister Lord Mulgrave, as Master-General of the Ordnance, to put the case for his father's retirement on half pay. Mulgrave, who seems to have borne no malice for his anti-government squibs, agreed, and Moore breathed a sigh of relief. '*Between ourselves,*' he wrote to Power, 'he never could have got it, had I not myself written to Lord Mulgrave on the subject.'[29]

With the worst of his worries behind him, he could now set off to London with the manuscript of *Lalla Rookh*. He arrived there on 5 March, and before the day was out, the printers were at work and the financial arrangements with Longmans were agreed. (Moore kept £1,000 of the £3,000 to pay his debts, leaving the other £2,000 on interest for his parents and unmarried sister Ellen.) He had already decided to give up the house at Mayfield for something close to London, from which he could see his poem through the press. Having fixed on a cottage in Hornsey, six miles north of the city, he rushed back home to collect his family. On the evening of 11 March, with bills settled, and the good wishes of their neighbours to accompany them, they took the coach to London. 'You will perceive that my poem is announced...' wrote Moore in a hasty note to his mother before leaving; 'I shall now have a most racketting time of it till I am published.'[30]

14

Lalla Rookh

Having spent the summer and autumn of 1816 travelling, Byron had settled in Venice for the winter and from there had begun to write to Moore again. Though battered and shaken by the storm of invective that had driven him from England, he had risen to adversity with characteristic buoyancy of spirit: 'the same instinct of resistance to injustice, which had first forced out the energies of his youthful genius...' wrote Moore, 'was now destined to give a bolder and loftier range to his powers.'[1] Immediate evidence of this was the third canto of *Childe Harold,* which appeared in November: 'The 3rd Canto of the Childe is magnificent – ' Moore wrote to Murray, 'no man living can write up to it.'[2]

Byron in his turn was taking a close interest in the progress of *Lalla Rookh*. 'I feel as anxious for Moore, as I could do for myself, for the soul of me,'[3] he wrote to Murray; and to Moore, on 24 December: 'When does your Poem of Poems come out?'[4]

It was the day before Christmas; on the 26th, the Venice carnival would begin:

But the Carnival's coming,
Oh Thomas Moore,
The Carnival's coming,
Oh Thomas Moore;
Masking and humming,
Fifing and drumming,

Guitarring and strumming,
Oh Thomas Moore.

Effervescent, witty, full of affection and shafts of insight, Byron's letters
to Moore from Italy show him at his most delightful. Most precious of all
are the verses that sometimes make their first appearance there, as in a letter
of 29 February, when Byron having 'just turned the corner of twenty-
nine' sent Moore his unforgettable lines.

So, we'll go no more a roving
So late into the night,
Though the heart be still as loving
And the moon be still as bright...

Moore, as usual, was a dilatory correspondent. 'I have now written to
you at least six letters, or letterets,' complained Byron on 25 March, 'and
all I have received in return is a note about the length you used to write
from Bury Street to St James's Street, when we used to dine with Rogers,
and talk laxly, and go to parties and hear poor Sheridan now and then.'[5]

This time Moore had every excuse. On arriving in London, they had
taken some time to settle into the cottage at Hornsey, where a plague of rats
and a smoking room had driven him into a fidget of nervous frustration.
Everything now depended on his having two months of peace and quiet
to get his poem through the press – a more than usually complex task, due
to the number of unfamiliar oriental names and the profusion of footnotes
on each page. At the same time he was trying to hold off James Power, who
was eager to get out the next number of the *Irish Melodies*. Moore was not
yet satisfied with what he had done. 'I feel quite sure you will not press me
now (in the crisis of my fate)...' he wrote to Power on 26 March. 'You may
depend however upon my doing every thing to have the Number out as
soon after the Poem as possible, but I am the more anxious to have it good,
from looking upon it as a *corps de reserve* for my Fame, in case the *main
attack* is unsuccessful.'[6]

By 13 May, after nearly two months of concentrated work, he was at
last on the home stretch. 'I am posting away, whip and spur, for the goal
which (you will have seen by the papers) I am to reach on the 22nd,'
he told his mother. 'Strange to say the work is not finished yet, but I
hope to give the last of it into the printer's before Saturday. I believe there
is a good deal of anxiety for it, and the *first* sale will, I have no doubt, be

rapid; but whether it will stick to that is the question, and I have my fears.'[7]

Despite his misgivings, *Lalla Rookh* was a success beyond Moore's wildest dreams. Within the first year it had run into seven editions, while the twenty-two songs included in the poem, with their music printed separately, were a unexpected bonus for James Power. In the long run it would prove to be one of the great publishing triumphs of the nineteenth century. Selling steadily for over thirty years, it repaid Longmans a hundredfold for their faith in Moore; Thomas Longman, said a wag, used to lick his lips whenever Moore's name was mentioned.

Lalla Rookh was very much a poem of its time. It appeared when poetry still commanded a wide audience of educated readers; Moore and Byron were among the last generation of poets to reach a public that novelists would soon claim as their own. It was fortunate too in coming out at a time when the fashionable appetite for orientalism – whetted, as Byron had foretold, by his own Eastern poems – was at its height. The domes and minarets of the Prince Regent's pavilion at Brighton reflected the growing interest in the glamorous East: a vague, rich region, in which Egypt, China, Persia, India and the Bosphorus were almost indistinguishable from each other, and on which Moore drew indiscriminately in his background reading for the poem.

Perhaps one reason that *Lalla Rookh* is virtually forgotten now, is that it drew its inspiration from the library, not as Byron's poems did, from the lived experience of his travels. Moore, however, was immensely proud of the comprehensiveness of his research. 'I have not forgotten how great was my pleasure,' he wrote in his *Poetical Works*, 'when told by the late Sir James Mackintosh, that he was once asked by Colonel Wilks, the historian of British India, "whether it was true that Moore had never been in the East?" "Never," answered Mackintosh. "Well, that shows me," replied Colonel Wilks, "that reading over D'Herbelot's [*Bibliothèque Orientale*] is as good as riding on the back of a camel."'[8]

Moore's painstaking researches provided the groundwork for a poem of some five and a half thousand lines, divided, like *The Arabian Nights*, into separate tales, and linked by a narrative in prose. The King of Lesser Bucharia, we are told in the opening prose section, has just given up his throne in favour of his son and has arranged that this son should marry Lalla Rookh (or Tulip Cheek), the daughter of the Emperor Aurungzebe of Delhi. The wedding ceremony is to take place in Cashmere. Lalla Rookh leaves Delhi with a numerous retinue, and whiles away the tedium of the journey every evening by listening to the stories of the young poet Feramorz, with whom she unwillingly falls in love.

The first tale, set in Persia, is that of 'The Veiled Prophet of Khorassan'. The satanic Mokanna, the protagonist, is the leader of a revolutionary religious sect, whose veil is said to hide the unbearable brightness of his countenance. The beautiful Zelica, driven to despair by the reported death of her lover, has joined the movement as his High Priestess, after pledging her allegiance to him in a gruesome ceremony in a charnel house. But her lover, Azim, has not been killed, and he escapes from imprisonment to join the Prophet's supposedly noble cause. The former lovers recognise each other, Zelica recoiling from him in horror as she is reminded of her oath to Mokanna. Azim changes sides at the realisation of Mokanna's crimes, and joins the besieging forces that defeat him. Mokanna, after poisoning all his chieftains at a ghastly banquet, plunges into a pool of burning acid, but not before revealing the disfigured face behind his veil. Zelica, seeking death, dons his veil as Azim's forces storm his stronghold, and is impaled on Azim's spear. After years spent in prayer by Zelica's tomb, Azim learns in a vision that Zelica's soul has been received into paradise; he dies content and is buried by her side.

Strong stuff, and so far removed from Moore's normal style, that it was hardly surprising that critics ascribed its morbidity to Byron's influence. But it has none of Byron's power or energy, and modern readers will be tempted to join the fastidious eunuch, Fadladeen, Grand Nazir or Chamberlain of the Harem, in his dismissal of the poem:

> The chief personages of the story were, if he rightly understood them, an ill favoured gentleman with a veil over his face; – a young lady, whose reason went and came, according as it suited the poet's convenience … and a youth in one of those hideous Bucharian bonnets, who took the aforesaid gentleman in a veil for a Divinity. 'From such materials,' said he, 'what can be expected? – after rivalling each other in long speeches and absurdities, through some thousands of lines … our friend in a veil jumps into a tub of aqua-fortis; the young lady dies in a set speech whose only recommendation is that it is her last; and the lover lives on to a good old age, for the laudable purpose of seeing her ghost, which he at last happily accomplishes, and expires.'

Moore's sense of humour was hard to suppress, even when it was at his own expense, and the chamberlain's sarcastic comments in the linking narrative are one of the pleasures of *Lalla Rookh*.

The second story, 'Paradise and the Peri', as Feramorz says, 'with an appealing look to Fadladeen', is in a 'lighter and humbler strain' than the first. Insubstantial and delicious as candy floss, it tells of a Peri who searches the world for the gift that will open the gates of Paradise, and finds it at last in the tears of a repentant sinner:

> Joy, joy for ever! my task is done –
> The gates are pass'd and Heav'n is won!

The third tale, 'The Fire-worshippers', was, as Moore wrote himself, the most home-felt of his inspirations. He had been drawn to it by reading of the struggle between the Ghebers, or ancient Fire-worshippers of Persia and their tyrannical Moslem masters; the story seemed an allegory of his own country's woes. 'The cause of tolerance,' he wrote, 'was again my inspiring theme; and the spirit that had spoken in the melodies of Ireland soon found itself at home in the East.'[9]

As in 'The Veiled Prophet', the theme was that of love versus duty. The Moslem heroine Hinda falls in love with Hafed, leader of the rebel Fire-worshippers, only to realise that their love is doomed. In the most often quoted (and parodied) lines of the poem, she laments the ruin of her hopes.

> Oh! ever thus, from childhood's hour,
> I've seen my fondest hopes decay;
> I never lov'd a tree or flow'r
> But 'twas the first to fade away.
> I never nurs'd a dear gazelle,
> To glad me with its soft black eye,
> But when it came to know me well,
> And love me, it was sure to die!

Worse is to come. Hafed is betrayed. Like Robert Emmet he dies fighting for the cause of freedom, his gallant struggle condemned by the victors as rebellion. In a burst of indignation, that seems to reflect his own feelings for his friend, Moore denounces the double standards by which he is judged.

> Rebellion! foul dishonouring word,
> Whose wrongful blight so oft has stain'd

The holiest cause that tongue or sword
Of mortal ever lost or gain'd.
How many a spirit, born to bless,
Hath sunk beneath that with'ring name,
Whom but a day's, an hour's success
Had wafted to eternal fame!

Hinda does not survive her lover; as his funeral pyre lights the night sky, she flings herself into the waters of the Caspian:

One wild, heart-broken shriek she gave;
Then sprung, as if to reach that blaze,
Where still she fix'd her dying gaze,
And, gazing, sunk into the wave, –
Deep, deep, – where never care or pain
Shall reach her innocent heart again.

Fadladeen, the eunuch, surprisingly abstains from criticism of the Fire-worshippers; in fact, he regards its subject matter as so subversive that he is biding his time till he can denounce the poet to the authorities. But he is vocal in his scorn for the poet's last story, which recounts how the Sultana Nourmahal, after quarrelling with her husband, wins back his love by her enchanting singing at the Feast of the Roses in Cashmere. 'The profusion, indeed, of flowers and birds…' he sniffs, 'not to mention dews, gems, & c. – was a most oppressive kind of opulence to his hearers; and had the unlucky effect of giving his style all the glitter of the flower garden without its method, and all the flutter of the aviary without its song.' It is hard not to sympathise with Fadladeen. There is something cloying about so much sweetness, and though, at the end of the narrative, the eunuch changes his tune when he discovers that the poet is none other than the King of Bucharia in disguise, the rest of us feel he has a point.

Although it has many incidental beauties – 'Paradise and the Peri' in particular – *Lalla Rookh* as a whole is almost unreadable today. This is not only because long poems have gone out of fashion but because Moore, in the end, was a writer of songs and lyrics, not an epic poet. For all its skill and virtuosity one senses the weariness from which he was suffering when he wrote the poem. 'The Fire-worshippers', indeed, has some real feeling as an allegory of Ireland's woes, but his *Irish Melodies* are a hundred times more successful in pleading the same cause.

At the time, however, there were few to criticise. Almost all the reviewers were in raptures. Jeffrey made up for his former strictures in the *Edinburgh Review*: *Lalla Rookh*, he wrote, was the best example of orientalism yet written in England, and recalling how the *Edinburgh*, with perhaps 'unnecessary severity' had chastised the younger poet for his licentiousness, hailed Moore as an 'eloquent champion of purity, fidelity and delicacy'. The *British Review*, it is true, dismissed the poem as 'mellifluous nonsense'; against this must be set the verdicts of the *Monthly Magazine*, which saw its publication as 'the rising of a sun which will never set', and the formidable John Wilson ('Christopher North') of *Blackwood s Magazine* who called Moore 'the most ingenious, brilliant and fanciful poet of the age'.

The poem was translated into almost every European language, and even, it was said, into Persian, thus prompting a delightful quatrain from the wit and poet Henry Luttrell:

> I'm told, dear Moore, your lays are sung,
> (Can it be true, you lucky man?)
> By moonlight, in the Persian tongue,
> Along the streets of Isphahan.[10]

In America where, in the words of Dr Hoover Jordan, 'it pushed forward with the the Bible into the frontier', its characters found their way into the Mardi Gras. The Crown Prince of Prussia slept with a copy of the poem under his pillow; the East India Company named a ship in its honour; a village priest in Ireland paid for repairs to his chapel by raffling a copy. In Berlin, at a masque to celebrate the visit of the Grand Duke Nicholas, later Nicholas I, in 1822, the future Tsar and Tsarina – resplendent in pearls and amber coloured satin – played the roles of Feramorz and Lallah Rookh and a hundred and fifty royal or noble personages took part in the accompanying tableaux, songs and dances.

'In this grand Fête, it appears,' writes Moore,

> originated the translation of Lalla Rookh into German verse, by the Baron de la Motte Fouqué... As soon as the performance, he tells us, had ended, Lalla Rookh (the Empress herself) exclaimed with a sigh, 'Is it then all over? are we now at the close of all that has given us so much delight? and lives there no poet who will impart to others and to future times, some notion of the happiness we have enjoyed this evening?' On hearing this appeal, a knight of Cashmere (who is no other than the

poetical Baron himself) comes forward and promises to attempt to present to the world 'the Poem itself in the measure of the original'; – whereupon Lalla Rookh, it is added, approvingly smiled.[11]

Byron was delighted by *Lalla Rookh*'s success. 'I am very glad to hear of its popularity,' he told John Murray, ' – for Moore is a very noble fellow in all respects – and will enjoy it without any of the bad feelings which Success – good or evil – sometimes engenders in the men of rhyme.'[12] But though he did not say so openly he was privately disappointed by the poem. His first reaction, after receiving extracts from the first two episodes of *Lalla Rookh*, had been encouraging. 'I am very much delighted with what is before me,' he wrote to Moore in July 1817, 'and very thirsty for the rest. You have caught the colours as if you have been in the rainbow, and the tone of the East has been perfectly preserved.'[13] Thereafter he did not write to Moore again till February, four months after he had received the completed copy, when he referred to it only in his postscript: 'I delight in the fame and fortune of Lalla, and again congratulate you on your well deserved success.'[14]

Significantly, he made no further comment on the poem. He could not bring himself to give pain to Moore, or even – except very mildly – to criticise him to others. But Moore must have drawn his own conclusions from his silence. Throughout the writing of *Lalla Rookh* he had been plagued by feelings of self doubt, and even when its triumph was assured he never allowed his head to be turned. Years later, writing to Thomas Longman junior, who had been rejoicing at its continuing sales, he correctly foretold the verdict of posterity. 'With respect to what you say about *Lalla Rookh* being the "cream of copyrights", perhaps it may in a *property* sense; but I am strongly inclined to think that, in a race into future times (if *anything* of mine could pretend to such a run), those little ponies, the "Melodies", will beat the mare, *Lalla Rookh* hollow.'[15]

The summer of 1817 must have been a pleasant one for Moore. He was now at the zenith of his fame as a poet, feted on all sides, but surprisingly unspoilt throughout. We catch a pleasing glimpse of him in Benjamin Haydon's diary at a farewell dinner for the great Shakespearean actor John Philip Kemble on his departure from the stage.

> A more complete farce was never acted … The Drury Lane actors flattered
> the Covent Garden ones, the Covent Garden ones flattered in turn the
> Drury Lane. Lord Holland flattered Kemble; Kemble flattered Lord
> Holland. Thomas Campbell the Poet, flattered Moore (whom I knew

he hated), but Tom Moore, like an honest, sensible genius, as he is, drank his wine and flattered no one. This gives me a higher opinion of Moore, would make me feel more inclined to know him, than any thing he has ever written.[16]

Bessy too was enjoying the pleasures of London life – there were visits to the opera and the theatre, and a stream of callers to their house in Hornsey. But the cottage was expensive (£90 a year), the bustle of engagements made work almost impossible, and they had already decided that they must look for something cheaper and quieter in the country. At a dinner at Lady Bessborough's that June, the Marquess of Lansdowne (whose father, as Lord Shelburne, had been one of *Anacreon*'s first subscribers) suggested that they might like to find a home near Bowood, his house in Wiltshire, and promised to see what was available. It was a flattering suggestion; meanwhile, however, Moore had been invited to visit Paris with Samuel Rogers, and he postponed his decision till he returned. He set off with Rogers in mid-July, and was joined there soon after by his musical collaborator, Sir John Stevenson – the composer, wrote Moore, was not at his best in Paris: 'the ice is too cold for his stomach, and he cannot get whisky-punch for love or money – accordingly he droops.'[17]

They had come there at a fascinating time, when the remnants of the old Napoleonic regime had not yet been banished by the return of the Bourbons, themselves representing the *ancien régime* of more than twenty years before. 'It was as if, in the days succeeding the deluge,' wrote Moore, 'a small coterie of antediluvians had been suddenly evoked from the deep to take command of a new and freshly starting world.'[18] It was a setting that Moore would use as the background for his farcical series, *The Fudge Family in Paris*, a year later. But he had only been in Paris three weeks when a letter from Bessy summoned him home with the news that their eldest daughter Barbara, now five, was dangerously ill after a fall.

It is impossible, given the state of medical knowledge at the time, to tell exactly what was wrong with Barbara. The doctors later said that the fall had only hastened an existing internal condition, from which she would have died in any case. She rallied briefly after Moore's return but it soon became clear there was no hope for her. On 20 September, he wrote to his mother. 'It's all over, my dearest mother; our Barbara is gone. She died the day before yesterday, and though her death was easy, it was a dreadful scene to us both.' It was hard to bear the sight of Bessy's anguish. 'Indeed my dearest mother', he added with unconscious egoism, 'you can only conceive what she feels by imagining *me* to have been snatched away from you at the age of Barbara.'[19]

The cottage in Hornsey was full of sad memories, and they determined it was time to move. The kindly Lady Donegal came to their rescue, sweeping them off to the comfort of her London house in Davies Street while they decided what to do. Lord Lansdowne, meanwhile, had renewed his suggestion that they should come and live near Bowood and invited Moore to stay there while he looked at houses in the neighbourhood. Moore accordingly set off to Wiltshire, where of three houses available, only one was within their means, a small thatched cottage with a pretty garden, near the village of Bromham, three miles away from Bowood. At first sight Moore thought it too humble for even their modest requirements, but Bessy, who went to look at it with James Power a few days later, declared herself not only satisfied but delighted with it. They arranged to take it furnished for £40 a year – 'this is cheap, God knows,'[20] wrote Moore – and in early November they moved in. The house was called Sloperton Cottage. It was to be their home for the rest of their lives.

15

Sloperton Days

It was a forlorn little party – Moore, his wife, their faithful maid Hannah and the three-year-old Anastasia – that arrived in Wiltshire in November 1817. Moore tried to work on the verses inspired by his visit to France, *The Fudge Family in Paris,* but found it hard to summon up the 'gaiety of imagination' needed. 'I suppose it is natural that Death's first visit among those dear to us should leave this desolate feel behind it,'[1] he wrote to Samuel Rogers sadly. For him, though not for Bessy, the loss of Olivia as a baby scarcely counted in comparison to that of the five-year-old Barbara.

Gradually, however, things began to improve. In the first place the cottage was the most comfortable they had yet possessed: 'even during these last and stormy days it has neither smoked nor let in water – *et c est beaucoup pour Slopperton,*' he told Rogers in December. Its closeness to Bowood was a further blessing. 'Lord Lansdowne's Library is within a moderate walk of me, and as most of my London friends come down to visit him in the course of the year, I shall have just those *glimpses* of society, which throw a light over one's solitude, and enliven it,'[2] he wrote to his friend James Corry.

It would be easy to label Moore as a hanger-on in great houses, but this would do him an injustice. He had, indeed, in the words of the critic George Saintsbury, 'a cat-like disposition to curl himself up near somebody or something comfortable'. But there was nothing remotely servile about him; as Saintsbury put it, 'it does not appear that Moore was any more inclined to put up with insulting treatment than the cat itself is'.[3] There was no question, in any case, of anything but consideration from Lord Lansdowne. Unlike Lord Moira, who had been of a different generation from Moore, Lansdowne was a year younger than Moore, and their relationship was far more equal. A devoted follower of Fox, he had served as Chancellor of the Exchequer during the short-lived Ministry of All the Talents. Since then, he had been in the political wilderness; Lansdowne House, like Holland House, remained a centre of Whig opposition and liberal thought. Although he supported Whig policies, particularly on Catholic emancipation, Lansdowne lacked great political ambitions; the list of his appointments – Trustee of the British Museum, President of the Zoological Society, the Statistical Society, the British Association for the Advancement of Science and the Royal Literary Fund – shows where his real interests lay. Patronage of the arts and sciences ran in the family. Lansdowne's father had subsidised Joseph Priestley in his scientific researches – Priestley made his discovery of oxygen while staying at Lansdowne House – and had gathered around him most of the leading intellectual figures of the day.

His son carried on the tradition. Bowood was a palace of the fine arts, where Moore could study at will in the library, and where his sparkling company was a prime attraction when there were guests. Bessy found it harder to adapt to such magnificence and, knowing none of the people present, spent her first evening there in a 'state of dignified desolation', which she was not at all desirous to repeat. But the Lansdownes came to call on her soon after, staying for lunch and a ramble through the fields, and their unaffected friendliness soon melted her reserve. 'We shall get on with them, I have no doubt, most comfortably,' Moore wrote to Samuel Rogers; 'and as they will only come like comets now and then into our system, we shall enjoy a little of their light and warmth without being dazzled or scorched by them.'[4]

Fortunately, there were other less daunting neighbours, the closest to their heart, perhaps, the Reverend William Bowles, vicar of the nearby village of Bremhill. Bowles was an antiquarian and a poet – Coleridge had addressed one of his first sonnets to him – who had become increasingly eccentric with the years. 'His parsonage house at Bremhill is beautifully situated,' wrote Moore; 'but he has a good deal frittered away its beauty with grottos, hermitages and Shenstonian inscriptions; when company is coming, he cries, "here, John, run with the crucifix & missal to the Hermitage, & set the fountain going." His sheep bells are tuned in thirds and fifths; but he is an excellent fellow notwithstanding.'[5]

Another local cleric and poet was George Crabbe, whose sturdy, realistic poems of rural life were much admired by Byron; an elderly widower, he was afraid at first that the Moores might find him boring. But he was quickly won over by Moore's admiration for his work, while pretty Bessy, 'the Fair Lady', as he called her, became a special favourite.

With these, and other neighbours, who included William Henry Fox Talbot of Lacock Abbey, notable for his discovery of the basic process of photography, the Moores soon had friends enough to enliven the monotony of country life. Bessy too began to busy herself with charitable activities, for outside the well-run Bowood estate there was great agricultural distress in the area. Moore supported her, not only with money and encouragement, but with practical help. The grandson of the Reverend William Goddard, Moore's landlord at Sloperton Cottage, recalled how once, when smallpox was raging in the village of Bromham, Moore sent all his household away and stayed behind to nurse the sick and dying.

Meanwhile, as the winter of 1817–18 wore on, he settled down to work once more. He had several literary projects under way. As well as *The Fudge Family in Paris*, he was working on the seventh volume of his *Irish Melodies*, and a new collection of songs, drawing on music from other countries, *National Airs*.

He had also been approached by John Murray, who, struck by his verses on Sheridan's death, had suggested he write a biography of the playwright. It was a tricky undertaking. Sheridan's character was many sided, and his high ideals of honour and independence were coupled with behaviour of the most devious kind. 'The more I think and the more opinions I receive about the life of Sheridan, the more I see reason to quake upon the subject,' he wrote. 'Truth will be deadly, and vague praise will be cowardly – so what am I to do.'[6]

Byron, however, was full of enthusiasm for the project. In a letter to Moore from Venice he gave what must surely be the final word on Sheridan's erratic, brilliant and ultimately tragic career:

> The Whigs abuse him; however he never left them, and such blunderers deserve neither credit nor compassion. As for his creditors – remember Sheridan *never had a shilling*, and was thrown, with great powers and passions, into the thick of the world, and placed upon the pinnacle of success, with no other external means to support him in his elevation. Did Fox *pay his* debts? or did Sheridan take a subscription? Was the Duke

of Norfolk's drunkeness more excusable than his? Were his intrigues more notorious than those of all his contemporaries? and is his memory to be blasted, and theirs respected? Don't let yourself be led away by clamour, but compare him with the coalitioner Fox, and the pensioner Burke as a man of principle, and with ten thousand others in personal views, and with none in talent for he beat them all *out* and *out*. Without means, without connexion, without character (which might be false at first, and make him mad afterwards from desperation) he beat them all, in all he ever attempted.[7]

It must be counted as one of Moore's virtues, writes his biographer L.A.G. Strong, 'that he somehow provoked Byron to write him some of the best letters in the language'.[8]

Despite some unresolved problems with Sheridan's son Charles over the use of his father's papers, Moore set about collecting materials for the *Life*. He was just planning a trip to Ireland to research Sheridan's early years, when on 1 April 1818, he received a summons to London to appear before the Doctors' Commons (the court dealing with Admiralty business) within fifteen days. Goodrich, his deputy in Bermuda, had absconded with the proceeds of a ship and cargo and Moore, as the official registrar, was legally responsible for the sum.

Strangely, he had had a premonition of disaster. 'I dreamt about a week ago,' he wrote to Lady Donegal, 'that I was walking home in full sunshine, and that suddenly a pitch-black cloud came all over the sky, like the forerunner of an earth quake that made me cower down to the very earth exclaiming, "Oh, my dear Bessy and child!" Is this what they call dreams being *out*?'[9]

It was an appalling blow, though at first sight the situation seemed to offer some glimmerings of hope. Goodrich had been recommended by his uncle, a rich merchant, Robert Sheddon, and though the sum involved – £6,000 – was far beyond Moore's means, there was a possibility that Sheddon would feel morally bound to honour his nephew's debt, or at least put pressure on him to pay. Meanwhile the case was deferred till 10 July the following year. Having despatched a power of attorney to possess any of Goodrich's property available in Bermuda, Moore could do nothing but wait.

He put a good face on his troubles to his friends, writing jokingly to Lady Donegal that he hoped she would use her influence to find him *two* rooms in prison. 'I don't know how it is,' he told her, 'as long as my conscience is sound and that suffering is not attended by delinquency, I doubt whether even a prison will make much difference in my cheerfulness.'

Meanwhile there were two new works of his appearing that month, *The Fudge Family in Paris* and his *National Airs*. The tunes for the latter were variously identified as Italian, Russian, Spanish, Indian, Neapolitan and others, but the best known of them, 'Oft in the Stilly Night', supposedly to a Scottish air, was very probably one of his own:

Oft in the stilly night
Ere Slumber's chain has bound me,
Fond Memory brings the light
Of other days around me;
The smiles, the tears
Of boyhood's years,
The words of love then spoken;
The eyes that shone,
Now dimm'd and gone,
The cheerful hearts now broken!
Thus, in the stilly night,
Ere Slumber's chain has bound me,
Sad Memory brings the light
Of other days around me.

When I remember all
The friends, so link'd together,
I've seen around me fall,
Like leaves in wintry weather;
I feel like one,
Who treads alone
Some banquet hall deserted,
Whose lights are fled,
Whose garlands dead,
And all but he departed!
Thus, in the stilly night,
Ere Slumber's chain has bound me,

Sad Memory brings the light
Of other days around me.

'O si sic omnia,'[10] exclaimed Tennyson on reading this lyric, lovely enough on its own, but still more beautiful when sung.

Very different in tone was Moore's *The Fudge Family in Paris*. In a series of humorous verse letters, supposedly edited by 'Thomas Brown, the Younger', it recounts the experiences of an Irish family visiting Paris for the first time after the fall of Napoleon: Biddy Fudge, the daughter, chiefly interested in clothes; her father, Philip Fudge, who writes his letters to C-st-r--gh [Castlereagh], the Foreign Secretary, praising Tory policy and the Holy Alliance; his son Bob, a would-be dandy, proud of his whiskers, his tight neckcloth and his shiny boots; Phelim Connor, his cousin and tutor, an Irish patriot who deplores the downfall of Napoleon.

True, he was false – despotic – all you please –
Had trampled down man's holiest liberties –
Had, by a genius, form'd for nobler things
Than lie within the grasp of *vulgar* Kings,
But rais'd the hopes of men – as eaglets fly
With tortoises aloft into the sky –
To dash them down again more shatt'ringly
All this I own – but still!

The liberal message, running through a light-hearted commentary on the follies and frivolity of Restoration Paris, was very clear, and was greeted with pleasure by Whigs and radicals alike. The Tory press, predictably, was quick to damn the book, but their abuse did nothing to damage its sales – 'five editions in less than a fortnight,' Moore told his mother cheerfully 'and my share for that time (I go half and half with Longmans) was £350.'[11] But for the shadow of the Bermuda claim hanging over him he had every reason to be cheerful.

At the end of May Moore made his postponed visit to Dublin to begin his researches on Sheridan, and was given a hero's welcome on arrival. On a visit to the theatre, where *Lalla Rookh* had been adapted as an opera, he was greeted with repeated bursts of applause, which he rose to acknowledge again and again. There was a public banquet in his honour, presided over by Lord Charlemont, and attended by most of the notables of Dublin, including Daniel O'Connell. Among the many toasts that evening was one to his father, who was present, and Moore got up to answer it on his behalf. 'If I deserve (which I cannot persuade myself) one-half of the honours which you have this day heaped upon me, to him and to the education which he struggled hard to give me I owe it all: yes, gentlemen, to him and an admirable mother – one of the warmest hearts even this land of warm hearts ever produced.'[12]

'Perhaps you may have heard of the dinner given to Tho. Moore in Dublin...' wrote the young John Keats to his brother and sister-in-law in America. 'The most pleasant thing that occurred was the speech Mr Tom made on his Farther's [sic] health being drunk.'[13] 'I like that Moore,' he had commented a month earlier, when Moore had been in London, 'and am glad I saw him at the Theatre before I left town.'[14] Sadly, the two poets never met, though Leigh Hunt tried to bring them together at his Hampstead cottage.

Back from Ireland, his head still in a whirl from his enthusiastic reception – 'even better than Voltaire's in Paris,'[15] he told Rogers – Moore continued his Sheridan researches. On 18 August, he made the first entry in the journal which he would keep for the rest of his active life: 'Went to Bath, on my way to Leamington Spa, for the purpose of consulting Mrs Lefanu, the only surviving sister of Sheridan, on the subject of her brother's life.'

The next entry, 20 August, begins: 'Breakfast in the coffee room. Found Mrs Lefanu – the very image of Sheridan, having his features without his carbuncles, and all the light of his eyes without the illumination of his nose.'

The tone of the journal was set. From then on, for over a quarter of a century, Moore would keep an almost daily record of his activities, whether the quiet domestic round of Sloperton, or his sorties into society, and in doing so provide one of the most detailed and attractive pictures of early nineteenth-century literary, political and social life we have. Although it makes absorbing reading, and its pages have been repeatedly pillaged by historians of the period, it is not an introspective document. Only occasionally do we catch a glimpse of Moore's inner feelings, and he seldom makes any profound reflection on characters or events. But his asides and anecdotes are often more telling than more serious judgements, and thanks to Professor Dowden, some of the most revealing, expunged in the interests of propriety by Lord John Russell, are now in print. A good few of them relate to Sheridan, and in reading Moore's journal we understand some of his difficulties in presenting him in a flattering light.

There is the story of Sheridan's elopement, for instance, a romantic tale in which he rescues the beautiful singer Elizabeth Linley from the unwelcome advances of the villainous Captain Matthews. In Moore's biography of Sheridan, Elizabeth's virtue is never in question; in his journal, however, he notes down Matthews' boast that 'she was the prettiest creature stript you ever saw',[16] and that he had possessed her again and again. Later, in following the course of Sheridan's turbulent marriage, he records a curious story of Lady Holland's, whom Sheridan had tried to seduce by threatening to obtain her letters to a person 'for whom I certainly did not care in the least'. When this failed, he tried 'another most extra-ordinary method': 'I was told one day that a servant had brought a message which he would deliver to no-one but myself, & before I could order him to be admitted, in rushed Sheridan, wrapped in a great watch coat, and after my servant had quitted the room rushed up to me & with a ferociousness quite frightful bit my cheek so violently that the blood ran down my neck – I had just sense to ring the bell & he withdrew.'[17]

She added that at the time that Sheridan was attempting to make love to her, Elizabeth was flirting with Lord Lorne, eldest son of the Duke of Argyll, but that 'both of them would willingly have given us up for each other, if they could have come to some kind of explanation between them'. Between love and infidelity and jealousy, noted Moore, their life was one continual scene.

The biography, of course, painted a blander picture of Sheridan's marriage, and Moore did his best too, to gloss over the financial irregularities, sometimes little better than swindles, with which his career was littered. Where he was at his best was in his discussion of Sheridan's political dealings in which so often it was Sheridan, rather than the idolised figure of Charles James Fox, whose judgement was the soundest. The book, as a result, would not be altogether welcome to the Whigs.

On 1 October the seventh number of Moore's *Irish Melodies* appeared. He had been unwilling at first, he explained in his preface, to add yet another volume to the series. But he had received so many 'old and beautiful melodies' from contributors that he had been persuaded to continue, 'though not without considerable diffidence of their success'. To some extent his diffidence was justified; with one exception, 'They may rail at this life', the songs did not quite reach the level of his earlier collections.

On 22 October, Moore called at Bowood, then returned home to dinner at four. 'Went to bed early,' he wrote, and was called up by Bessy at half-past eleven o'clock: sent for the midwife, who arrived between one and two, and at a quarter before four my darling Bessy was safely delivered of a son (and heir in partibus) to my unspeakable delight for never had I felt half such anxiety about her. I walked about the parlour by myself, like one distracted; sometimes stopping to pray, sometimes opening the door to listen; and never was gratitude more fervent than that with which I knelt down to thank God for my dear girl's safety, when all was over – (the maid, by the by, very near catching me on my knees.) Went to bed at six o'clock.[18]

The child was called Tom, or Thomas Lansdowne Moore in full, for Moore had asked Lord Lansdowne to be his godfather, and the latter had willingly agreed. The other godparents were Mary Godfrey, and the learned Dr Parr, a 'Whig Dr Johnson' as he was once described: an early friend of Sheridan's, whom he had taught at Harrow, he had been particularly helpful to Moore in his researches. By this stage Moore was making good progress with the narrative: 'Have got Sheridan fairly married at last,' he wrote on 29 October, 'and now enter into a new region of his life.'[19]

Bessy recovered quickly from Tom's birth; Moore hovered over her solicitously, reading aloud to her in the evenings – *Joseph Andrews* was their current reading – and trudging off across the fields to engage a wet nurse when her supply of milk ran out. On New Year's Eve they gave their first party at Sloperton: there were lobsters, oysters and champagne sent down expressly from London, and the dancing went on till four in the morning. 'A gay beginning to the new year,' wrote Moore in his journal. 'Heaven send it may so go on.'

16

The Blow Falls

Among the literary highspots of 1818 had been the series of lectures on the English poets by Hazlitt at the Surrey Institute; his criticism, thought Keats, was 'one of the three things to rejoice at in this Age'. His final lecture was 'On the living poets', and Moore, of course, was one of those he dealt with. He began by comparing him to the Scottish poet, Thomas Campbell, of whom he had just been speaking: 'Tom Moore is a poet of a quite different stamp. He is as heedless, gay and prodigal of his poetical wealth, as the other is careful, reserved and parsimonious. The genius of both is national. Mr Moore's Muse is another Ariel, as light, as tricksy and as humane a spirit...An airy voyager on life's stream, his mind inhales the fragrance of a thousand shores, and drinks of endless pleasures under halcyon skies.'

His chief fault, in Hazlitt's view, was too much facility: 'The graceful ease with which he lends himself to every subject...prevents him from giving their full force to the masses of things, from connecting them into a whole. He wants intensity, strength and grandeur...His pen, as it is rapid and fanciful, wants momentum and passion.'

For this reason *Lalla Rookh*, if not a failure, was a disappointment to the public's expectations:

> Mr Moore ought not to have written Lalla Rookh, even for three thousand guineas. His fame is worth more than that...Fortitude of mind is the first requisite of a tragic or epic writer. Happiness of nature and felicity

of genius are the pre-eminent characteristics of the bard of Erin. If he is
not perfectly contented with what he is, all the world beside is. He had
no temptation to risk anything in adding to the love and admiration of
his age, and more than one country.[1]

If the musical dimension, which added so much, is excluded, it would
hard to find a more sympathetic assessment of Moore's poetic qualities.
Moore would certainly not have quarrelled with Hazlitt's view of *Lalla
Rookh*. Later, for reasons that will become clear, Hazlitt turned violently
against him, dismissing his *Irish Melodies* in a devastating phrase: 'Mr Moore
converts the wild harp of Erin into a musical snuff-box!'[2] At the time,
though they had never met, the two men were on the best of terms. Moore,
who thought highly of Hazlitt's political journalism, presented him with
an inscribed copy of his *Fudge Family in Paris*; while Hazlitt, in his lecture,
'On the Comic Writers of the Last Century', the following year, welcomed
Moore as Sheridan's future biographer: 'His character will ... soon be drawn
by one who has all the ability and every inclination to do him justice; who
knows how to bestow praise and how to deserve it; by one who himself is
an ornament of public and private life; a satirist, beloved by his friends; a wit
and a patriot to boot; a poet and an honest man.'[3] Moore read the lecture,
with its 'warm eulogium' on himself, in the *Morning Chronicle* of 8 January
1819. It was a welcome compliment at a moment when he was beginning
to feel his powers were waning. The reviews of the *National Airs* and the
seventh volume of his *Irish Melodies* had been mixed. 'A remark in one of
these articles struck me with a sort of chilling consciousness,' he wrote
on 11 January. '"We can perceive the coming of age in the calmer fires of
the modern Anacreon" – alas! it is but too true.'[4]

He was further discouraged by the poor reception of his new political
satire, *Tom Crib s Memorial to Congress*, published by Longmans that month.
Written once more in boxing slang, it made fun of the political leaders of
the day: the Prince Regent, for instance, being knocked about the ring by
the Tsar. Although it was published anonymously, few reviewers were
deceived. So hostile was the general reaction, including that of friends
like Lady Donegal, that Moore resolved never to have anything to do
with satire again: 'It is a path in which one not only strews but gathers
thorns and nothing but the most flourishing success can enable one to
brave & laugh at all the emnity it produces.'[5] He was just preparing to
write a 'Farewell to Satire' when he heard that the first two editions had

sold out, and that a third was being advertised. He decided to postpone his farewell.

At the end of January, Moore was called to London to sign affidavits for his Bermuda case, which was still in limbo, though Toller, his proctor, was optimistic that it would be settled. While he was there he was called into the discussions over the publication of the first canto of Byron's *Don Juan*. Both Hobhouse and Murray were convinced that it could not be published as it stood; Byron suggested that they should show it to Moore and two others, Hookham Frere and Stewart Rose, for a decision.

'Went to breakfast with Hobhouse in order to read Lord Byron's Poem – ' wrote Moore on 31 January. He found it 'full of talent & singularity', with 'some highly beautiful and some highly humourous passages' but thought it too outspoken to be published as it stood. 'Don Juan's mother is Lady Byron – and not only her learning but various other points about her ridiculed…He talks of her favourite dress being dimity (which is the case) – dimity rhyming very comically to sublimity…and the conclusion to one stanza is "I hate a dumpy woman" – meaning Lady B again…There is also a systemised profligacy running through it which would not be borne.'[6] Moore had not spent eighteen years being castigated for immorality without knowing the risks of flouting public opinion.

Not surprisingly, Thomas Little was one of those quoted by Byron in defence of his own poem: 'If the objection be to the indecency, the Age which reads the "Bath Guide" and Little's poems…may bear with that; – if to the poetry – I will take my chance.'[7] But he agreed that the poem should be published anonymously and that some offensive lines on Southey and Castlereagh – who could not challenge him since he was abroad – should be cut. Beyond giving his opinion to Hobhouse, Moore took no part in these decisions. But he noted that Samuel Rogers, taking fright at the possible outcry *Don Juan* would arouse, had toned down some flattering references to Byron in his latest poem.

While he was in London Moore signed a new agreement with James Power for £500 yearly for the next six years. The two brothers, William in Ireland, and James in London, had fallen out. 'Heartily, most heartily sorry am I…' wrote Moore when the quarrel first broke out, 'that you are indeed become belligerent *Powers*.'[8] He had tried to remain neutral in their legal wranglings. but finally came down on the side of James. Since Stevenson, in Dublin, took the part of William, a new composer, Henry R. Bishop, was hired to arrange the music for future numbers of the *Irish Melodies*.

On 1 February, he set out for home: 'In the Coach at 1/2 past six ... arrived at eight in the evening and found the dear wife and her little ones well, and all smiles to see me.'[9] It was a happy beginning to what, had he only known it, would be his last untroubled period with his family for three years. 'One day so like another, that there is little to distinguish their features – and these are the happiest – ' he wrote of his life there; 'true Cottage days, tranquil and industrious.'[10]

By May he was forced back to London in search of further information on Sheridan, the Hollands, of course, being one of his most fruitful sources. Others he interviewed included Henry Grattan, William Lamb (later Lord Melbourne), Creevey and Sheridan's sister-in-law, Sukey Ogle. 'Like all those of the friends and relatives of Sheridan I have met,' he wrote, '[she was] full of enthusiasm about his memory, his fame & c ... whilst in almost the same breath they gave me proof of his being one of the most selfish men that ever lived – what am I to do?'[11]

In the middle of May, Bessy and the children, with their maid Hannah, joined him in London, en route to Edinburgh, where Bessy's sister Anne was marrying the manager of the Theatre Royal. After two days of shopping and amusements – and a visit to Barbara's grave – Moore waved them goodbye on the boat to Scotland, then plunged again into a round of interviews and visits. There were still problems over the biography – one of them being that, having been given the use of Sheridan's papers by his son Charles, Moore might be open to a claim from Sheridan's creditors unless a guarantee could be arranged.

Meanwhile, he had gone to Murray's offices to read the proof sheets of the second canto of *Don Juan*. 'The poem will make a great sensation...' he noted in his journal. 'Young Hadee [sic] is the very concentrated essence of voluptuousness and will set all the women wild.' He was shocked, however, to be shown a letter from Byron to Murray, 'the bookseller, a person so out of his caste', describing his current intrigue with the daughter of a nobleman – 'entering into such details as it would be dishonourable to communicate even to the most confidential friend ... for the edification of Mr Murray & all the visitors of his shop'.[12] It is hard to defend this snobbish view of Murray (though expressed in the privacy of his journal); but his concern at Byron's reckless indiscretions is more defensible.

The Bermuda court case was due to take place on 6 July. Toller, Moore's proctor (or lawyer) was optimistic. There were 'evident signs of collusion in the adverse party', sufficient to place the legal responsibility elsewhere.

With no great feeling of worry, Moore went home to Sloperton for two weeks – finding it lonely without Bessy – before returning to London to meet her boat from Scotland and to await the results of the trial. On 7 July, he saw Bessy and the children off on the coach to Calne, and stayed up till three watching fireworks and supping with James Power. 'Have not heard from Toller today, so take it for granted my Cause did not come on yesterday',[13] was the last sentence of his journal entry for that day.

Two more days passed, Moore assuming that since he had not heard from Toller all was safe. On 10 July reality hit him 'like a thunderclap'. Toller's letter to him had been misdirected; on 6 July, judgement had been given against him. In two months from that date an attachment would be put in force against him for £6,000: a sum he had not the slightest hope of paying.

It has been suggested that Moore's frequent attacks on the Tory government may have helped to influence the court's decision; certainly though he was legally responsible for his sub-agent's debts there was no ethical case against him, and since Goodrich, the defaulter, was still solvent and living in Bermuda, it seems extraordinary that he was not the one pursued. To make matters more complicated Goodrich's father, Edward, had been deputy Marshal of the Prize Court in Bermuda and thus in a position to cover up for his son; it may well have been Edward Goodrich's death in 1817 that brought the whole affair to light.

Whatever the rights and wrongs of the matter, Moore was legally responsible; Sheddon, when approached, had nothing but sympathetic noises to contribute. Moore's only chance of escaping imprisonment for debt was to leave the country before two months were up. His first thought was to take refuge in Ireland; Lord Holland also made enquiries, through his Scottish librarian Allen, whether he might be safe from arrest in Edinburgh. But neither alternative was altogether free of risk; the only really safe solution was to cross the Channel.

News of Moore's misfortune was quickly public knowledge. Offers of help flooded in from all sides. An unknown lady offered her house as a place of concealment, but begged him not to let her husband know; another offered him the royalties from a book of poems she was hoping to publish. Jeffrey, Rogers and Power each offered to lend him £500 for an indefinite period. Perry of the *Morning Chronicle* suggested starting a subscription, enthusiastically supported by Leigh Hunt who announced, wrote Moore, 'that he would sooner sell & will actually sell the Piano-forte which had so often resounded with my music than not contribute his mite to keep such a man from going to prison'.[14] Moore refused both the loans and the offer of a subscription. He had always been too proud to accept charity from friends and was not going to change his attitude now. He was equally adamant in refusing an offer from Sir Francis Burdett to appeal to the Crown, one of the three claimants against Moore, to relinquish their share of the claim. 'I would rather bear twice the calamity,' he told him, 'than suffer the least motion to be made towards asking for me the slightest favour from the Crown.' He was much happier to accept the help of Longmans, who offered to advance him any sum he wished on business terms until some solution could be found: 'This is very gratifying, and this is the plan I mean to adopt as the most independent & most comfortable to my own feelings.'[15]

Back in Wiltshire, Moore found a letter from Lord Lansdowne, offering to stand security for any sum he wished, and to help him in any way he could. 'This is real friendship,' he noted in his journal, 'and should make me pause a little in my conclusions with respect to the hollowness of the Great – It is more valuable, from Lord Ls. being a man who measures every step he takes.'[16] Moore refused the offer of a loan, but saw the Lansdownes almost every day during his last weeks at Sloperton; since Bessy was still shy about encountering a large party at Bowood, the Lansdownes, with their children and Lord John Russell, walked over to see her instead. Other friends and neighbours did their best to cheer and entertain the Moores. There were picnics and country dances, and at last a farewell party at their cottage. 'Did not separate till near three in the morning –' wrote Moore; 'on their drinking my health at supper, made them a short speech alluding to the probability of my soon being obliged to leave them, which drew tears from most of the women.'[17]

The moment of departure was fast approaching. After long discussions with Bessy, Moore had decided to go to France alone. Hopefully matters in England would soon be cleared up; if not Bessy and the children would join him there later. On 24 August, he left for London, where there were business arrangements to be completed – his Sheridan manuscript, for instance, lodged with John Murray – and a passage to France to be booked. Fortunately a new friend, Lord John Russell, was planning to cross the Channel with his parents, the Duke and Duchess of Bedford, and offered him a place on their boat. Bessy came up to London – though it was hard for her to leave the children – to spend two last nights with him. He saw her off on the coach at six in the morning: 'God send I may meet her again in health & in happiness – a nobler-hearted creature never breathed,'[18] he wrote that evening. At seven in the morning the next day – 4 September 1819 – he set off with Lord John for Dover.

Lord John Russell, the future Prime Minister, and eventual editor of Moore's journals, was twenty-seven at that time, a diminutive figure with the air of 'a pettifogging attorney', but with a brilliantly incisive mind. Recently elected an MP and a prominent member of the Whig opposition, he also had literary ambitions and may well have been flattered to travel with a poet so renowned as Moore. Both he and his brother Lord Tavistock had wanted to contribute to a subscription for him – if Moore had been willing to accept one, his debts would have been paid off overnight – but as we have seen, he was determined to work his own way out of trouble.

The journey to Dover went pleasantly – it would be hard to imagine a better travelling companion, wrote Lord John. Their friendship, begun at Holland House and Bowood, would cement itself on this first trip together. The Bedfords too were delighted by Moore's company. When they separated at Calais – the Bedfords going on to the Rhine – the Duchess said sadly that she 'wished they had someone with them like Mr Moore, to be agreable when they got to their inns in the evening'.[19]

Moore and Lord John were headed for Paris, where Lord John planned to spend some time researching in the libraries, and where Moore, who had promised Longmans to write a series of 'poetical epistles' on his journey, would seek what inspiration he could find. In Paris, Moore was greeted as a celebrity. A poem announced his arrival in Galignani's magazine *The Messenger*, the same publisher, Moore discovered, had just brought out a complete edition of his works. 'Cruel kindness this,' wrote Moore, 'to rake up all the rubbish I have ever written in my life, good, bad and indifferent, it makes me ill to look at it.'[20] In those days before international copyright agreements, he could not even expect any royalties.

After ten days of sightseeing, parties and visits to the theatre, the two friends set off for Italy. Travelling by stages of about seventy-five miles a day, they arrived at the Jura and reached the village of Le Vattay just as the sun was sinking. Going ahead on foot, Moore caught his first sight of Mont Blanc. 'It is impossible to describe what I felt – I ran like lightning down the steep road that led towards it, with my glass in my eye, and uttering explanations of wonder at every step.'[21] It was a moment he recaptured in his *Rhymes on the Road*, his poetical epistles for Longmans:

Mighty Mont Blanc, thou wert to me,

That minute, with thy brow in heaven,

As sure a sign of Deity

As ere to mortal gaze was given...

There were further scenic wonders as they crossed the Simplon Pass. 'Nothing was ever like it – ' Moore wrote in his journal,

> at the last stage before we reached the barrier on the summit, walked on by myself & saw such a scene by sunset as I shall never forget – that mighty Panorama of Alps whose summits there, indistinctly seen, looked like the tops of gigantic waves, following close upon each other – the soft lights falling on those green spots which cultivation had conjured up in the midst of this wild scene & the pointed top of the Jung Frau, whose snows were then pink with the setting sun – all was magnificent to a degree that quite overpowered me.[22]

They arrived in Milan on 1 October, where to Moore's disappointment he found no letter waiting for him from home. But they were greeted by Byron's friend, Lord Kinnaird, who acted as their guide while they were there, and read them a poem he had written in imitation of *Don Juan*: 'unfortunately,' noted Moore in his journal, 'it has all the profligacy of that wonderful work without any of its beauty.'[23] After three days in Milan Moore and Lord John parted company, Lord John to go on to Rome, Moore to visit Byron in Venice. After passing through Verona, Vicenza and Padua, in a 'crazy little caleche'[24] he had bought as a bargain for the journey, he arrived at La Mira, Byron's villa near Fusina, on 7 October. It was over five years since he had seen his friend.

I7

Venice, Rome and Paris

Moore's description of his meeting with Byron in Italy is one of the great moments in his biography of the poet, and thanks to the publication of his uncut diaries, we catch a few uncensored comments on his visit too. The so-called daughter of a nobleman, for instance, of whose seduction Byron had boasted to Murray, was in fact 'an ugly little ill-made girl', and the balcony he claimed to have climbed no more than 'a portal at the side of the hall door'.[1] His new love Teresa Guiccioli, thought Moore, was an equally unfortunate choice: 'It would have been far safer to stick to his Fornarinas.'[2] Byron himself seemed inclined to agree. 'I say, Tom,' he remarked on their first evening, 'you might have been my salvation – for if you had come here a little sooner, I'll be damned if I would have run away with a red-haired woman of quality.'[3]

Moore arrived at La Mira at about two o'clock. Byron had just got up and was still in his bath, but sent a message that if Moore would wait till he got dressed, he would accompany him to Venice. He soon came down, 'and the delight I felt in seeing him once more ...' wrote Moore, 'was not a little heightened by observing that his pleasure was to the full, as great... It would be impossible, indeed, to convey to those who have not, at some time or other, felt the charm of his manner, any idea of what it could be when under the influence of such pleasurable excitement as it was most flatteringly evident he experienced at this moment.'[4]

Moore was struck by the change in Byron's appearance; he was fatter and bewhiskered, with long hair, and a coat and cap of foreign cut, and the 'refined and spiritualised' look of his earlier days had been replaced by 'an expression of arch, waggish wisdom', better suited to Don Juan than Childe Harold. 'He was still, however, eminently handsome... while by the somewhat increased roundness of the contours, the resemblance of his finely formed nose and chin to those of the Belvedere Apollo had become even more striking.'

After a hasty breakfast – a meal he rarely took before three or four o'clock – Byron introduced Moore to Countess Guiccioli, 'blonde & young... but not very pretty,' noted Moore in his journal. They then set off for Venice, Moore's ricketty caleche groaning under the extra weight of Tito, Byron's mustachioed gondolier, who sat in front. By the time they embarked from Fusina, the sun was just setting across the Lagoon: 'It was an evening such as Romance would have chosen for a first sight of Venice,' wrote Moore, with memories of Byron's lines on Venice in his mind:

I stood in Venice on the Bridge of Sighs;

A palace and a prison on each hand;

I saw from out the wave her structures rise

As from the strokes of the enchanter's wand...

Byron's mood, however, was anything but romantic, and 'our course was I am almost ashamed to say,' wrote Moore, 'one of uninterrupted merriment and laughter till we found ourselves at the steps of my friend's palazzo on the Grand Canal'.

Byron was living at La Mira with Countess Guiccioli, so could not stay with Moore in Venice. He insisted, however, on lending him his palazzo, and promised to come and dine with him every day. Moore's spirits sank at the first sight of Byron's damp-looking mansion, and he began to hint that it might be less trouble if he stayed at a hotel. But Byron would not hear of it, and after groping their way through the dark hall, amid cries from Byron of 'Keep clear of that dog', and 'Take care or that monkey will fly at you', led him upstairs to his own apartment. The door, however, was locked, and seemed to have been so for a long time, for no key could be found. Moore was beginning to think longingly of a hotel once more, when Byron burst the door open with a vigourous kick, revealing a spacious and elegant set of rooms, in total contrast to the gloom outside.

Byron had ordered dinner from a nearby trattoria, and while waiting for it – and a bachelor friend, Alexander Scott – to arrive, he and Moore stood on the balcony to watch the last of the sunset. A few clouds were still bright in the west; Moore began to remark on their rosy hue, when Byron, clapping his hand on his mouth, said laughingly, 'Come, d--n it, Tom, *don t* be poetical,' Scott joined them for an agreeable dinner, full of laughter and reminiscences, then Byron left them for La Mira, while Moore and Scott went on to see a play by Alfieri. (Moore's Italian, like his French, was fluent, a tribute not only to his early studies but to the quickness of his ear.)

The ensuing evenings followed much the same pattern, Byron arriving to dine with Moore, Scott then taking him on to the theatre, or some evening party. Byron read Moore what he had written of the third canto of *Don Juan* and talked of writing a tragedy about the sixteenth-century Doge, Marino Faliero. But his chief subject when they were alone was his marriage, and the wave of scandal that had driven him from England. He admitted his own faults freely, but felt the injustice of his punishment, so out of proportion to his offences, bitterly. What haunted him especially was his fear that the 'fixed hostility' of his persecutors would continue to blacken his memory even after he was dead. 'So strong was this impression upon him,' wrote Moore, 'that during one of our few intervals of seriousness, he conjured me, by our friendship, if, as he both felt and hoped, I should survive him, not to let unmerited censure settle on his name, but while I surrendered him up to condemnation where he deserved it, to vindicate him where aspersed.'[5]

Moore had hoped that Byron might come with him to join Lord John Russell in Rome. But the complications of his position with Countess Guiccioli made it impossible for him to leave her and Moore resigned himself to going on alone. On his last day in Venice, Byron told him, with all the glee of a schoolboy given a holiday, that Countess Guiccioli had agreed that he and Moore should 'make a night of it'. They accordingly went to the opera – the leading singer, said Byron, was renowned for having stilettoed one of her favourite lovers – then had supper in St Mark's Square, where they sat drinking hot brandy punch and laughing over old times till the clock struck two. After this Byron took him in his gondola to see Venice by moonlight.

'Nothing could be more solemnly beautiful than the whole scene around,' wrote Moore,

and I had for the first time the Venice of my dreams before me. All those meaner details which so offend the eye by day were softened down by the moonlight into a sort of visionary indistinctness; and the effect of that silent city of palaces, sleeping, as it were, upon the waters, was such but could not but affect deeply even the least susceptible imagination. My companion saw that I was moved by it, and though familiar with the scene himself, seemed to give way to the same strain of feeling; and, as we exchanged a few remarks suggested to us by that wreck of human glory before us, his voice, habitually so cheerful, sunk into a tone of mournful sweetness, such as I had rarely heard before from him, and shall not easily forget.

The mood was only momentary. 'Some quick turn of ridicule soon carried him off into a totally different vein, and at about three in the morning, at the door of the palazzo, we parted laughing, as we had met.'[6]

Moore was to have dinner at La Mira after leaving Venice the next day. He arrived at three o'clock, catching a glimpse of Byron's little girl Allegra with her nursemaid in the hall. Shortly before dinner Byron went out of the room and came back with a white leather bag. 'Look here,' he said, holding it up, 'this would be worth something to Murray, though *you*, I dare say, would not give sixpence for it.' It was the manuscript of his memoirs, or Thoughts and Adventures, as he called them. 'It is not a thing that can be published during my lifetime,' he told Moore, 'but you may have it – if you like – there, do whatever you please with it.'[7] He added that Moore might show the manuscript to any of their friends he thought worthy of it. Overwhelmed by the gesture, Moore thanked him as best he could. 'This will make a nice legacy for my little Tom,' he added, 'who shall astonish the latter days of the nineteenth century with it.'

Countess Guiccioli joined them for dinner – 'looked prettier than she did the first time,' noted Moore – and at Byron's request wrote him a letter of introduction to her brother in Rome. Byron tried to delay Moore for a day or two, in order to visit Petrarch's tomb at Arqua, but Moore had got it into his head that he must get to Rome as soon as possible, and refused – a circumstance, he wrote later, 'I never can think of without wonder or self reproach'.[8] When Moore left the villa, Byron decided to go with him for the first few miles, and ordering his horses to follow went with him in his carriage as far as Strá – 'where, for the last time' – wrote Moore, 'how little thinking it was to be the last! – I bade my kind and admirable friend farewell.'

After the fun and gaiety of his Venetian visit – 'Moore and I did nothing but laugh,'[9] Byron told Murray – Moore's spirits took a dip. In Ferrara, the next day, it was raining too hard to distract himself at the theatre, and he spent a 'very, very gloomy evening… wishing myself at my own dear cottage with that dear wife & children, who alone make me truly happy'.[10] Then his unreliable caleche broke down twice, and he had to overpay each time to have it mended. He was bitten all over by 'fleas, bugs and all sorts of vulgar animaletti' in a series of bad inns on the way to Florence. By the time he arrived there one of the bites at the back of his leg had become infected, and was so inflamed that he was forced to take to his bed. Fortunately the surgeon Sir Charles Morgan, husband of the Irish novelist Sydney Owenson, was living in Florence at the time, and came to examine him at once. Resting up on his advice, Moore did less sightseeing than usual, but was able to dine with them and various friends. 'I never saw Moore gayer or pleasanter… What elasticity, what everlasting youth!'[11] wrote Lady Morgan to her sister Lady Clark in Dublin, and told her to tell Moore's mother how well her son was surviving his difficulties.

On 24 October, his leg healed, Moore set out for Rome, arriving there three days later, to find a letter from Bessy – 'more precious to me than all the wonders I can see'[12] – awaiting him. There was also one from Lord John Russell, explaining that Parliament had been summoned unexpectedly and that he had had to go back to England. 'I was very sorry not to have you with me on my journey,' he wrote to Moore when he reached London, 'and I felt grievously the difference of the going and returning.'[13]

Moore spent a pleasant three weeks in Rome. Still optimistic that things in England would soon be settled, he bought trinkets for Bessy and more than a hundred books to be sent home. Rome, out of bounds during the long period of the Napoleonic wars, was now a magnet for English artists. Moore met Turner, Thomas Lawrence, the sculptor Francis Chantrey and others, and sat for his portrait by the young English painter John Jackson. He visited the workshop of Canova, and on one memorable occasion accompanied him, with Lawrence, Jackson, Turner and Chantrey, all four Royal Academicians, to see the academy of painting where Canova had first studied – 'saw the naked model – a very noble figure of a man who threw himself into the attitudes of various Antient statues with striking effect'.[14] His stay in Rome gave him a taste for the company of artists – and they for his – which never left him.

By 17 November, sated with sightseeing, Moore was ready to leave Rome. Travelling with Jackson and Chantrey, he spent a week in Florence, where he sat for his bust by Bartolini; then he and his fellow travellers set

off by gradual stages for Paris. After crossing Mont Cenis they paused in
Chambéry to see the house where Rousseau had stayed with Madame de
Warens. Jackson did a sketch of the house, and Moore, who shared Dr
Johnson's view – 'Rousseau, Sir, is a very bad man' – was inspired to write
a poem on the subject:

> Strange power of Genius, that can throw
> O'er all that's vicious, weak and low,
> Such magic lights, such rainbow dyes,
> As dazzle even the steadiest eyes!...

The three travellers arrived in Paris on 11 December, and Moore, with a
beating heart, rushed to see if there were any letters waiting for him.
There was a cheerful one from Bessy, saying all was well at Sloperton, but
from Longmans came the unwelcome news that nothing had been settled
about the Bermuda business, and that it was still not safe to come home.

It was a bitter disappointment. Moore had treated his travels in Italy
as an extended holiday. Now he found himself doomed to an indefinite
exile. His first action was to send for Bessy and the children: 'wherever they
are will be a home & a happy one for me.'[15] But there were delays in bringing
them over; the baby, Tom, was ill; Bessy must pack up Sloperton, and
settle all her local bills, the obliging Longman acting as her banker in
Moore's absence. Moore awaited their arrival in a fever of frustration and
impatience. Jackson and Chantrey (who had kindly arranged for Moore's
books to be shipped to England with his sculptures) left for London.
Christmas came and went, and at last, on 27 December, he heard from
Bessy that she was planning to leave Wiltshire that day. He set off to Calais
to meet her. 'Arrived after two nights travelling at Calais about seven
o'clock this morning' – he wrote in his journal for 30 December; 'went to
bed at eight – rose again a little after ten & heard there were two packets seen
at a distance – breakfasted & went down to the pier, where I remained till
the Packet entered the harbour – numbers on Deck but no Bessy – at last
the dear girl & her little ones made their appearance.'

One can picture the scene, the windy harbour side, the small figure of
Moore anxiously scanning the horizon, the happiness of their reunion.
The children looked well, though Moore was momentarily shocked by
Bessy's appearance. She had broken her nose in a fall from a pony some
weeks before and her face was still swollen as a result. 'She never told me
of this accident, but it was a severe one...' he wrote. 'What an escape! her

beautiful nose too, that might have vied with Alcina's own, to have been so battered.'

They set out for Paris in the mail coach that evening – 'myself, Bessy, the two young ones & our excellent servant Hannah all inside' – wrote Moore, 'a cold, cold night, with the ground as slippery as glass from the frost!' After two days of travelling, 'in constant alarms from the slipperiness of the roads',[16] they arrived in Paris on New Year's Day.

Moore had taken lodgings for the family in the rue de Chantereine, and the next few days were spent settling in. Since Bessy spoke no French, Moore had to translate for her – 'indeed, housekeeping, millinery, everything falls upon me just now,' he complained, '& I fear there is but little leisure for writing'.[17] Despite these minor irritations, his pleasure at seeing her again was obvious. 'Every one speaks of your conjugal attention,' a friend remarked comically to Moore, '&, I assure you, all Paris is disgusted with it.'[18]

Just at a time when he most needed to make money to settle his debts, Moore found it exceptionally difficult to work. 'Paris,' he wrote, 'swarming throughout as it was at that period, with rich, gay, and dissipated English, was to a person of my social habits and multifarious acquaintance, the very worst place that could have been resorted to for even the semblance of a quiet and studious home,'[19] Besieged by visitors and invitations, tormented by a 'harridan' of a landlady, they decided to move out to a cottage near the Champs Elysées, then still entirely rural, where they were less accessible to callers. But it was not until the summer when some Spanish friends, the Vilamils, lent them a cottage on their country estate near Sèvres that he was able to settle to a steady routine. There, at last, wrote Moore, 'we contrived to conjure up an apparition of Sloperton, and I was able for some time to work with a feeling of comfort and home. I used frequently to pass the morning in rambling alone through the noble park of Saint Cloud, with no apparatus for work but my memorandum book and pencils, forming sentences to run smooth and moulding verses into shape.'[20]

Only two years after the success of *Lalla Rookh*, Moore was beginning to feel he was losing ground with the public. 'It is somewhat discouraging now to write, when the attention of all the reading world is absorbed by two writers, Scott & Byron –' he noted in his journal, 'and when one finds such sentences as the following in the last Edinburgh Review, "These novels (Scott's) have thrown evidently into the shade all contemporary prose and even all recent poetry, except perhaps those inspired by the Genius – or Demon – of Byron."'[21]

The truth was that his unsettled life, the distractions of Paris and the worry of the Bermuda business, had nibbled away at his creative energies. Almost none of his projects for that year, 1820, went well. The second volume of his *National Airs*, imperfectly printed due to his hasty departure from England, had to be corrected for a new edition before he could begin on a new collection for the following year. The Sheridan biography was in abeyance till he could return to England. The rhyming epistles on his Italian journey, intended to be a companion volume to *The Fudge Family in Paris*, had to be abandoned on his publishers' advice: with the Bermuda settlement still unresolved, it was no moment to attack the government. (They later appeared as *Rhymes on the Road*.) He was also contemplating a poem with an Egyptian theme – stimulated perhaps by the discoveries of the *savants* who had accompanied Napoleon on his Egyptian campaign. He had barely begun his researches, however, when a demand from James Power for the eighth number of the *Irish Melodies* – which was already being advertised, and of which he had not yet written a word – set him working against the clock. By the end of the year he had completed the twelve *Melodies* required. Despite the haste with which they were written, they included some of his most memorable songs. Among them was the exquisite 'Echo', its eighteenth-century air rearranged by Moore to include two echo effects in the accompaniment.

> How sweet the answer Echo makes
> To music at night,
> When, rous'd by lute or horn, she wakes,
> And far away, o'er lawns and lakes,
> Goes answering light.
>
> Yet Love hath echoes truer far,
> And far more sweet,
> Than e'er beneath the moonlight's star,
> Of horn, or lute, or soft guitar,
> The songs repeat.
>
> 'Tis when the sigh, in youth sincere,
> And only then, –
> The sigh that's breath'd for one to hear,

Is by that one, the only dear,
Breath'd back again!

Equally memorable was the dirge, 'Oh ye Dead!', its slow, halting rhythm reflecting the melancholy of the words. James Joyce loved this song, which, according to his brother Stanislaus, gave him the theme of his story 'The Dead', in The *Dubliners*. Its first stanza is strangely Joycean in feeling:

Oh, ye Dead! oh, ye Dead! whom we know by the light you give
From your cold gleaming eyes, though you move like men who live,
Why leave you thus your graves,
In far-off fields and waves,
Where the worm and the sea-bird only know your bed,
To haunt this spot where all
Those eyes that wept your fall
And the hearts that wail'd you, lie dead.

It was no wonder that Moore would stake his claim to future fame on those 'little ponies', the *Irish Melodies*. It was only when his words were linked to Ireland's music – the music he had done so much to revive – that his lyrical gifts found their truest expression. In the midst of all his cares and worries it was clear that they could do so still.

18

Homecoming

After a peaceful summer in the country, the Moores moved back to Paris for the autumn. Among the English travellers passing through was Wordsworth, a poet Moore had never met but whom he regarded as 'one of the very few real and original poets'[1] of the age. On hearing Wordsworth had been enquiring for him, he and Bessy went to call on him and Mrs Wordsworth – 'who requires all the *imaginative* powers of her husband to make anything decent of her,'[2] noted Moore. He met Wordsworth again the following evening at a dinner given by George Canning. 'I see he is a man to *hold forth*,' he wrote, 'one who does not understand the *give & take* of conversation'[3] – an opinion confirmed two days later when Wordsworth called on Moore for breakfast before leaving Paris. 'Talked a good deal so very smugly,' wrote Moore. 'Spoke of Byron's plagiarisms from him – the whole third Canto of Childe Harold's founded on his style & sentiments – the feeling of natural objects, which is there expressed not caught by B. from Nature herself, but from him, Wordsworth, and spoiled in the transition – Tintern Abbey the source of it all.'[4]

Moore does not record his own comments; he probably let Wordsworth sweep on uninterrupted. But Byron was much in his mind that year. He had shown the manuscript of his memoirs to a number of selected friends in Paris, as well as to the Hollands and the Lansdownes while he was in London. (Lady Holland was apparently displeased by a derogatory reference to her in the MS.) Byron had also offered to show the memoirs to his wife, but she indignantly refused to read them or to countenance their future publication. 'For my own sake,' she wrote, 'I have no reason to shrink from publicity – but...I should lament some of the *consequences*.'

Byron sent her letter on to Moore, together with his reply, which he asked him to copy before forwarding it. 'To the mysterious menace of the last sentence – whatever its import may be...' he told her, 'I could hardly be sensible even if I understand it – as before it could take place, I shall be, where "nothing can touch me further".'[5]

As Byron's letter made clear, there was no question of the memoirs being published in his lifetime. But he was anxious to help Moore in his financial difficulties, and in December 1820, he sent him a further instalment of the memoirs with the suggestion that he might be able to raise money on them by way of a reversion. 'Would not Longman or Murray advance you a certain sum *now*,' he wrote, 'pledging themselves *not* to have them published till after *my* decease, think you? – and what say you?'[6] It was an idea that seemed increasingly attractive as the months of Moore's exile dragged on. Without a substantial sum to offer, he could not negotiate to settle the Bermuda claims. In the end, with Byron's full agreement, he arranged to sell the memoirs to John Murray for 2,000 guineas, with the condition that, if he survived Byron, he himself should edit them.

In late September 1821, travelling under the name of Dyke, and taking a pair of false moustaches in case a disguise was needed, he set out for England with the memoirs. His aim was to finalise terms with Murray, and use the money towards settling his Bermuda claims. Murray agreed to advance him £1,000 at once, but to Moore's amazement Thomas Longman, who had been handling the Bermuda negotiations for him, seemed curiously reluctant to take it. 'Said I had better let matters go on as they were,' wrote Moore, '& appeared labouring under some mystery...at length, after much hesitation acknowledged that a thousand pounds had been placed at his disposal, for the purpose of arranging matters when the debt could be reduced to that sum, and that he had been under the strictest injunctions of secrecy with regard to this deposit, which nothing but the intention I had expressed of settling the business in another way could have induced him to infringe.'

The unknown benefactor, as Moore immediately guessed, had been Lord Lansdowne: 'How one such action brightens the whole human race in our eyes! – [Longman] entreated of me still to leave the settlement of the business in Lord L's hands – but of course will not.'[7]

With Longman's assurances that the claim was well on its way to being settled, Moore decided to visit his parents in Dublin, travelling again under the name of Dyke, and enjoining all his friends there to strictest secrecy. After a happy reunion with his family, he returned to London on 22 October. His host was Samuel Rogers, and he was just preparing to sneak out, still incognito, to dine with a friend, when Longman's partner, Owen Rees, arrived with the joyful news that his thousand pounds had been accepted as a settlement, and he was now a free man once again. 'God bless you, my own free, fortunate, happy *bird*,' wrote Bessy on hearing of his release, 'but remember your cage is in Paris & that your mate longs for you.'[8]

There were still details to be settled. Together with Thomas Longman, Moore went to see Goodrich's uncle, Robert Sheddon, to see if he was prepared to contribute anything towards the thousand pounds. 'His conduct all along shabby and shuffling,' noted Moore,

> & now, when brought to the point ... his agony at the prospect of being made to *bleed* quite ludicrous. Upon my rising from my seat & saying with a sort of contemptuous air, 'Since Mr Sheddon does not seem inclined to give anything but advice, Mr Longman, I think we may take our leave' – he with much stammering proposed to give two hundred pounds, and upon Longman saying that really this was not worth while talking about, he was at last, with much pain and groaning delivered of three hundred.[9]

Moore decided to pay the balance of the debt with Lansdowne's money – 'in order that his generous purpose should not be wholly frustrated'[10] – and then repay him immediately with a draft from Murray. It might seem strange that Moore should refuse money from the immensely wealthy Lord Lansdowne, and accept a gift worth 2,000 guineas from Byron. But he thought too much of his own independence and his reception at Bowood to place himself at a disadvantage vis-à-vis the Lansdownes. Byron's memoirs, on the other hand, were in the nature of a legacy, on which, thanks to Byron's generosity, Moore could raise money while he was still alive. However, as Lady Byron's letter had shown, they were likely to be a controversial property.

The cottage at Sloperton had been let, and it would be nearly a year before the Moores could repossess it. They spent most of that period in Paris, their return to England delayed when in February 1822, there was a further claim of £1,200 from Bermuda – 'an afterclap of that thunderstorm'.[11] It was not until September, after long negotiations, that Longman's partner Rees was able to tell him that the matter had been resolved for another £200 and that it was finally safe to come home.

In the midst of these new worries Moore began the long poem that would become *The Loves of the Angels*, based on a passage in the Book of Enoch: 'It happened, after the sons of man had multiplied in those days, that daughters were born to them, elegant and beautiful; and when the angels, the sons of Heaven beheld them, they became enamoured of them.' It was a subject that he had long contemplated, and on which he had already written a story in prose, but the news that Byron was writing a poem on a similar theme, the *Deluge* or *Heaven and Earth*, seems to have galvanised him into action. It would be too much to be pre-empted once again.

'This Poem,' he wrote in the preface to the first edition,

somewhat different in form and much more limited in extent, was originally designed as an episode for a work, about which I have been at intervals, employed during the last two years. Some months since, however, I found that my friend Lord Byron had, by an accidental co-incidence, chosen the same subject for a Drama; and, as I could not but feel the disadvantage of coming after so formidable a rival, I thought it best to publish my humble sketch immediately, with such alterations and additions as I had time to make, and thus, by an earlier appearance on the literary horizon, give myself the chance of what astronomers call an *Helical rising*, before the luminary, in whose light I was to be lost, should appear.

Any question that Moore and Byron were still on an equal footing in the eyes of the public was long past. Byron was now a legend throughout Europe, and the scandal created by *Don Juan* and then by philosophical poems such as *Cain* (in which, as in *Paradise Lost*, the devil has all the best lines) had only added to his fame.

Moore had been bowled over by *Cain*; it was 'wonderful – terrible – never to be forgotten,'[12] he told Byron. But he was alarmed at the damage it had done to Byron's reputation – Murray had narrowly escaped prosecution for blasphemy – and he hoped that his future thunderbolts would be reserved for politics rather than religion. In the same spirit he strongly opposed Byron's plan to collaborate with Leigh Hunt, who had just arrived

in Italy, and Shelley, in the publication of a reformist magazine, *The Liberal*.
'*Alone* you may do any thing,' he wrote; 'but partnerships in fame, like
those in trade, make the strongest party answerable for the delinquencies
of the rest, and I tremble even for *you* with such a bankrupt Co. They are
both clever fellows, and Shelley I look upon as a man of real genius; but
I must say again *you* could not give your enemies...a greater triumph
than by forming such an unequal and unholy alliance.'[13]

Byron, with typical indiscretion, showed the letter to Shelley and Hunt,
but whereas Shelley, who admired Moore, accepted that he was acting out
of concern for Byron, Hunt took violent offence. Moore would have no
inkling of this till much later; in fact he was always sympathetic to Hunt,
and when Byron withdrew from the journal in 1823, suggested that he
should give Hunt the profits of anything he had published there. But
Hunt, impecunious and aggrieved, felt that Moore had been actuated
by snobbery, that he considered Byron was demeaning himself by the
association. The cry was taken up by Hazlitt after Byron's death. A
passionate admirer of Rousseau, he had been infuriated by Moore's lines
against him in *Rhymes on the Road*. The episode with Hunt added fuel to
the fire. In a reversal of his earlier friendly attitude, he rounded on Moore
in his collection of essays *The Plain Speaker*, portraying him as an abject
snob, darting backward and forward 'from Mr Longman's to Mr Murray's
shop in a state of ridiculous trepidation, to see what could be done to
prevent this degradation of the aristocracy of letters'.[14] Moore had lived
so long among the great, he sneered, that he fancied himself one of them.

Luckily Moore had no idea of the indignation he was arousing. Far from
rushing from Longman's to Murray's – how could he since he was still in
Paris at the time? – he was working against the clock on his poem, and
trying, not very successfully, to resist the endless invitations that came his
way. When the time came to leave Paris, Bessy going before him to
put Sloperton in order, fifty of his friends arranged an elaborate farewell
dinner for him. Lord Kinnaird presided, Grattan's son composed a song,
appropriately titled 'Farewell to the Bard', and the Reverend Archibald
Douglas, in toasting Mrs Moore, remarked that it was altogether fitting for
Moore to be writing a poem on the subject of angels since he was living
with one at home.

When Moore reached Sloperton on 28 November, he found that Bessy
had surpassed herself in putting the cottage in order, and that she had
thrown two rooms into one to make a larger study for him: 'a wonderful

improvement,'[15] wrote Moore. He spent the next few weeks revising and correcting his *Loves of the Angels* for the press. The poem appeared on 23 December; the first part of Byron's verse drama was published nine days later in the *Liberal*.

The *Loves of the Angels*, running to some two thousand lines, was Moore's last long poem. Unlike *Lalla Rookh* in which he had tried for effects of terror and grandeur, it was written well within his usual range. Apart from his satires and humorous verse, his favourite themes were love and patriotism; in the *Loves of the Angels* it is love that has the upper hand. The protagonists are three fallen angels who have forfeited heaven for the love of mortal women. Each tells the story of his love,

> The history of that hour unblest,
> When, like a bird, from its high nest
> Won down by fascinating eyes,
> For woman's smile he lost the skies...

Inevitably Moore's poem was compared with Byron's *Heaven and Earth*, but as Hazlitt, writing in the *Edinburgh Review*, and still well disposed to Moore at this point, observed, Moore had no need to worry that Byron would extinguish him. 'An aurora borealis need not fear an eruption of Vesuvius. Moore appeals to the gay, the witty, the happy, Byron to the galled, the cankered, the unhappy. Moore has some tinsel lines but also some excellent ones ("She moved in a light of her own making") and never writes a line that would not pass for poetry.'

Other critics were less kind. The fact that Moore's poem had a semi-religious theme roused the bigot and the prude in a variety of commentators. The old charge of immorality – this time more pernicious since veiled in religious sentiment – was brought out again. He was accused of impiety, of 'making light of the book of Enoch', a text that had never even been admitted to the Apocrypha; 'one might as well talk of making light of the Arabian Nights,'[16] wrote Moore crossly.

More distressing was the fact that some of his friends – Lady Donegal in particular – were shocked by his mingling of earthly and angelic love – though others, like the Lansdownes, praised the beauty and purity of the poem. By the time the fifth edition was in preparation, Moore was so weary of being damned for being irreligious, that he suggested to Longmans that the poem should be set in an Islamic, rather than a Christian heaven. God was transformed into Allah, a few names changed, and the preface was abandoned for a learned disquisition on Persian mythology. But the change came too late to make much difference; 6,000 copies of the poem had already been sold, and when it came to be published in later editions of Moore's works, it was returned to its Christian setting with no further comment.

Today it is almost harder to put oneself into the mind-set of those who condemned the poem for its impiety than to understand the enthusiasm of its admirers. Yet they were many and distinguished. Among them was Moore's fellow Irishman, O'Connell, who, in the thick of his political efforts that year, found time to write to his wife: 'Moore's *Loves of the Angels* is come out. I got it a while ago and read it in half an hour. It is only an account of three angels that fell in love with three ladies, and although the subject is not very promising... it is really an exquisitely beautiful little poem... a mere trifle for such a poet but exquisitely sweet and not stained with a single indelicate thought. The poetry is full of Moore's magic.'[17] For most readers today the magic has evaporated. Still more than *Lalla Rookh*, *The Loves of the Angels* was a poem for its time; graceful and mellifluous, but without the power or inspiration to keep it alive for later generations.

Far more accessible, because in a lighter vein, was Moore's next collection of verses, *Fables for the Holy Alliance and Rhymes on the Road &c.* Dedicated to Byron, under Moore's old pseudonym of Thomas Brown, it contained a number of semi-libellous attacks on the various crowned heads and statesmen of Europe, poems on his travels, and a series of miscellaneous verses, including a reprint of his 'Lines on the Death of Sheridan'. For those interested in omens, the most significant item was his poem, 'The Torch of Liberty', describing the passage of freedom's flame from country to country till at last it reaches Greece:

> Shine, shine for ever, glorious Flame,
> Divinest gift of gods to men!
> From Greece thy earliest splendour came,
> To Greece thy ray returns again.

By May 1823, when the volume first appeared, Byron was already planning to leave for Greece. Moore's lines, so reminiscent of Byron's on the Isles of Greece, were an *envoi* to his friend.

Moore was now settling back into his usual English routine, long periods of work and family life at Sloperton, occasional visits to London. In May Bessy gave birth to their fifth and last child, a boy christened Russell for his godfather Lord John Russell. She quickly recovered from the birth and according to Moore had seldom been in better looks. 'How *very* pretty she is!' remarked Lady Lansdowne; 'it is quite refreshing to see anything so pretty.'[18]

At the end of July, with Bessy's reluctant agreement, Moore accepted an invitation to join the Lansdownes on a tour of their estates in Ireland. It was a chance to see his parents in Dublin and, apropos of this, to introduce Lord Lansdowne to them without the embarrassment of an actual visit. The little episode has long delighted Moore's detractors; let us give it as he writes it: 'My mother, expressing a strong wish to see Lord Lansdowne, without the fuss of a visit from him, I engaged to manage it for her. I told him that he must let me show him to two people who considered me the greatest man in the world, and him as the next, for being my friend. Very good-naturedly allowed me to walk him past the windows, and wished to call upon them; but I thought it better thus.'[19]

From Dublin, Moore travelled some of the way with the Lansdownes to their estates in County Kerry, peeling off at Cork to pay a visit to his sister Kate and her husband at Cove (Cobh). He went there by river and there is an amusing description by the newspaper editor John O'Driscoll of the crowds that gathered on the quay to see him leave. Neatly dressed in a brown frock coat, white hat, grey trousers and yellow waistcoat, Moore was looking, he thought, particularly well, but there was a general feeling of disappointment when he first appeared:

That's he – 'the little chap'...' Well to be sure if that's all of him, what lies they do be telling about Poets – sure I thought I'd come out to see a great *joint* [giant] as big as O'Brien, at any rate – for wasn't Roderick O'Connor roaring and bawling through all the streets last night that the Great Poet had come amongst us from foreign parts.' 'Oh then Roderick was drunk, sure enough.' 'Well, 'tis a darling little pet at any rate.' 'Be dad, isn't he a dawny creature, and dosn't [sic] he look just like one of the good people.'[20]

Protected in his childhood, Moore had never been exposed to the full extent of Irish miseries before, and he was shocked by the poverty he encountered on his travels. In Callan, outside Kilkenny, he saw 'for the first time in my life some real specimens of Irish misery and filth; three or four cottages together exhibiting such a naked swarm of wretchedness as never met my eyes before'. It was a relief to hear that the Lansdownes were considered model landlords, but such individual instances could not counter 'the degradation and enslavement of the great mass of the Irish people',[21] the harshness of the land laws or the blatant injustice of the tithe. There were stories of secret organisations among the peasantry, and a mysterious figure, 'Captain Rock', who was said to be their leader. Staying with Lord Kenmare in Killarney, Moore met O'Connell and his brother. They talked of the unrest in the countryside, and O'Connell recalled his dialogue with a certain Judge Day who asked him what cure there was for Ireland's miseries.

O.C. 'I could tell you some, but you would not adopt them.' J.D: 'Name them' O.C. 'A law that no-one should possess an estate in Ireland who has one anywhere else.' J.D. 'I agree to that.' O.C. 'That tithes should be abolished.' J.D. 'I agree to that.' O.C. 'That the Catholics should be completely emancipated.' J.D. 'I agree to that.' – 'That the Union should be repealed.' – J.D. 'I agree to that.' – O.C. 'Very well, since that is the case take a pike and turn out, for there is nothing else wanting to qualify you.'[22]

It would be interesting to know more of Moore's conversation with O'Connell, whose plans to rouse a mass movement for reform in Ireland through the creation of the Catholic Association were just taking shape. But, whether or not Moore was influenced by their meeting, the misery he had met with on his journeys had been enough to renew and deepen his indignation at his country's treatment, and no sooner had he returned to England than he set to work to express them in an extended polemical pamphlet, *The Memoirs of Captain Rock*. Its effect, at a time when O'Connell's mass meetings were beginning to alarm the authorities and to shake long-held prejudices, was electric. If Moore's *Irish Melodies* had helped to create a vague poetic sympathy for Ireland's cause, his Captain Rock – in a scathing, mordantly ironic history of his country's wrongs – demanded justice in more immediate terms. It was O'Connell's leadership and genius that steered Ireland towards the goal of Catholic emancipation, but Moore's *Memoirs of Captain Rock* – though virtually forgotten now – played a major part in preparing the way.

19

The Destruction of the Memoirs

On returning to England at the end of August, Moore set Sheridan aside in order to concentrate on *Captain Rock*, or to give the full title, *The Memoirs of Captain Rock, the Celebrated Irish Chieftain, with Some Account of his Ancestors.* It was published in April 1824. For those accustomed to the dulcet tones of Moore's songs and poetry, the hard-edged, almost Swiftian prose of the pamphlet came as a complete surprise. Taking the mythical rebel leader Captain Rock as his hero, Moore followed him and his ancestors through the long years of British misrule from its first enactments under Henry II. He comments ironically on the righteous zeal of Cromwell, whose soldiers, piously acting on his orders that 'the Irish were to be treated as the Canaanites were by Joshua', followed the scriptures to the letter. 'All the spoils of the cities and the cattle they took for a prey unto themselves, and every man they smote with the edge of the sword, until they had destroyed them; neither left they any to breathe.'[1] Of the poet Alexander Pope, a Catholic born in England, he remarks that 'if Pope had been born a Munster Papist, instead of a London one, by Act 7 William and Mary, and 2 Anne, he would have been voted an irreclaimable brute, and hunted into the mountains'.[2] As to recent Protestant concessions: 'The courteous address of Lancelot to the young Jewess, "Be of good cheer, for truly I think thou art damned", seems to have been the model upon which the Protestant Church has founded all its conciliatory advances towards Catholics.'[3]

To reproach a country, long accustomed to such violence from its rulers, for its lack of peaceful moderation was like Mercury in Aeschylus, 'coolly

lecturing Prometheus, on the exceeding want of good temper and tractable-
ness he exhibits – while the only grievance, forsooth, he has to complain
of, is being riveted by his legs and arms to a rock and having a wedge of
eternal adamant driven into his breast!'[4]

The broad facts of Ireland's tragic history had not yet been staled by
too much repetition, and Moore's extended account of them (376 pages)
had the force of novelty as well as indignation. Not surprisingly it aroused
strong reactions from the diehards. Moore's neighbour, the Reverend
William Bowles, was so horrified by the extracts that he had seen, that he
refused to read it; the *British Review* described Moore as a 'popist bigot'
heading a conspiracy to undermine the Protestant faith; the *Literary Chronicle*
blamed Ireland's people, rather than its government, for its troubles: 'The
country contains a factious party and a barbarous peasantry, who are as
remote from civilisation as the New Zealanders. We know no country
whose annals are so stained with crime as Ireland.' But it was greeted with
huge enthusiasm by the Catholics in Ireland, poverty-stricken peasants
clubbing together with their sixpences and shillings to buy copies. The
Whig press, too, were ecstatic; Sydney Smith, whose doughty battles for
Catholic emancipation gained added force from his status as an Anglican
clergyman, acclaimed it in the *Edinburgh Review*. The picture drawn of
Ireland, he wrote, was 'piteous and frightful', exciting shame and abhorrence
at England's 'steady baseness, uniform brutality, and unrelenting oppression',
and he praised Moore as a 'steady friend of all that is honourable and just'.
Other papers followed the same tune. 'The love of justice, humanity and
liberty,' wrote the *Times*, 'breaks out through every apostrophe of the author,
however he may affect to veil his emotions under sarcasm, levity or scorn.'

The public flocked to buy the book. The first edition sold out on the first
day, and the second, of another thousand copies, was gone before Moore's
corrections, sent post haste from Sloperton, could arrive. 'Success! Success!'
wrote Lord John Russell. 'Your Captain is bought by all the town … and has
given all the Orangemen the jaundice with spleen and envy.'[5] Meanwhile,
O'Connell's Catholic Association, supported by the so-called 'Catholic
rent' of a penny a month, was gathering numbers daily. When an alarmed
government brought a bill dissolving secret societies the following year,
O'Connell simply transformed the association into another, and continued
to agitate for Catholic emancipation in strict conformity with the law.

Much cheered by the success of *Captain Rock*, Moore set off for London
at the beginning of May, with the ninth number of his *Irish Melodies* ready

for the printer. Though not of such a consistently high standard as some of the earlier volumes, the collection contained at least one gem, a melancholy lyric much admired by Edgar Allan Poe:

I wish I was by that dim lake,
Where sinful souls their farewells take
Of this vain world, and half-way lie
In Death's cold shadow, ere they die.
There, there, far from thee,
Deceitful world, my home should be;
Where come what might of gloom and pain,
False hope should ne'er deceive again.

The lake in question, a traditional place of pilgrimage and penitence, was Lough Derg in County Donegal.

Moore's other object in coming to London was to see John Murray, with whom he had revised his agreement over Byron's memoirs two years earlier, stipulating that if Murray's 2,000 guineas were repaid they could be redeemed by himself or Byron: in effect turning Murray's original payment into a loan. He had now come to feel it would be safer to have the memoirs back in his own hands, and had arranged to borrow the money from Longmans to redeem them.

Byron had left for Greece on 24 July 1823. Writing to Moore from Cephalonia on 27 December of that year, he announced his impending departure for Missolonghi, and his intention of marching with the Greek forces. 'If any thing in the way of fever, fatigue, famine, or otherwise, should cut short the middle age of a brother warbler...' he wrote, 'I pray you to remember me in your "smiles and wine".'[6] His last letter to Moore, from Missolonghi, on 4 May, described himself as having had an attack of apoplexy or epilepsy, but slowly recovering, despite having been nearly bled to death.

On 13 May Moore dined with Longman's partner, Owen Rees, who asked him if he had completed his arrangements to buy back the memoirs, and advised him to lose no time about it. Moore was planning to do so as soon as possible when, on calling at Colbourn's Library the following morning, he heard the shocking news that Byron was dead.

At first he could not believe it, though the contents of Byron's last letter made him fear the worst. As he rushed out of Colbourn's, he met

Lord Lansdowne who confirmed 'this most disastrous news'. Speaking of Moore's unfinished arrangements with Murray, he told him, 'You have nothing but Murray's fairness to depend on'.[7] Moore, at the time, was not too worried over this, believing that his agreement with Murray gave him the option to redeem the memoirs for three months after Byron's death. After calling in at the *Morning Chronicle* to verify the news once more, he hurried round to Murray's offices, and finding him out, left him a note asking to meet as soon as possible. He then went on to see Samuel Rogers, who had not yet heard the news. Rogers advised him to do nothing about the memoirs till he heard from Murray, but to consult the well-known lawyer Henry Brougham, meanwhile. Moore dined alone at a local inn, having cancelled his dinner engagement for the evening – the only indication in his journal entry of how much he had been shaken by the news of Byron's death. On returning home he found a letter from Byron's executor and friend, Douglas Kinnaird, anxiously asking in whose possession the memoirs were, and offering £2,000 for them on Lady Byron's and the family's behalf.

Byron's other executor, John Cam Hobhouse, was another who had the memoirs on his mind. He had always resented Byron's gift to Moore and, far more censorious than Moore – he had bitterly opposed the publication of *Don Juan* – was determined to prevent any harm to Byron's reputation the memoirs might cause. How far his motives were coloured by unconscious jealousy of Moore is difficult to establish; he seems to have genuinely believed he had a duty to protect Byron's posthumous reputation. He had talked matters over with Kinnaird, whose letter to Moore that evening, offering to buy back the memoirs for the Byron family, was the result of their discussion.

The following morning Moore went round to see Kinnaird who repeated his previous offer. Moore refused any suggestion of repayment, insisting that the responsibility for redeeming the memoirs was his alone. He would submit them, not to Lady Byron, but to a chosen group of other people. If they, after examining them, decided they were unfit to publish, he would destroy them. He then went off in search of Brougham, who advised him to apply for an injunction if Murray attempted to appropriate the memoirs.

After this he saw Hobhouse, who told him that Murray was prepared to put the manuscript at the disposal of the Byron family, and that Wilmot Horton, a relative, was ready to redeem the memoirs for them. Moore reminded Hobhouse of his agreement with Murray, insisting that he alone had the right to decide what should be done. He was willing to place the memoirs at the disposal of Byron's half-sister, Augusta Leigh, but not of Lady Byron – for this, they both agreed, would be treachery.

Moore and Hobhouse then returned to Kinnaird, who thought, as Hobhouse did, that Augusta ought to burn the memoirs. 'I endeavoured,' wrote Moore, 'to convince them that this would be throwing a stigma upon the work, which it did not deserve.'[8] But Hobhouse, who had not been shown the memoirs – a cause for resentment in itself – and Kinnaird, who had, but felt that Moore had 'sold his Lordship to the booksellers',[9] were both strongly in favour of destroying them.

Overridden by the two men – both in a far stronger financial and worldly position than himself – Moore reluctantly agreed to sign a paper agreeing to meet Murray and Mrs Leigh at her rooms in St James's Palace on Monday (17 September), pay Murray £2,000, and give the manuscript to Mrs Leigh for her absolute disposal. 'I said,' he wrote, 'that as to the burning, that was her affair, but all the rest I would willingly do.'[10]

The next day, Saturday, Moore began to have second thoughts about relinquishing the memoirs and determined to do his best to save them. He called on Hobhouse who reported that Murray had accepted his claim to them, at the same time pointing out that the sum due was in guineas not pounds, with the addition of interest and expenses. With his rights to the manuscript confirmed, Moore then went on to Henry Luttrell, a good friend of Byron's, who had already read the memoirs. They both agreed that in giving them to Mrs Leigh they should strongly protest against their being destroyed. Luttrell suggested going to see Wilmot Horton, Mrs Leigh's representative in the matter. They found him at home, and explained their concern about the fate of the memoirs, and 'the injustice we thought it would be to Byron's memory to condemn the work wholly, and without even opening it, as if it were a pest bag'.[11] Nothing would be lost by first examining the manuscript, Horton on the part of Mrs Leigh, Lady Byron's representative, Colonel Doyle, on hers, together with anyone else the family might choose, They could then reject any passages that gave offence, while what was innocuous and creditable to Byron – 'of which I assured him,' wrote Moore, 'there was a considerable proportion' – could be preserved. Horton fully accepted this idea, and promised to speak to Mrs Leigh proposing that the manuscript should be placed in a banker's hands till its future had been decided.

Alas, it was too late. Hobhouse had already seen Mrs Leigh, and won her over to his point of view. A confused and suggestible person, she had a position at court – as a Lady in Waiting to Queen Charlotte – to maintain; she had already suffered from the outcry against *Don Juan*, and was terrified that the memoirs would cause her further scandal and embarrassment. Even without Hobhouse's persuasions, she would probably have insisted on their destruction. Meanwhile Moore had called on Colonel Doyle, and repeated his earlier suggestion to Horton. Doyle seemed sympathetic, though he said that the Byron family thought the whole of the manuscript should be burned. He added that he could answer for Lady Byron's readiness to repay Moore for the memoirs. Moore's touchy pride – a poor man's pride – flared up at this. He told Doyle that this was out of the question, he had already refused a similar offer from Kinnaird, and was determined to persist in his refusal.

Horton had arranged that the meeting on Monday should take place at Murray's, rather than Mrs Leigh's, fixing the time for 11 am. On Monday morning, Moore sent a note to Hobhouse telling him the change of plans, then set out for Longmans to collect the money. It was half past ten before the notes – two for £1,000, one for £200 – arrived from the bank. (Moore had borrowed the extra money for interest and expenses from Rogers.) Already a little late, Moore set off to Luttrell's chambers in Albany Place to beg him to come to Murray's with him. On his way he met Hobhouse, whose rooms were in the same building. Hobhouse had just been talking to Horton and was full of indignation at Moore's suggestion of 'a less summary method of proceeding'. 'Nothing less than the immediate & total destruction of the MS' would do, he insisted. Moore repeated again and again that he stood by his promise to put the memoirs at Mrs Leigh's disposal. Hobhouse, however, accused him of breaching his signed agreement, adding ominously that if the matter were ever publicly discussed 'he must say what he thought'.

Accompanied by Luttrell, they then went on to Murray's lodgings, and found him, wrote Moore, in 'an equal state of excitement against me'. Murray claimed he had not read the memoirs, but said they had been seen by William Gifford of the *Quarterly*, who had pronounced them as only fit for a brothel. (Gifford's opinion would have meant more if he had not said exactly the same about *Don Juan*.) Murray, in any case, was also determined on the destruction of the memoirs. 'A good deal of loud talking,' wrote Moore, 'during which Murray threatened to burn the MS himself, and applied some impertinent epithet to my conduct, which induced me to say with a contemptuous smile "Hard words, Mr Murray – but, if you chuse to take the privileges of a gentleman, I am ready to accord them to you." As near as I can recall this was what I said – but whatever it was, he saw its meaning and was more courteous.'

The four men – Moore, Hobhouse, Luttrell and Murray – then adjourned to Murray's house in Albemarle Street, and the first floor drawing room, which was also his publishing office. Horton and Doyle were waiting for them. Horton had seen Mrs Leigh in the meantime, and had completely come over to her side: he was now insistent that the memoirs should be destroyed at once. Hobhouse, triumphantly, accused Moore of misrepresenting Horton; it was only when Luttrell corrected him that Horton admitted he had changed his mind. Moore continued to argue the case for a stay of execution amid taunts and angry barracking from Hobhouse. When Moore, in pointing out the injustice they were doing to Byron's memory in condemning the work unread, mentioned 'as a minor consideration', the injustice they were also doing to him in denying him the benefit of the parts that were not objectionable, Hobhouse exploded: 'This is letting the author predominate over the friend.' He repeatedly held up the paper Moore had signed, insisting loudly, 'We must keep him to his bond – we must keep him to his bond.' 'On one of these ejaculations of his,' wrote Moore, 'I pointed smilingly at him and said "Look at Shylock".'[12] Hobhouse looked nettled for a moment, but returned to the attack, insisting – despite all Moore's protestations to the contrary – that he had broken his agreement.

In the end no arguments could save the manuscript. Augusta's wishes, as represented by Horton, and backed by Murray and Hobhouse, overrode the objections of Luttrell and Moore, though Moore went on protesting to the last. Even when the memoirs, and the only copy that existed of them, had been brought into the room and were about to be thrown into the flames, he continued his remonstrances, saying '*Remember I protest against the burning as contradictory to Lord Byron's wishes and unjust to me.*'[13] It was Horton and Doyle who tore up the pages, and flung them into the fire, both Murray and Hobhouse declining to take part. The fireplace in Albemarle Street, a mute witness to one of the greatest acts of literary vandalism in history, remains unchanged to this day; Byron's portrait hangs above it.

Once the burning was over and Moore had signed a paper confirming there were no other copies of the memoirs, a relative calm descended on the company. There now came the question of finding Moore's original agreement with Murray, preparatory to handing him the money. It was some time before the agreement could be found; when it was, Moore discovered to his consternation that the clause giving him the right to redeem the memoirs within three months of Byron's death did not exist. Careless as always about business, he had not bothered to read the finished document, having dictated the clause, as he thought, at the time it was drawn up. Murray seemed equally surprised; in legal terms it was his property, not Moore's, that had been destroyed. 'I hinted something of this at the moment,' wrote Moore, 'but was luckily not attended to. I say "luckily" because I should never have felt comfortable if the money had been paid by anyone but myself.'[14]

Murray himself seemed to feel the awkwardness of the situation, saying, when Moore offered him the money, 'I do not feel I have the right to take this'. Luttrell, however, reminded Moore that he had borrowed the money from Murray, and Moore's touchy pride, and determination not to seem self interested, made him insist. Murray finally agreed to take the money, at the same time telling Hobhouse, as Byron's executor, that he thought the Byron family should see that Moore was repaid.

Hobhouse, his main aim achieved, now came up laughingly to Moore, saying 'Well, my dear Moore, I hope you will forgive anything I have said that angered you', and asked him to agree that Murray had acted perfectly well and honourably. Murray too came up, and apologised to Moore for the offence he might have given, repeating several times, 'Shoot me, but forgive me.' 'Him, however,' wrote Moore, 'I received with more coldness.'

Horton and Doyle had already left. Hobhouse, Moore and Luttrell now moved off, laughing and joking with the exhilaration that often comes after moments of high emotion. They parted at Albany Chambers, Hobhouse calling after Moore and Luttrell, who were still laughing over something, 'You merry undone dogs.' Moore's high spirits quickly subsided after he left them. Byron was dead; the precious gift of his memoirs had been destroyed; his insistence on his right to dispose of them had plunged him 2,000 guineas into debt. He called at Longmans to report what had happened. 'It was evident to them, as well as to me,' he wrote bitterly, 'that Murray's violent anxiety for the total destruction of the MS arose from his fears that any part of it should find its way into their hands, and so far he had triumphed.'

'Felt altogether very uncomfortable,' he continued,

> – had been treated by none of the parties in this business as I deserved ... The insulting looks & manners of Hobhouse, too, recurred

to me, and though I had given away to his good humoured advances at the end, I felt now I ought not to have done so, and [as] if the easiness of my temper had compromised my self respect. These thoughts so gained upon me, in the state of nervousness into which the whole transaction had thrown me, that I would have given worlds at that moment to have been placed hostilely face to face with Hobhouse with a pistol, not from any hostility to him but from feeling that nothing else could now set me right with myself.

So strongly did he feel this that as soon as he had returned to his lodgings, he sat down and wrote a note to Hobhouse. It was the second time in the day – the first was in his exchanges with Murray – that he had envisaged the possibility of a duel. 'Though it may be difficult to believe (particularly after the friendly manner in which we parted) that you could seriously mean to insult me today, yet some of your looks and phrases, which seemed so very like it … haunt me so uncomfortably that it would be a great satisfaction to me to be assured by yourself that you had no such intention, and I trust you will lose no time in setting my mind at rest on the subject.'

He then went out to a dinner party but feeling 'not at all well & happy' returned home early. He spent the night worrying about what would happen to his family if he were killed but felt unable to withdraw his letter.

There was no answer from Hobhouse the next morning, 'which I was not surprized at' – wrote Moore; 'felt I had acted most irregularly in making this call upon him, after our having parted so amicably, yet, at the same time, felt that I must follow it.'[15]

Fortunately he found a mutual friend, Sir Francis Burdett, to whom he put the case. Burdett assured him that though Hobhouse could often be impetuous and overbearing, he knew he had a high opinion of Moore, and could not possibly have meant to insult him. He added that it would be a shocking thing if Hobhouse and Moore should fight about their common friend Lord Byron, and asked him who else had been present at the time. Moore told him Luttrell, adding that he was perfectly ready to meet Hobhouse on friendly terms if he felt his honour could be satisfied. He then went on to arrange to a life insurance to cover his debt to Longmans – a necessity with a duel in prospect. Fortunately, however, soon after he had returned home, Burdett called to tell him that Hobhouse had also been to see him, and that both men had consulted Luttrell as a witness to the previous day's proceedings. Luttrell's opinion was that Hobhouse's manner during the discussion was certainly rather – 'I forget the epithet,' wrote Moore – but that his way of speaking afterwards showed that he was really sorry for it, and that Moore could be perfectly satisfied by this.

This was enough to soothe Moore's ruffled feelings and after thanking Burdett warmly for his intervention he hurriedly got dressed for luncheon – 'having been invited this week past to meet the Princesses [George III's daughters] at Lady Donegal's'. In the flattering company of royalty, his songs applauded and 'chorussed' by the princesses, he could briefly escape the painful emotions of the last few days.

20

A Visit to Scotland

The news of Byron's death, in the words of the *Morning Chronicle*, 'came upon London like an earthquake'. The reverberations were felt all over Europe. The story of the burning of the memoirs, so quickly after Byron's death, sent further shock waves. Ironically enough, in view of his desperate efforts to save them, it was Moore who was generally regarded as responsible for their destruction, for the most part with approval. As far away as Russia, Pushkin could write: 'Why do you regret the loss of Byron's notes? The devil with them! Thank God they are lost. He made his confession in his verses, in spite of himself, carried away with the rapture of poetry. In cool prose...he would have been caught in the act, just as Rousseau was caught in the act – and spite and slander would have triumphed again... Moore's deed is better than his *Lalla Rookh*.'[1]

What had been lost in the memoirs? Their contents were hardly a state secret. A number of Moore's friends, including Lady Holland and Lord Lansdowne, had read the first part, and none had been especially shocked, though the second part, according to Moore, contained some coarser passages. In the opinion of Lord John Russell, who had read almost all of them, 'three or four pages of it were too gross and indelicate for publication; and the rest, with few exceptions, contained little traces of Lord Byron's genius and no interesting details of life'.[2] Moore's own summing up, at the end of his biography of Byron, was probably the most accurate statement of the case:

For the satisfaction of those whose regret at the loss of that manuscript arises from some better motive than the mere disappointment of a prurient curiosity, I shall here add, that on the mysterious cause of the separation, it afforded no light whatever: – that, while some of its details could never have been published at all, and little, if any, of what it contained personal to others could have appeared till long after the individuals concerned had left the scene, all that materially related to Lord Byron himself was (as I well knew when I made that sacrifice) to be found repeated in the various Journals and Memorandum-books which... were, as the reader has seen from the preceding pages, all preserved.[3]

In the immediate aftermath of the burning of the memoirs, however, Moore was in a state of great trouble and confusion. It was doubtless gratifying to be told by the Duke of Gloucester, at a large assembly at Lansdowne House: 'You have done the handsomest and finest thing that ever man did',[4] but he was far from feeling the same himself. He was a little consoled by the fact that Hobhouse had told him that, when he last saw him, Byron had expressed regrets at having lost control of the memoirs; it was only out of delicacy towards Moore that he had not tried to recall them. 'This, if I wanted any justification to myself for what I have done,' wrote Moore, 'would abundantly satisfy me as to the propriety of my sacrifice.'[5]

Having placed himself seriously in debt over the memoirs, it was particularly irritating to find that in several of the papers, it was Murray who was credited with the sacrifice. With the help of Hobhouse, Horton and Luttrell, Moore wrote a correction for the press, making it clear, however, that Murray had been ready to take the loss himself. Both Horton and Doyle, on behalf of Mrs Leigh and Lady Byron, tried to persuade Moore to take the money for the memoirs back, but he felt that he would lose all moral credibility if he accepted payment, and refused.

Several of his friends thought his refusal too quixotic. Rogers told him that while he himself would not take the money, he thought that Moore's having a wife and children made all the difference. When Moore assured him that 'more mean things have been done in this world... under the shelter of "wife and children" than under any other pretext', he at last surrendered smilingly: 'Well, your life may be a good *poem*, but it is a damned bad matter of fact.'[6] And so Moore may have ruefully felt, as he returned home to the treadmill of his work on Sheridan.

Although he was desperate to finish the biography he set it aside to go back to London for Byron's funeral on 12 July. At half past nine that morning he and Rogers set off for Great George Street, Westminster, where Byron's body had lain in state; from there the funeral cortege would leave on the long journey to Newstead Abbey where Byron was to be buried. A vast crowd accompanied the procession, but few of the aristocracy attended. The social ostracism Byron had experienced in his lifetime continued after his death, though a number of empty coaches had been sent out of deference to Hobhouse and his friends. Only the three first mourners' carriages were occupied, Hobhouse and others in the first, Moore with Rogers, Campbell, Stanhope, the agent of the London Greek Committee and Orlando, the Greek deputy, in the third. 'When I approached the house,' wrote Moore,

> and saw the crowd assembled, felt a nervous trembling come over me, which lasted till the whole ceremony was over; thought I should be ill. Never was at a funeral before, but poor Curran's. The riotous curiosity of the mob, the bustle of the undertakers & c., and all the other vulgar accompaniments of the ceremony, mixing with my recollections of him who was gone, produced a combination of disgust and sadness that was deeply painful to me...Left the hearse as soon as it was off the stones, and returned home to get rid of my black clothes, and to try to forget as much as possible, the wretched feelings I had experienced in them.[7]

Once in London, Moore spent a further week there, talking much about Byron with Stanhope, the Hollands and others, and collecting last minute information about Sheridan. Rogers, for instance, recalled how Sheridan, having suffered miseries at being called an actor's son at Harrow, said he had never seen Garrick on the stage, and would never see a play all through. It was the kind of detail that often makes Moore's diary entries about Sheridan more revealing than his biography.

To the biography, however, Moore returned, devoting most of the next eight months to completing it: 'hard at work on Sheridan' was a familiar refrain in his journal. By the beginning of April 1825, the first proofs had arrived, though he continued to revise and introduce new material for several months longer. On a visit to London in June, to discuss the engraving of Sheridan for the frontispiece, he was received by Lady Holland with the discouraging remark, 'This will be a dull book of yours, this "Sheridan"

I fear'. But then she had recently told Lord Porchester 'I am sorry to hear you are going to publish a poem. Can't you suppress it?'[8]

Moore came to London again in August for some final questions about Sheridan, and to discuss arrangements for the next number of his *National Airs*. In the course of this visit he saw Augusta Leigh for the first time. They met at Holland House, where Augusta, having asked to be introduced to him, talked pleasantly of her brother and even invited Moore to see a miniature she had of him. Although she did not at all resemble him, there was something about her that reminded Moore strongly of Byron: 'I felt it difficult to keep the tears out of my eyes as I spoke with her.'[9] He could not know that Augusta, ambivalent about visiting Holland House in the first place, was referring to him in her letters as 'that detestable *little* Moore' and would write a few weeks later, 'Thank Heaven I did not see him when he called'.[10] For Augusta, he would always be the man who knew too much.

By early September Moore had virtually reached the end of his Sheridan task. The misery of Sheridan's last days made painful writing and reading. Burdened with debt and knowing that only his own health and efforts lay between him and a similar fate for his family, he broke down one evening from sheer exhaustion and wept. The biography had been a consistently uphill task, complicated in its final stages by the fact that Sheridan's son Charles, wanting to help the family of his widowed sister-in-law, had demanded to be paid for the use of his father's papers. When Murray refused to offer more than the £1,000 agreed as Moore's fee, Longmans had taken on the book instead, contracting to give Charles Sheridan half the profits after the first 2,500 copies had been sold, as well as making up Moore's £1,000. The negotiations, which had taken place two months before the drama of Byron's memoirs, were resolved on apparently amicable terms, Moore repaying Murray the £350 he had so far spent. But they may well have had a bearing on Murray's determination to keep the memoirs out of Longmans' hands.

On 26 September, Moore sent in the final proofs to Longmans and caught the coach home. On 6 October, having spent the night at Bowood, he came down to breakfast to find the morning papers full of extracts from his life of Sheridan: 'Fidgeted exceedingly by seeing people reading them, at which they were not a little amused'. The following day he had a letter from Charles Sheridan expressing his admiration and gratitude in the warmest terms: 'a most seasonable relief to my mind,' wrote Moore, 'as I have been even more anxious about his opinion than that of the public.'[11] The day after, better still, came 'a triumphant letter from Longmans'[12] congratulating him on the perfect success of the book, which was already selling very well. They added that they were placing a further £300 to his credit, beyond the original payment of £1,000.

Here was a happy send-off for a work that had involved him in so much labour and self doubt. To understand something of his achievement, one must remember that, apart from Boswell's *Life of Johnson* thirty-four years earlier, there was no established model of biography to follow. Moore was writing in what was still a relatively new genre, his task made more difficult by the widely differing opinions of Sheridan he had met with in his interviews with his friends, acquaintances and enemies; it was impossible to avoid offending some, if not all of them, in the course of his biography.

Not surprisingly, the book is at its most successful in depicting Sheridan's youth, when there were fewer controversial matters to address. It gives a delightful picture of a lively young scapegrace, involved in an elopement and two incredible duels, and of his brilliant successes as a playwright. It is illuminating too in its discussion of Sheridan's literary methods, and Moore quotes at length from the many drafts of *The School for Scandal*, which Sheridan was still refining and correcting when the play had already been announced. A note at the bottom of the final page – 'Finished at last. Thank God! R.B. Sheridan' – had a heartfelt postcript from the prompter – 'Amen! W. Hopkins.'

Sheridan, as Moore shows, would follow the same laborious methods of preparation when it came to his great feats of parliamentary oratory, above all his speeches at the trial of Warren Hastings. But it is in the second half of Sheridan's life, when politics were his central interest, that the narrative slows down. Moore's prose takes on something of the ornateness of the political debates of the time, and is marred by elaborate figures of speech. At times they can be memorable – Burke for instance is characterised as a Whig 'who took his perch at all times on [the] loftiest branches, as far as possible away from popular contact'[13] – but at others they obstruct the story. One reviewer was reminded of Curran's observation, 'If you can't talk sense talk metaphor'.

Sheridan's personal life, probably for reasons of discretion, is largely ignored in the second half of the book, and Moore weaves his way delicately through the ramifications of his business dealings. In following Sheridan's long political career, however, he gives an admirably balanced history of the period, more Whig than Tory in its outlook, but far from being an apologia for all Whig policies. Throughout the book he emphasises how consistently Sheridan spoke for Ireland, protesting vainly against the Act of Union and refusing to accept office in a government opposed to Catholic emancipation. He quotes movingly from one of Sheridan's final speeches in the House of Commons: 'If they were to be the last words I should ever utter in this House, I should say, "Be just to Ireland, as you value your own honour; – be just to Ireland as you value your own peace."'[14] It was a warning that would echo down the century.

Moore's painstaking habits of research, his use of primary documents, and his many interviews with living witnesses, make his book essential reading for all later biographers of Sheridan. But his interpretation of recent history provoked considerable controversy at the time. As he noted in his preface to the fifth edition: 'The Tory, of course, is shocked by my Whiggism; – the Whigs are rather displeased by my candour in conceding, that they have sometimes been wrong, and the Tories right, while the Radical, in his patriotic hatred of both parties, is angry with me for allowing any merit to either.'

Moore refused to be shaken by his critics. He had written the book as honestly as he knew how, and if there were murmurings among the grandees of the Whig party, not all of whom accepted his version of events, they were not enough to spoil his pleasure in its success. Exhausted by months of unremitting work, he now felt that he deserved a holiday.

His first idea was to join the Lansdownes on a trip to Paris, but the expense, and the thought of leaving Bessy for too long, decided him on a trip to Scotland instead. His first stop was at Abbotsford, where he had an open invitation to stay with Walter Scott. He arrived there on 29 October, after a two-and-a-half-day journey, and was greeted with a hearty welcome. The two men had only met once before in London, but they hit it off immediately, and as soon as Moore had been introduced to Scott's family, they set off on a walk together. The conversation soon turned to Byron, whom Scott had always liked and admired. They talked of *Don Juan* – its last Cantos, thought Scott, were the best things he ever wrote – and deplored a report that Lady Byron was about to marry a man called Cunningham. 'No – no,' said Scott, 'she must never let another man bear the name of husband to her. Being even a W[hore] would be better, perhaps, than that!'[15] They also discussed Moore's sacrifice of the memoirs. Scott told him that though he was well aware of the honourable feelings that dictated it, he doubted whether he would have agreed to it himself. When Moore pointed out the circumstances – the strong pressure from Byron's sister and two most intimate friends, and above all, Hobhouse's assurances that Byron had regretted giving Moore the manuscript – Scott agreed that he had had no choice. He thought, however, that Moore had a strong claim on the Byron family for help if he wished to write the poet's life.

Moore spent three days with Scott at Abbotsford, where they walked and drove and drank and talked of poetry and poets, and though totally differing in politics – Scott a Tory, Moore a Whig – were delighted with each other's company. It is interesting to compare the two poets' opinions of each other, Scott noting in his diary some weeks later:

> I was curious to see what there could be in common betwixt us, Moore having lived so much in the gay world, I in the country... Moore a scholar, I none; he a democrat, I an aristocrat – with many other points of difference... Yet there is a point of resemblance, and a strong one. We are both good humoured fellows, who rather seek to enjoy what is going forward than to maintain our dignity as Lions; and we have both seen the world too widely and too well not to condemn in our souls the imaginary consequence of literary people, who walk with their noses in the air, and remind me always of the fellow whom Johnson met in an alehouse, and who called himself *'the great Twalmly – inventor of the flood-gate iron for smoothing linen'*.[16]

And here is Moore, in his diary, on the Wizard of the North: 'Could not help thinking, during this quiet, homely visit, how astonished some of those foreigners would be, to whom the name of Sir Walter Scott is encircled with so much romance, to see the plain quiet neighbourly manner with which he took his seat among these old maids & the familiar ease with which they treated him in return – no country squire, with but half an idea in his head, could have fallen into gossip of a hum-drum visit more unassumingly.'[17]

From Abbotsford, Moore went on to Edinburgh where he stayed with Bessy's sister Ann and her husband, the actor-manager William Murray. He spent ten days there, seeing friends from the *Edinburgh Review*, and being wined and dined so much that he actually fell ill – the culprit, he thought, was some 'sour *Presbyterian* claret',[18] which made him sick for several days. On the night before his departure, duly recovered, he went to the theatre with Walter Scott. Word had got about that he was coming and when they appeared in their box the whole pit got up and began applauding loudly. Scott pushed Moore to the front of the box saying 'It is you – it is you – you must rise & make your acknowledgement'. 'I hesitated for some time,' wrote Moore, 'but on hearing them shout out "Moore, Moore", I rose & bowed my best for two or three minutes – The scene was repeated after the next two acts & the Irish Melodies were played each time by the orchestra.' Scott was delighted by Moore's reception – he had been similarly greeted in Dublin and said several times, 'This is quite right – I am glad my country-men have returned the compliment for me.'

'Home very tired with my glory,' wrote Moore, 'and had to pack for my journey.'[19]

2 I

Negotiations

Moore had only been back at Sloperton a fortnight when a letter arrived from his sister Ellen in Dublin telling him that his father, who had been seriously ill for some time, was dying. He set off for Ireland as quickly as he could, making the twelve-hour crossing from Holyhead in a howling gale. He was lying sick and prostrate in his berth when he overheard someone asking the steward whether Moore was on board, and saying: 'His father is...' Moore could not hear the final word but immediately assumed that his father had died; 'it is a proof of the power of the mind over even sea-sickness,' he wrote, 'that though I was just then on the point of being sick, the dread certainty which these words conveyed to me quite checked the impulse.'

He arrived in Dublin to learn that his father was still alive, but unconscious and feeling no pain. Having taken a room at a hotel, he hurried round to see his mother and sister. Knowing his extreme sensibility in the face of death or illness, both women urged him not to see his father, as there was nothing he could do and it would only upset him unnecessarily. For Moore this was a great relief: 'I would not for worlds have the sweet impression he left upon my mind when I last saw him, changed for one which would haunt me.'[1] The next morning, when he went round to his parents' house, he heard that his father had died a few hours earlier.

His father's half pension died with his death, but Philip Crampton, the doctor who had attended him in his last illness, was on good terms with the Lord Lieutenant, the Marquess of Wellesley, and approached him to see if it could be continued on behalf of his wife. Despite his friendship with the King, and Moore's opposition views, the Marquess generously agreed to keep it on. But this would have changed a pension into a government subsidy, and true to his principles to accept no favours from the Tories, Moore politely refused it, though 'God alone knows,' he wrote, 'how I am to support all the burdens laid on me.'[2]

Moore was dismayed to find that his mother could not live, as he had hoped, with his married sister Kate, since she did not get on with her overbearing son-in-law, John Scully; Kate also warned him that Scully could do nothing to help the family financially. It was not Kate's fault – her husband had completely worn her down – but Moore found it hard to understand how Scully could give balls and keep five servants, yet had nothing to spare for his wife's family. Meanwhile the admirable Bessy had been planning economies to help his mother and, knowing how miserable he was feeling, had been writing to him every day.

Moore's father's funeral had been expensive, there were other bills to be paid, and the future of his mother and his unmarried sister Ellen to be considered. Almost in despair, he had written to Longmans before he left to know whether he might draw on his balance with them on the Sheridan account. He knew, he wrote, 'that I had no right to draw it, as everything ought to go into that chasm of debt that was open between us, but that I could not help it'. He received a letter from them shortly after his arrival in Dublin, begging him to draw on them for whatever he wanted 'without reference to the amount'.[3] It was a typical example of their generous attitude towards him – and of their faith in his abilities.

Having done the best he could for his family, Moore returned to England in time for a belated Twelfth Night party with his children, then settled back to work again. He had various irons in the fire, among them his Egyptian story, begun in Paris, then set aside, and several new collections of songs for Power. The most ambitious of these, *Evenings in Greece*, consisting of a series of songs, linked by a 'thread of poetical narrative', included a moving farewell to Byron.

> Thou art not dead – thou art not dead!
> No, dearest Harmodius, no.
> Thy soul, to realms above us fled,
> Though, like a star, it dwells o'erhead,
> Still lights this world below...

'You will perceive,' Moore wrote to Power, 'that "Thou art not dead" alludes (under the name of a celebrated antient Greek) to Lord Byron.'[4]

Byron continued to be central to Moore's thoughts. Despite Hobhouse's assurances – for which, incidentally, there was not the slightest evidence in Byron's letters – that Byron had wished to take the memoirs back, Moore could not help feeling he had betrayed him by allowing the memoirs to be destroyed. To write his biography would be an act of reparation; it also offered his best chance of repaying the ruinous debt with which he had burdened himself.

He had already written to Hobhouse from Ireland, asking him, as Byron's executor, whether he had any objections to Moore writing his biography. Hobhouse's answer was stiff and unfriendly. 'I do not see what good end can be answered by writing a life of our late friend – and I do see a good many objections to it... You will write, there can be no doubt, a very clever and a very saleable book. But I shall be most agreably surprised if you accomplish those higher objects which you must propose to yourself by becoming the Biographer of such a man as Lord Byron.'[5]

Moore swallowed Hobhouse's letter as best he could. Though secretly irritated by its superior tone, he had everything to gain by a conciliatory reply. No-one, he told Hobhouse, could think more humbly of his talents than himself: 'nothing but the want of means from any other source could have induced me so long to avail myself of even that "saleable" quality (as you describe it) which, however undeservedly, my writings have hitherto possessed... But until I can discharge, in some other way, the heavy obligations I am under, I must at least seem to entertain the intention.'[6]

Hobhouse was somewhat mollified by this show of humility, and grudgingly admitted the justice of Moore's arguments. He wrote back in a milder tone, suggesting that they meet in London to discuss an alternative plan – in fact a collection of Byron's letters, with a critical preface by Moore. By the time they met in May 1826, however, Moore had already determined on a full-length biography, whatever the objections of Byron's friends and family. (Augusta and Lady Byron, in particular, were resolutely opposed to the idea.) Hobhouse could do nothing to prevent it but consoled himself with the thought that, on the whole, Moore would treat the subject fairly, and that Byron had certainly intended his memoirs to benefit him. That being so, he wrote, 'I cannot but assist him to gain his £2000 out of Lord Byron's memory'.[7]

Hobhouse's assistance did not go very far, but he promised to speak to Lady Melbourne's daughter, Lady Cowper, to ask if Moore could see

Byron's letters to her mother. He also encouraged Moore to make his peace with Murray, to whom he had not spoken since their angry exchanges on the day of the burning of the memoirs. Hobhouse saw Murray, rather than Longmans, as the natural publishers for a life of Byron, and knowing Murray well, felt he would be better able to influence what appeared.

Moore was happy enough to be reconciled with Murray – he felt he had been wrong in not accepting his apologies at the time. He was already planning to call on him, when he happened to see him passing in the street. He immediately ran after him and accosted him, saying, 'Mr Murray, some friends of yours & mine seem to think that you & I should no longer continue upon these terms – I therefore proffer you my hand and most readily forgive, & forget all that has passed'. Murray seemed startled at first but he soon brightened up and they walked on together very amicably. On parting at Charing Cross he shook Moore's hand warmly, repeating 'God bless you, Sir, God bless you, Sir'.[8] It was hard to stay enemies with Moore for long.

The way was now open for an agreement with Murray for the biography, the great advantage to Moore being the number of letters from Byron in Murray's possession. (Byron had deliberately used his correspondence with Murray, a leading figure in literary circles, as a means to keep his name before the public.) Longmans behaved with their usual generosity: 'Do not let us stand in the way of any arrangements you may make,' they told him; 'it is our wish to see you free of any debt, and it would only be for this one work we should be separated – put us therefore out of the question, nor let us in the least degree fetter you in the business.'[9] Although no formal contract was signed, Murray's suggestion was that Moore should be paid by the discharge of his debt to Longmans, together with half the profits from the book. He promised to collect his Byron materials together as soon as possible – 'near to filling a Quarto volume,'[10] he told him.

Moore spent a cheerful month in London, as usual 'swallowed up' by engagements. He sat for his portrait to Gilbert Newton – Sydney Smith, who called to see the work in progress, asking the artist gravely, 'Couldn't you contrive to throw into his face somewhat of a stronger expression of hostility to the Church Establishment?'[11] He was feted at the annual dinners of the Literary Fund and the Artist's Benevolent Fund; saw much of Rogers, the Lansdownes and Lady Donegal; went to the opera and the Royal Academy; and attended the anniversary dinner of the Madrigal Society, where the singing was so bad that Wesley, the composer, whose music was being sung, got up crying, 'Oh, for God's sake gentlemen, no more – I cannot bear it' after the first three bars.

Although he was committed to writing Byron's life, Moore had received no money in advance. The research would be a long and painstaking process: 'biography,' he once told Rogers, 'is like a dot engraving, made up of little minature points, which must all be attended to, or the effect is lost.'[12] There was the question of what to live on in the meantime and among his other projects he was greatly relieved to find a new source of income when the editor of the *Times*, to which he had been contributing satires for some time, offered him £400 for a series of further poems.

It was good to be back in the political fray, and his humorous squibs, published anonymously over the next few years, were soon the talk of

Study for Moore's portrait: by Gilbert Stuart Newton, 1826.

London. Dependent on the political events and personalities of the time, they have inevitably lost most of their bite but some of them, especially those on Ireland, still hit the mark. Here, for instance, are the opening verses of 'The Petition of the Orangemen of Ireland':

> To the people of England, the humble Petition
> Of Ireland's disconsolate Orangemen, showing –
> That sad, very sad, is our present condition;
> Our jobbing all gone, and our noble selves going: –
>
> That, forming one seventh, within a few fractions,
> Of Ireland's seven millions of hot heads and hearts,
> We hold it the basest of all base transactions,
> To keep us from murd'ring the other six parts…

And when in 1827, after a motion for Catholic emancipation had been defeated in the House of Commons, the government sent five million cartridges to the Irish garrisons, Moore marked the occasion with his 'Pastoral Ballad by John Bull':

> I have found out a gift for my Erin,
> A gift that will surely content her; –
> Sweet pledge of a love so enduring!
> Five millions of bullets I've sent her.
>
> She asked me for Freedom and Right,
> But ill she her wants understood; –
> Ball cartridges morning and night,
> Is a dose that will do her more good.

Before starting his biography of Byron, Moore had his Egyptian novel, *The Epicurean*, to finish for Longmans. Published in 1827, and excessively slow moving by modern standards, it delighted its nineteenth-century readers; George Eliot, for one, declared herself 'enchanted as completely as if I had been in the clutches of the Egyptian priests'.[13] The story is that of a Greek Epicurean of the fourth century AD who is inspired by a dream to travel to Egypt in search of immortality. In seeking to penetrate the Egyptian mysteries he falls in love with a young priestess, who has secretly become a Christian, and is finally martyred for her faith. He himself becomes a convert; his story, written in the first person, is supposedly found by a traveller among a heap of old Greek manuscripts in a desert monastery. The book, which sold steadily for many years, had the honour of being illustrated by Turner (1839), translated into French by Théophile Gautier (1865) and re-issued in 1900, when the success of Rider Haggard's *She* provoked a controversy as to whether it had been partly plagiarised from Moore. It was Moore's only attempt at a novel, its religious and philosophic theme the sign of a new seriousness in his outlook.

Other works to appear that year included a trio of articles for the *Edinburgh Review*, a set of glees for Power, and the sixth and final number of the *National Airs*. The biography of Byron, meanwhile, was hanging fire. Since his meeting with Murray the previous summer, he had heard nothing more of the Byron papers he had promised him. When he visited London in February he found to his intense irritation that Murray had decided to keep the letters as a legacy for his children and would not allow him to use them. Since Moore's only object in switching publishers had been to pool resources with Murray, he went back to Longmans, who of course received him with open arms. He still had to finish *The Epicurean*, however, and it was not till July that he began to gather biographical data in earnest.

One of his first contacts was with Mary Shelley, the poet's widow. Shelley had always been an admirer of Moore's. 'One of the first things I remember with Shelley,' Mary Shelley told Moore, 'was his repeating to me one of your *gems* with enthusiasm.'[14] He had dedicated his political satire, *Peter Bell the Third*, to 'Thomas Brown, the Younger', and most memorably of all, had linked Moore with Byron – 'the Pilgrim of Eternity' – as one of the poets who, 'with others of less note', mourn Keats in *Adonais*:

...from her wilds Ierne sent
The sweetest lyrist of her saddest wrong
And Love taught Grief to fall like music from his tongue.

Mrs Shelley had read the first part of Byron's memoirs before he had given them to Moore and promised to write down what she remembered of them, and to help him in any way she could. The two got on well, Mrs Shelley, lonely and poor, relaxing in Moore's sympathetic company, Moore unburdening himself – as he seldom did to others – of his anxieties and self doubts. He was particularly touched when she showed him a letter to her from Byron in which he wrote that he had never felt real friendship, except for one man, Lord Clare, and 'perhaps,' he added, 'Thomas Moore'.[15]

(It was Hobhouse's angry suspicion that Byron preferred Moore to himself, a far older friend, that coloured so many of his dealings with Moore.)

There was no information to be expected from Lady Byron or Augusta – incidentally, Mary Shelley told Moore (in a passage suppressed by Russell in his edition of Moore's journals) that Byron had told her all about his sister. But he had fruitful interviews with many of Byron's early friends, including his first love, Mary Chaworth; with travellers whom he had known in the Near East; and those like Samuel Rogers, the Hollands and Lady Jersey, who had been part of his social circle in London. Mary Shelley put him in touch with Bowring, the Secretary of the Greek Committee, and more importantly, with Countess Guiccioli, whose memoir Moore described as 'perfection', though he knew he must be circumspect in using it.

It was not until he had worked through several months of interviews and copying correspondence, that he wrote to Hobhouse about his promise to obtain Byron's letters to Lady Melbourne. Hobhouse, however, had reverted to his old position of intransigence, and reported in his diary: 'After a great deal of deliberation I wrote to *repeat* that I could not be a coadjutor in his work, and he could not consult the letters to Lady Melbourne...I told him that I found Barry and Me Guiccioli had been told I was assisting him, and that I was piqued at it.'[16]

Moore's answer, wrote Hobhouse, was in 'proper terms', though he may not have seen its underlying irony:

> It is very possible that some expressions of mine relative to your kindness & c., may have been construed by Mr Barry and others into a boast of your sanction and co-operation. But be assured that I did not mean them to be so taken & that I shall do my utmost to remove the impression. Indeed, the simple fact that my book is likely to appear without a single contribution of either paper or anecdote from any one of Lord Byron's immediate friends or relatives will sufficiently absolve them all from any share of responsibility for it.[17]

While Byron's two great friends, both fundamentally decent men, were sparring, a third and less scrupulous figure, Leigh Hunt, had decided to enter the fray. His two-volume memoir, *Lord Byron and Some of his Contemporaries*, appearing in January 1828, was a vicious attack on Byron in which, while portraying himself as noble and hard done by, he painted Byron as a monster of vanity, avarice and envy. Not for nothing was Hunt depicted as

Harold Skimpole in *Bleak House* – having sponged on Byron for two years in Italy, he was now cashing in on him after his death. Even before the book came out there had been extracts from it in the papers. Moore had always been sympathetic to Hunt – and some years later would subscribe to a fund for his relief – but this act of treachery was too much. Roused to fury on Byron's behalf, he gave vent to his indignation in a scathing set of verses for the *Times*,

> Next week will be published (as 'Lives' are the rage)
> The whole Reminiscences, wondrous and strange,
> Of a small puppy-dog that once lived in the cage
> Of the late noble Lion at Exeter 'Change…
>
> Though he roared pretty well – this the puppy allows –
> It was all, he says, borrowed – all second hand roar;
> And he vastly prefers his own little bows-wows
> To the loftiest war-note the Lion could pour…
>
> Nay, fed as he was (and this makes a dark case)
> With sops every day from the Lion's own pan,
> He lifts up his leg at the noble beast's carcass,
> And – does all a dog so diminutive can.
>
> However the book's a good book, being rich in
> Examples and warnings to Lions high-bred,
> How they suffer small mongrelly dogs in their kitchen,
> Who'll feed on them living, and foul them when dead.

One good result for Moore from the publication of the book was that Murray, infuriated at the venom and inaccuracy of Hunt's account, now changed his mind about the publication of his Byron papers, and wrote to Moore, saying he had submitted a new offer to Rogers (who fully approved it) and suggesting that they should meet as soon as possible. Moore was coming up to London anyway, since he and Bessy wished to consult a surgeon about their daughter Anastasia, aged fourteen, who had been suffering from a painful abscess on her thigh, and whose health was causing them concern. Moore called on Murray the day after his arrival, and heard his new proposition in a few words – Murray was to place all his Byron papers at his disposal and offered him 4,000 guineas for the *Life*. 'Told him,' wrote Moore,

> that I considered this offer perfectly liberal, but that he knew how I was situated with the Longmans, and that I certainly could not again propose to take my work out of their hands without having it in my power to pay down the sum that I owe them – 'They would, I suppose (he said) be inclined to give some accomodation for the payment?' – 'I cannot answer for that, Mr Murray (I replied) – I must have it in my power to offer them the payment of the debt' – 'Very well, Sir (he said) you may do so.'[18]

Moore went to see Longmans the next day who, behaving with their usual graciousness agreed to the arrangement. 'Nothing could be more frank, gentlemanly and satisfactory than the manner in which this affair has been settled on all sides,'[19] reported Moore with satisfaction. In fact, his interest payments, both to Murray and Longmans, together with the heavy travelling expenses involved in his researches, meant that he would have very little left from Murray's advance. In Longmans' opinion, Murray could have been far more generous.

Moore now had all Byron's letters to Murray, together with a hundred and forty two of his own; by the time the book was published two years later he had gathered together five hundred and sixty one letters in all. He had already decided that Byron should speak for himself in the biography; its title gives the format: *Letters and Journals of Lord Byron: With Notices of his Life by Thomas Moore*. Weaving his narrative round Byron's own inimitable words, Moore sets the documents in context, and though discretion and the prudery of the age inevitably led to many omissions, his book is still the best, as well as the first, of all full-length lives of Byron. Written by a poet, imbued with the romantic spirit, it is, in the words of the Byron scholar Thérèse Tessier, a 'kind of...polyphonic composition, in which the leading voices, Byron's and his biographer's, are heard in a powerful duo'.[20] For Moore the biography was a labour of love. It is common to dismiss him, as does for instance Doris Langley Moore, as shallower and less feeling than Byron's other great friend Hobhouse. The book, if any evidence were needed, is a flat refutation of this view. Into no other work of prose did Moore ever put so much effort and such heart. The result is one of the masterpieces of nineteenth-century biography, but it was written, as we shall see, against a background of tragedy that almost broke his buoyant spirit.

22

Bereavement and Biography

The Moores' daughter Anastasia had been her father's pet since Barbara's death, and when the time had come for her to go to boarding school in Bath he had missed her sorely. But now she had come home; the abscess in her thigh had not cleared up and she was growing visibly weaker. The year 1828 was one of hopes and fears for her parents; the lameness persisted, spreading to her knee and ankle, and at times she was so weak that she could only walk on crutches. They consulted doctors in London and Devizes, but none of them seemed able to diagnose her illness – which was probably some form of tuberculosis – and beyond draining the abscess at intervals there was little they could do.

With the cloud of Anastasia's illness hanging over him, Moore set about the enormous task of assembling his Byron material, and setting it in chronological order; in July he began the actual work of writing. It was a year fraught with drama on the political front. On 9 January, the Duke of Wellington, a staunch opponent of Catholic emancipation, had become Prime Minister. In July, at a by-election in County Clare, Daniel O'Connell stood against the sitting candidate, Vesey Fitzgerald; although Fitzgerald himself was in favour of emancipation, O'Connell was returned with an overwhelming majority. The resulting agitation – since O'Connell as a Catholic, could not take his seat in the House of Commons – brought the country to the brink of civil war. By August Wellington had become convinced that the Catholic claims could no longer be resisted; something must be done 'to restore to property its legitimate influence'. It was the work of another six months to bring round George IV – as irrationally opposed to emancipation as his father – and to convince the die-hard members of his party, but on 5 February 1829, it was announced in the King's Speech that he would be asking Parliament to end the disabilities against Catholics.

For Moore it was the achievement of a lifelong dream; for the last twenty-five years he had been advancing Catholic claims, and had sacrificed much – including the continuance of his father's pension for his mother – in their cause. But the news left him almost cold. 'Could I ever have thought that this event under any circumstances, would find me indifferent to it,'[1] he wrote. It was now clear that Anastasia was dying. 'Lucky for me that I am *obliged* to work, as it in some degree distracts my thoughts,' he wrote a few days later. 'The dreadful moment is that interval at night, when I have done working and am preparing for bed. It is then that everything most dreadful crowds upon me, and the loss not only of this dear child, but of all that I love in the world, seems impending over me.'[2]

In the midst of this agony he had a letter from Murray, calling him up to London. The first chapters of the Byron biography were now completed, and there were urgent details to discuss. Murray, who had just been reading the MS, pronounced himself highly delighted by it. 'Publishers, like picture dealers,' wrote Moore, 'are sharpened into taste by their interest, and acquire a knack of *knowing* what is good without understanding it.'[3] He called on O'Connell who was savouring his triumph but had to confess that he felt too wretched to share in the general rejoicing. 'Faith and you were up to it as early as any man I knew,'[4] said a Trinity College friend, O'Gorman, in an attempt to cheer him. When Moore arrived home after five days' absence, he had not the courage to go round to the front door of the cottage, but tapped at the kitchen window to know what to expect. 'Our poor child much the same,' he wrote, 'found her upstairs in the room she was never again to leave while *alive*.'

Moore's journal for the next fortnight was a chronicle of the last days of his 'darling child'. Both he and Bessy did their best to appear calm and cheerful. They spent the time playing drafts or checkers, or going through children's books and books of sketches. One evening, when her mother was putting her to bed, she asked if she should sing. 'Do, love,' said her mother. She immediately sang a line from one of her father's songs, 'When in death I shall calmly recline' – without, however, her mother was sure, having any idea of applying it to her own situation. Towards the end of the second week, she became so weak that they expected to lose her any moment. On the Friday evening, 6 March, she played a game of draughts with her father, but was so exhausted afterwards that Bessy, who had been sleeping in her room for the last month, sat with her up most of the night. The end came two days later, recounted in harrowing detail in Moore's journal:

On Saturday morning she was so weak that we thought it better not to move her from her bed and she dozed away most of the day, occasionally teazed by her cough but without any other suffering – That evening she expressed a wish that Mamma and I should play a game of cribbage together, and she would listen to us, but she remained in a drowsy state the whole of the time – As she did not appear to me much weaker than last night, I entreated Bessy to take a little sleep that she might be better able to go through what was yet before her – but though she did not say so, I saw that she would sit up – Next morning (Sunday, the 8th.) I rose early & on approaching the room heard the dear child's voice as strong, I thought, as usual, but on entering I saw death plainly in her face. When I asked her how she slept she said 'pretty well' in her usual courteous manner, but her voice had a sort of hollow & distant softness not to be described, and when I took her hand on leaving her, she said (I thought significantly) 'Goodbye, Papa'. I will not attempt to tell what I felt at all this.

In attempt to spare him, Bessy begged him not to go into the room again, though he went to listen at the door at intervals. At about noon she called him, and he came and took his daughter's hand, while Bessy leant her head between the dying child and him so that he should not see her face. As he staggered from the room, the agonised Bessy ran after him with smelling salts, exclaiming 'For God's sake don't *you* get ill'. About a quarter of an hour later she came to tell him all was over.

'I could no longer restrain myself, – he wrote,

the feelings I had been so long suppressing found vent and a loud fit of violent sobbing seized me, in which I felt as if my chest was coming asunder. The last words of my dear child were 'Papa – Papa' – her mother had said, 'my dear I think I could place you more comfortably – shall I?' to which she answered 'yes', and Bessy, placing her hand under her back gently raised her – That moment was her last – she exclaimed suddenly 'I am dying, I am dying – Papa, Papa!' and expired.

MEMOIRS,

JOURNAL & CORRESPONDENCE,

OF

Thomas Moore

VOL. VI.

Moore's Residence at Sloperton.

LONDON
LONGMAN, BROWN, GREEN, & LONGMANS,
PATERNOSTER ROW

Sloperton Cottage, from a contemporary engraving.

Anastasia was buried in Bromham churchyard. The last thing her mother did before the coffin was closed the night before was to pick some snowdrops from the garden and place them within it. Neither parent could bear to be present at the funeral ceremony and Moore ordered a chaise to drive them around for two hours till all was over. 'And such is the end of so many years of fondness & hope,' he wrote that evening; '& nothing is now left to us but the dream (which may God in his mercy realise) that we may see our pure child again in a world which is more worthy of her.'[5]

For Bessy, the only solace lay with her other children, the ten-year-old Tom and Russell, aged nearly six. She tried her best to hide her own feelings for her family's sake though her calm, wasted looks, wrote Moore, showed the effort she was making. He himself found what escape he could in work – 'work I *could* not put off and which is of a nature to *force* my mind to it'.[6] But a few weeks later, when he sat down at the piano to sing for the first time since he had played to the dying Anastasia, he was overcome by emotion, and burst into convulsive sobs. It was several months before he could sing in public without breaking down.

For some time the cottage at Sloperton had been in a state of disrepair. Originally a labourer's dwelling, its walls were bulging from defects in the plaster, the kitchen door let in water, which flooded the floor whenever there was heavy rain, the thatch was rotting, the fences were falling down. With the health of Bessy and the two remaining children an ever present source of anxiety, Moore decided that the house must either be remodelled or that they must move. After many discussions and negotiations he arranged with his landlords, the Goddards, that in return for repairing the house, adding a wing to the south end, and replacing the thatch with slate, they would rent him the house for fifty years at ten pounds a year, he himself being responsible for the taxes and maintenance on the property. In the long run it was an ideal arrangement; but for the next six months, he and Bessy and the children were obliged to stay with friends and neighbours, spending the summer at the Lansdownes' villa in Richmond, where Lady Lansdowne, in anticipation of their arrival, had laid out a store of toys for little Russell.

By November, thanks to Bessy's tireless efforts, the house was ready for reoccupation; the labourer's dwelling now 'a cottage of gentility', with trellised doorways, a terraced walk, and a commodious first-floor study lined with books. There had been new furnishings to buy; at a carpet shop in Bath the proprietor was so excited at seeing Moore's signature on the cheque, that he asked to shake Moore's hand. 'What a nice old man!' said Bessy as they left. 'I was very near asking him whether he would like to shake hands with the poet's *wife* too.'[7]

They had hardly moved into Sloperton when they heard that Tom, who had just gone to Charterhouse, was very ill with scarlatina. Bessy rushed up to London to bring him home, weak and 'pale as death'[8] but fortunately out of danger. Then Moore had to go up to London to discuss the final changes to the first volume of his *Life of Byron*, which was now at the printers. Murray, already foreseeing a great success for the book, had commissioned a portrait of Moore by Thomas Lawrence – the painter's only condition being that Moore should sit still long enough for the canvas to be completed. The portrait, one of Lawrence's last works, still hangs in the Murrays' drawing room in Albemarle Street. Moore returned home on Christmas eve after 'a deuce of a journey',[9] the road across the Marlborough Downs blotted out by drifting snow, and the coach in imminent peril of being over-turned. His journal entry for the first three days of the new year was laconic: 'Busy at my Second Volume'.[10]

On January 1830, the first volume of Moore's *Life of Byron* appeared. 'At work – loads of letters every day about my book & most flaming eulogies of it in the Sun, Atlas, Court Journal, Northern Whig & c &c.' he wrote in his journal for 19–27 January. Its success, he wrote a month later, had far surpassed his greatest expectations. But there was trouble brewing from Lady Byron. Though his references to her in the *Life* were few and respectful, far too much so according to Hobhouse, he did venture to suggest that the public outcry against Byron over his marriage had been largely undeserved. Lady Byron's refusal to comment on the causes of the separation – 'from motives, it is but fair to suppose, of generosity and delicacy,'[11] wrote Moore demurely – had left the way open for the wildest excesses of abuse and calumny. Time and justice, he was convinced, would soften the harsh judgement of the world.

This was not at all to the liking of Lady Byron, who liked to regard herself as faultless in the whole affair. Although her friends all told her there was nothing to object to, she decided to issue a pamphlet, 'Remarks on Mr Moore's Life of Lord Byron', in reply. Ostensibly defending her parents from a charge of having advised the separation, it was in reality a work of self-justification, implying in veiled terms that Byron's offences were such as to make reconciliation impossible. Her unfortunate sister-in-law Augusta, whose earlier relations with Byron may have been the excuse for the separation, was the chief victim of these insinuations.

Moore sensibly declined to enter these deep waters; in the climate of the time there was no way he could have referred to Byron's incestuous love for his sister, or indeed his homosexual practices, the other possible reason for the separation. He simply included Lady Byron's 'Remarks' in an appendix to the second volume, thus taking the wind out of her sails more effectively than any amount of discussion could have done.

By mid-July, after six months of concentrated work, Moore had the proofs of the second volume of his *Life of Byron* in his hand. Its closing tribute, one of the great finales in biography, was a fitting farewell to a friendship that, through all its ups and downs, reflected nothing but credit on them both:

> The arduous task of being the biographer of Byron is one…on which I have not obtruded myself: the wish of my friend that I should undertake that office having been more than once expressed, at a time when none but a boding imagination like his could have foreseen much chance of that sad honour devolving to me…Of any partiality, however, beyond what our mutual friendship accounts for and justifies, I am by no means conscious; nor would it be in the power, indeed, of the most partial friend to allege anything more particularly favourable of his character than the few simple facts with which I shall here conclude, – that, through life, with all his faults, he never lost a friend; – that those about him in his youth, whether as companions, teachers or servants, remained attached to him to the last; – that the woman, to whom he gave the love of his maturer years, idolises his name; – and that, with a single unhappy exception, scarce an instance is to be found of any one, once brought, however briefly, into relations of amity with him, that did not feel towards him a kind regard in life, and retain a fondness for his memory.[12]

The second volume of the biography appeared in January 1831. There is much that can be said against it, the strongest criticism from the point of view of modern scholarship being the free and easy way with which Moore cut, and sometimes ran together Byron's letters and, whenever discretion seemed called for, his tantalising use of asterisks in place of proper names. But this would be judging Moore by standards that simply did not apply at the time. What shines through the biography is its fidelity to its subject. 'The great charm of the work to me, and it will have the same to you,' Mary Shelley wrote to Murray, 'is that the Lord Byron I find there is our Lord

Byron – the fascinating – faulty – childish – philosophical being – daring the world – docile to a private circle – impetuous and indolent – gloomy, and yet more gay than any other – I live with him again in these pages.'[13]

Even the grudging Hobhouse was forced to recognise Moore's achievement. When Murray gave him a copy of the first volume, he spent three days reading it. 'As to Byron's character, he has, on the whole, portrayed it fairly,' he noted in his diary, at the same time hinting darkly at Byron's homosexuality: 'Moore has dilated on B's unequal friendships such as for Ed[d]lestone and Rushton. He little knows on what grounds he treads.'[14] Later he annotated both volumes of the *Life of Byron*, scattering his comments in the margins. At first they are largely dismissive. When Moore, in his preface, writes that 'to have left [Byron's] works without the commentary which his Life and Correspondence afford would have been … an injustice to himself and to the world', Hobhouse adds, 'Which however T.M. would not have done if he had not had £3,500'. And when he writes of Byron's lack of friends on first coming to London Hobhouse sneers: 'In fact he had no *friend* till he knew Mr Tom Moore.' But gradually the appreciative comments begin to outweigh the hostile ones – 'Excellent!'; 'Admirable!'; 'Very true!'; 'This is the man himself!'[15] From now on the two men, though never friends, remained on amicable terms, and Hobhouse, some years later, offered Moore's son Russell a cadetship at Addiscombe College, a training centre for the East India Company.

Hobhouse had been won over, but a life of so controversial figure as Byron was bound to attract a wide variety of reactions. Hunt, still smarting from Moore's poem in the *Times*, quoted Byron in the *Tatler* as joking that 'Tommy loves a lord'[16] – a remark for which we have only Hunt's authority, but which has been used against Moore ever since. The poet Thomas Campbell decided to espouse the cause of Lady Byron, attacking Moore and Byron simultaneously in his paper *The New Monthly*: 'Keep off your sentimental mummeries from the hallowed precincts of the widow's character … You said, Mr Moore, that Lady Byron was unsuitable to her Lord … A woman to suit Lord Byron !!! Poo! Poo! I could paint you the woman that could have matched him, if I had not bargained to say as little as possible about him.'[17]

Other reviews made a point of emphasising Byron's immorality. How could Moore have associated with 'a rebel to God and a slanderer of God's creatures – infesting the world with the outpouring of blasphemy and vice', demanded the *British Critic*. There were various others in this vein; one reviewer trembled to think of sisters or 'aged relatives' reading the book; in revealing Lord Byron's sins, wrote another, Moore was putting the chastity of his own wife and children at risk.

It was left to Macaulay to treat the hypocrisy and cant that had almost destroyed Byron with the scorn that they deserved: 'We know of no spectacle so ridiculous as the British public in one of its periodical fits of morality,' he declared in his famous review of the book for the *Edinburgh Review*. In a long and searching essay on Byron and the cult of Byronism, he had nothing but praise for Moore's biography – 'one of the best specimens of English prose our age has produced' – and for his self-effacing role as author.

> It would be difficult to name a book which exhibits more kindness, fairness and modesty. It has evidently been written, not for the purpose of showing, what, however it often shows, how well its author can write, but for the purposes of vindicating, as far as truth will permit, the memory of a celebrated man, who can no longer vindicate himself. Mr Moore never thrusts himself between Lord Byron and the public. With the strongest temptations to egotism, he has said no more than the subject absolutely required.

Moore himself was quietly satisfied with his achievement. 'I assure you,' he wrote to Murray five months after the second volume had appeared, 'that, convenient as money is to me, no sum of money could give me half as much real pleasure as the consciousness that I have by this book done a service to poor Byron's memory... In this I am convinced that you will rejoice as much as I do.'[18]

23

Irish Initiatives

With the achievement of Catholic emancipation, Moore considered his role as a political campaigner was at an end: 'Anything of a secondary class – anything short of seven millions of people...is beneath my notice,'[1] he told Lord John Russell jokingly. But his interest in Ireland had not abated, and no sooner had he finished his *Life of Byron* than he started on a biography of the hero of the Irish rising of 1798, Lord Edward Fitzgerald, this time with Longmans as his publishers. He began with the encouragement of Lord Holland, whose father, the second Lord Holland, had been Lord Edward's first cousin. Other relations came forward to help: Lord Edward's son, Henry, brought him a collection of his father's papers; William Ogilvie, the family tutor, who had married Lord Edward's mother after the Duke of Leinster died, sent further material; and Moore's Wiltshire neighbour Colonel Napier, another first cousin of Lord Edward's, gave him details of Fitzgerald's death, which he and his brother Charles had put together at the time.

The next stage was a trip to Ireland where he and Bessy and their two boys set out in August 1830, and where, among others, Moore interviewed Lord Edward's nephew, the Duke of Leinster, his daughter, Lady Campbell, and the man who had shot and arrested him, Major Sirr, now seventy-five years old. It was a chance, too, to see his mother and his sisters, and to receive his usual rapturous welcome when he showed himself in public; since the passing of Catholic emancipation he had become a symbol of his country in a way that few poets have ever experienced. Moore had never met Lord Edward, but, as already mentioned, he had seen him once a year before his death, when, 'on being told who he was as he passed, I ran anxiously after him, desirous of another look at one whose name had, from my school days, been associated with all that was noble, patriotic and chivalrous'. Some of the hero worship of this brief encounter was carried through into the biography of Lord Edward. Once again, he used letters and journals to illuminate his narrative wherever possible, and as in his *Life of Byron* – but not, alas, of Sheridan – his style was lucid and unadorned.

It was a romantic story, beginning with Lord Edward's service as a soldier in the American War of Independence, his travels among the Red Indians on his way to join his regiment and his adoption as an honorary member of the Bear Tribe. His return to Europe, and his growing involvement in Irish politics, triggered by a visit to revolutionary Paris in 1792, were recounted with the measured indignation of one who had shared the emotions of the time, when Ireland's hopes of reform were dashed by the obduracy of the British government and their ruthless policy of repression. Moore did not condone Lord Edward's actions but – in a paragraph that has not lost its relevance – he left the question of their justification open:

Of the right of the oppressed to resist, few in these days, would venture to express a doubt – the monstrous doctrine of passive obedience having long since fallen into disrepute. To be able to fix however, with any precision, the point at which obedience may cease, and resistance begin, is a difficulty which must for ever leave vague and undirected the application of the principle; – a vagueness, of which the habitual favourers of power adroitly take advantage, and while they concede the right of resistance, as a general proposition, hold themselves free to object to every particular instance of it.[2]

As Moore proceeded with the biography even those, like Lord Holland, who had first encouraged it, began to have second thoughts. In June 1830 George IV had died, to be succeeded by his brother William IV. In November, after thirty-four years in the wilderness, the Whigs returned to power under Lord Grey. Lord John Russell was Paymaster General, Lord Holland Chancellor of the Duchy of Lancaster, and Lord Lansdowne Lord President of the Council. From the viewpoint of government, Irish affairs looked very different, especially since new troubles had broken out there since the passing of the Catholic Relief Bill. The immediate cause was the raising of the voting qualification from forty shillings to ten pounds in the wake of the bill, a measure that had disfranchised some 160,000 Irish freeholders. In the longer term, agitation for repeal of the Act of Union led by O'Connell was gathering pace, with mass meetings and associations to support him springing up across the country.

Lord Holland was one of the first to voice his doubts about the perils of publishing the book in the 'present ticklish state of Ireland'. 'I owned that it *was* rather an unlucky moment...' wrote Moore, 'but that it was not of *my* choosing, as I had begun the work before any of this excitement had occurred and it now must take its chance.'[3] Others soon echoed Lord Holland's objections. The Duke of Leinster wrote on behalf of Lord Edward's daughter, Lady Campbell, urging him to postpone publication; Lord John Russell had been against it from the first. Only Lord Lansdowne, despite his responsibilities as a member of the government, did not put pressure on him. 'If anything, indeed, could make me sacrifice my own views & (in some respects) my character,' Moore noted, 'It would be the gentle & considerate delicacy with which he has refrained, not only from urging but even hinting, what I know to be his anxious wishes on the subject.'[4]

Moore was still hard at work on the biography when, in February 1831, he received a letter from his sister Ellen telling him that his mother was dangerously ill. The news brought on one of those violent fits of sobbing to which he had been prone since Anastasia's death, though he was calmed by a letter from his mother's doctor shortly after saying that, after twenty-four hours between life and death, his mother had rallied and there were good hopes of recovery. He set out for Ireland nonetheless, consoled when he boarded the boat at Holyhead by the fact that there was nothing in the Irish papers about her death: 'And yet to come in for the last scene would be more painful than I could well bear – the suspense, altogether, dreadful.'[5]

Luckily he found his mother far better than he could have hoped, very weak but full of concern at having brought him over unnecessarily. He spent five days with her and his sisters and was able to collect more facts on Lord Edward while he was there. When he left his mother gave him her wedding ring, which she put onto his finger herself, and bade him a cheerfully matter of fact goodbye: 'Now, my dear Tom, don't let yourself be again alarmed about me in this manner, nor hurried away from your home and business.'[6] It was the last time he would ever see her.

By July 1831 *The Life and Death of Lord Edward Fitzgerald* was ready for the printers. To the continuing objections of Lord John Russell and others,

Moore replied that he could not, in justice to himself, give up the book; it would be said, especially in Ireland, that he had withdrawn it simply because his friends were now in power. But he promised that his preface would set the work in perspective, making it clear that it was one of history not politics; Ireland's greatest grievance had been righted with Catholic emancipation and the change of government gave hopes that other problems would be peacefully resolved.

This was the line Moore followed when the book came out in September, though it did not prevent some Tory critics, Southey among them, from denouncing it as incendiary and revolutionary. On the whole, however, it was well received by the press, and though the Duke of Leinster and Lady Campbell did not acknowledge the copies he sent them, his friends in office, increasingly involved in the battles leading up to the passing of the Reform Bill, had other things to think about. The book remains the classic account of Lord Edward's life, a simple and touching story whose final pages, recounting the agony of his family and their vain attempts to save him during his last days in prison, are impossible to read without emotion.

Moore had now written three biographies, each ground-breaking works, and none of them disposed to show their aristocratic readers in a particularly flattering light. Sheridan, shabbily treated by the Whigs; Byron, ostracised by society; Lord Edward, a traitor to his caste: these were subjects that can have brought them little satisfaction. For one who supposedly 'loved a lord', Moore had certainly not pulled his punches. It was a tribute to his brilliance, wit and charm that he continued to be sought after in the grandest houses, his singing still adding the final enchantment. Let us pause for a moment to see him on one such occasion, somewhat battered by the years – 'a superannuated cherub' as Greville called him – but still as much a star as ever. The scene, recorded by the gossipy writer E.P. Willis, took place at Lady Blessington's, where his very arrival was an event.

'Mr Moore,' cried the footman, at the bottom of the staircase;

'Mr Moore,' cried the footman at the top; and with his glass at his eye, stumbling over an ottoman between his near-sightedness and the darkness of the room, enters the poet...Sliding his little feet up to Lady Blessington, he made his compliments with a gaiety and an ease combined with a kind of worshipping deference that was worthy of a prime minister at the court of love. With the gentlemen, all of whom he knew, he had the frank, merry manner of a confident favourite, and he was greeted like one. He went from one to another… and to every one he said something which, from any one else would have seemed particularly felicitous, but which fell from his lips as if his breath was not more spontaneous… It would be difficult not to attend to him while he is talking, though the subject be but the shape of a wine glass.

After dinner, he was persuaded to take his place at the piano:

He makes no attempt at music. It is a kind of admirable recitative, in which every shade of thought is syllabled and dwelt upon, and the sentiment of the song goes through your blood, warming you to the very eyelids, and starting your tears, if you have a soul or sense in you. I have heard of a woman's fainting at a song of Moore's… We all sat around the piano, and after two or three songs of Lady Blessington's choice, he rambled over the keys awhile, and sang 'When first I met thee,' with a pathos that beggars description. When the last word had faltered out, he rose and took Lady Blessington's hand, said good night, and was gone before a word was uttered. For a full minute after he was gone, no-one spoke.[7]

In contrast to these glowing public appearances Moore's private life was full of sorrows at this time. To the loss of Anastasia had been added the loss of other relations and friends: Bessy's sister Ann, with whom he had stayed in Edinburgh; Mary Dalby, wife of the Rev. John Dalby, a dear friend since his early days at Donington; the poet George Crabbe; the benevolent Lady Donegal. Then, in May 1832, came a letter from his sister, telling him that his mother was gravely ill again. Before he had time to leave for Dublin, he heard the news that she had died. 'It is like a part of ones life going out of one,'[8] he wrote in his diary, recording his reaction as being less one of violent shock than of a deep and continuing depression.

The passing of the Reform Bill, in which so many of Moore's noble friends were leading actors, was the great issue of 1831–1832. On 21 March 1831 the bill, introduced by Lord John Russell, was passed in the House of Commons by one vote, only to be defeated in committee. In the struggle that ensued, marked by uproar in both houses, and riots and demonstrations across the country, Moore's attitude towards the proposed reforms was surprisingly lukewarm. He agreed with the Whigs *in principle*, he told Lord Lansdowne, but shared the Tory fears that things might go too far. Despite this he wrote a number of verses in support of the reformers, concentrating his fire on the House of Lords who, having thrown out the bill on its second reading, were being threatened with the creation of new peers to force it through. In his 'Musings of an Unreformed Peer' he made fun of the outrage this had caused:

Of all the odd plans of this monstrously queer age,

The oddest is that of reforming the peerage;

Just as if we, great dons, with a title and star,

Did not get on exceedingly well, as we are.

And perform all the functions of noodles, by birth,

As completely as any born noodles on earth.

But his heart was not really in the struggle. His real interest, as ever, was in Ireland, and he was already embarked on a new book with an Irish theme, *The Travels of an Irish Gentleman in Search of a Religion*. This time its subject was theology – one is constantly amazed by the variety of Moore's interests – which took as its starting point the Catholic Relief Bill of 1829. Its hero is a student of Trinity College, and we first see him, sitting in his chambers, up two flights of stairs, on the day that the news of the royal assent reached Dublin. 'Being myself one of the seven million thus liberated,' he writes, 'I started suddenly, after a few minutes reverie, from my chair and taking a stride across the room as if to make trial of a pair of emancipated legs, exclaimed, "Thank God! I may now, if I like, turn Protestant!"'

Moore's interest in theology had begun with his readings from the early fathers in Bishop Marsh's Library over thirty years before; his own library, later bequeathed to the Royal Irish Academy, was rich in books on the subject. He now put his studies to good use in a semi-serious, semi-comic examination of the claims of the Catholic Church. As the Protestants argued they had restored the primitive Christian faith, he ironically set his Trinity student to find out how such Popish corruptions as 'Transubstantiation, Relics, Fasting, Purgatory, Invocation of the Saints & c. &c.' had set in, only to discover they belonged to the earliest traditions of the Church. This was a setback for his hero, who was hoping to marry the sister of an absentee landlord's agent, who had hinted that he might inherit the rich living at her brother's disposal if he became a Protestant: 'never before,' he wrote, 'were Cupid and Calvin so indistinguishable from each other'. Still hoping to be persuaded, the student goes to Germany, the chief source of Protestant theology, where he falls under the influence of the learned Dr Scratchenbach, whose lectures carry German rationalism to its logical conclusion, the erosion of Christianity altogether. At the end of his researches – and twelve chapters of theological argument – he returns to Dublin a better Catholic than he left it, content to forego the 'fleshpots of Ballymadrugget', the Anglican living in question, for the sake of 'popery and poverty'.

Had Moore stuck to his humorous and ironic tone, the book would have been a satirical masterpiece, but it was too weighed down with learning to be an easy read; in today's terms it suffered from information overload. Its dedication was defiant: 'To the people of Ireland, this defence of their ancient national faith is inscribed by their devoted servant, the author of Captain Rock.' It was not like Moore, a lifelong believer in religious tolerance, to become involved in doctrinal controversy. But he had written the book, he noted in his journal, in 'disgust at the arrogance with which most Protestant parsons assume to themselves and their followers, the credit of being the only true Christians, and the insolence with which weekly from their pulpits they denounce all Catholics as idolaters and anti-Christ'.[9] Although the legal disabilities of Catholics had been relieved, the social and religious prejudices against them were as strong as ever.

On 4 June 1832, after its third reading in the House of Lords, the Reform Bill was passed by 106 votes to 22: the threat of creating new peers had forced the hardline Tories to abstain from voting. ('I never saw so many shocking bad hats in my life,' said Wellington when the reformed House of Commons assembled.) Meanwhile there was a movement afoot that Moore should stand for an Irish seat in the new Parliament. Several seats were suggested, the most persistent offer coming from the election committee in Limerick, who in November 1832, sent a deputation to Sloperton, consisting of two brothers, Gerald and Daniel Griffin, to try and persuade him to stand. Moore had already refused their offer, pleading poverty and his dependence on his writing to survive. When they suggested buying him an estate that would provide the necessary income, he had refused again: he was grateful for their generosity but he could not compromise his independence by going into politics as their paid representative.

The Griffin brothers' visit was a last attempt to make him change his mind, and though he politely refused, their meeting is memorable for the picture Gerald Griffin gives of Moore at home. They found the poet in his study:

a table before him, covered with books and papers, a drawer half opened and stuffed with letters, a piano also open at a little distance, and [Moore]

…himself, a little man, but full of spirits, with eyes, hand, feet, and frame for ever in motion, looking as if it would be a feat for him to sit for three minutes quiet in his chair…young as fifteen at heart, though with hair which reminded me of 'Alps in the sunset'…finished as an actor, but without an actor's affectation; easy as a gentleman but without some gentleman's formality; in a word…a hospitable warm-hearted Irishman, as pleasant as can be himself and disposed to make others so.

'Need I tell you,' wrote Griffin, 'that the day was spent delightfully, chiefly in listening to his innumerable jests and admirable stories…and how we did all we could, I believe, to get him to stand for Limerick, and how we called again, the day after, and walked with him about his little garden…and how we came in again and took luncheon…and how he walked us through the fields and wished us a "goodbye", and left us to do as well as we could without him.'[10]

After so many years of fighting Irish battles, so many, too, of being excluded from the very possibility of standing for Parliament, it must have cost Moore a pang to turn down the chance to follow in the footsteps of Sheridan and Grattan and continue the battles they had fought. But apart from other considerations – his commitment to his writing, Bessy's distaste for London – the financial obstacles were insuperable. 'Were I obliged to choose which should be my direct paymaster, the Government or the People,' he wrote in his answer to the Limerick Union, 'I should say without hesitation the People; but I prefer holding on my free course, humble as it is, unpurchased by either; nor shall I the less continue, as far as my limited sphere of action extends, to devote such powers as God has gifted me with to that cause which…was my first inspiration and shall be my last – the cause of Irish freedom.'[11]

Moore was probably well out of politics. His role was that of a bard and a satirist, not an infighter in the squabbles and compromises of parliamentary life. Nor would he have got on well with O'Connell, whose populist views he distrusted, while O'Connell in his turn was probably relieved he would not have to deal with a rival celebrity. But although the two were temperamentally opposed, the 'great Dan' was too generous not to recognise the influence of Moore's *Irish Melodies*, declaring at a meeting of the Dublin Political Union shortly after: 'I attribute much of the present state of feeling, and the desire for liberty in Ireland to that immortal man – he has brought patriotism into the private circles of domestic life.'[12]

Ironically, despite their popularity, the *Irish Melodies* were causing Moore considerable trouble and irritation at the time. On a visit to London in April 1832, he had asked James Power to draw up a statement of the longstanding account between them. Power's manner, he thought, had been 'sly and unsatisfactory',[13] but it was not until several weeks later, when the account arrived at Sloperton, that he saw to his dismay that far from being in credit, as he had imagined, he was in debt to the tune of £500. What had happened was that Power had been regularly deducting £125 a year, as well as various additional expenses, from Moore's annual fee of £500, to pay their new composer, Bishop, for arranging the music for the *Melodies*. When Moore expostulated that he had never agreed to give more than £50 from his £500 for the arrangements, Power wrote back smoothly to say that as Bishop's total fee was £300, he had 'concluded' – '"*concluded*" indeed!'[14] fumed Moore – that Moore would not think it too much to pay half. Without saying anything to Moore, and with not a word in writing, he had been subtracting between £150 and

Thomas Moore in his study at Sloperton Cottage.

£200 from Moore's total fee each year, and coolly presenting him with the bill.

On the face of it, Power had not a leg to stand on, but financial matters are seldom simple, and Moore's carelessness in business, and the cheerful way he had drawn on Power whenever he needed money, had left him very ill protected in the legal battle that ensued. In the end, after two years of wrangling, with the ever helpful Rees of Longmans to hold his corner, it was agreed that Moore should write sixteen songs for the tenth volume of the *Irish Melodies*, release all the copyrights of his previous songs to Power, and be paid £350. The tenth volume would therefore be his last.

Moore had written one hundred and twenty four *Irish Melodies* in all, their quality inevitably varying over the years, but their underlying themes remaining much the same. No-one perhaps has caught their essence better than John Betjeman in his affectionate tribute to the poet, 'Ireland's Own or the Burial of Thomas Moore', written after a visit to Moore's grave in 1953:

The critics may scorn you and Hazlitt may carp
At the 'Musical snuff box' you made of the Harp;
The Regency drawing rooms that thrilled to your song
Are not the true world to which now you belong.

No! the lough and the mountain, the ruins and rain
And purple blue distances bound your demesne,
For the tunes of the elegant measures you trod
Have chords of deep longing for Ireland and God.

24

Farewell to Poetry

The Travels of an Irish Gentleman in Search of a Religion appeared in the spring of 1833, received with enthusiasm by Catholics in Ireland, but predictably arousing the ire of Protestant divines, one of whom, the Reverend Mortimer O'Sullivan, devoted a whole book – some 350 sanctimonious pages – to refuting Moore's theology and warning him against the 'shipwreck of his soul'. Moore would get his revenge two years later in his satire, *The Fudges in England*, in which O'Sullivan, thinly disguised as the Reverend Mortimer O'Mulligan, complains that he and his fellow clergy are suffering a new form of persecution by the Catholics,

> Martyrs, not quite to fire and rack,
> As Saints were, some few ages back,
> But – scarce less trying in its way –
> To laughter, whereso'er we stray…
> Lowering the Church still more each minute,
> And – injuring our preferment in it.

The Fudges in England, a sequel to *The Fudge Family in Paris*, was Moore's last extended essay in light verse, less witty than the first, but still with some amusing moments. Longmans had also suggested that he should write a long poem on a serious subject to follow his *Loves of the Angels*, but he felt that the moment for such things had passed, and perhaps the necessary inspiration too. For all his fame, he had never regarded himself as one of the 'great guns of Parnassus'; a few years earlier, when Murray had suggested that he should write a running commentary for a collected edition of Byron's works, he had refused on the grounds that it would be presumptuous for a 'rhymer' like himself to criticise the work of such a poet.

There was something disarming about Moore's self deprecation, an irreducible core of modesty and common sense. We see him in this context, with Wordsworth, a poet he greatly admired, on an evening at which he had sung some of his own songs and as usual, had been rapturously applauded. The story, so characteristic of both poets, is told by Edmund Gosse: 'Wordsworth was asked if he also did not admire these songs, and he replied: "Oh! yes, my friend Mr Moore has written a great deal of agreeable verse, although we should hardly call it *poetry*, should we Mr Moore?" To which the bard of Erin, sparkling with good nature, answered, "No! indeed, Mr Wordsworth, of course not!" without exhibiting the slightest resentment.'[1]

Whatever the truth of Wordsworth's judgement, it certainly had not affected Moore's popularity with the public. (Wordsworth's sales were never more than a fraction of Moore's.) The *Irish Melodies* continued to sell steadily, the tenth and final volume, dedicated to Sir John Stevenson's daughter, appearing in 1834. When Moore went to Ireland the following year to see his sister Ellen, the visit became a triumphal progress. In Dublin, the whole house rose to greet him when he visited the theatre, the people hurrahing and throwing up their hats, 'trusting to Providence to return them',[2] and the pressure of dinners and receptions was so great that he collapsed for two days from exhaustion.

From Dublin he set out on a tour of Wicklow and Wexford. They paused in the vale of Avoca, the scene of one of Moore's earliest *Irish Melodies*, 'The Meeting of the Waters':

There is not in the wide world a valley so sweet,
As that vale in whose bosom the bright waters meet.

He could not help feeling a a little proprietorial, 'feeling that my property in it might be perhaps as durable as the waters'.[3] So far he has been proved right; thanks to its association with Moore, Avoca is still a famous tourist spot today.

Moore's host for his journey was a Mr Boyce, who had planned a grand reception for him at his home town of Bannow. On the way they stopped in Wexford, to visit the home of Moore's maternal grandfather, Tom Codd. 'Nothing...could be more humble and mean than the little low house which remains to tell of his whereabouts,' Moore wrote in his journal, 'and it shows how independent *Nature* is of mere localities is that one of the noblest-minded as well as the most warm-hearted of of all God's creatures (that ever it has been my lot to know) should be born beneath this lowly roof.' Moore's memories of his mother were ever green.

In Bannow, Moore was greeted like a hero. As their carriage, drawn by four post horses, approached the town, a calvalcade of horsemen, bearing green banners and surrounded by people on foot, came out to meet them. They were the advance party of a great multitude of people and carriages, which formed up in a procession behind them. A series of triumphal arches had been erected, with a decorated car beside the first one, containing the Nine Muses – 'some of them,' Moore noted, 'remarkably pretty girls'. One of them placed a crown on Moore's head, and Moore invited her and two companions to join him in his open carriage. As they proceeded slowly along with a band, 'smart young fellows in blue jackets, caps and white trousers', playing some of the best known *Irish Melodies* at each stop, Moore said to the pretty Muse behind him, 'This is a long journey for you'. '"Oh, Sir", she exclaimed, with a sweetness and kindness of look not often found in artificial life – "I wish it was three hundred miles!"'[4]

He spent the night with Boyce – where his host had given him his own bedroom. The next day there were deputations and speeches, and in the evening, a fete, with bonfires, music and dancing, in the grounds of the house. A large flag on the roof displayed the words '*Erin go bragh* and Tom Moore for ever', and a green balloon with the words 'Welcome Tom Moore' was launched above the dancers' heads. 'The music being very inspiring,' wrote Moore, 'I took out my young Muse … and after dancing down a few couples surrendered her (very *unwillingly* I own) to her former partners.'[5]

Going through Wexford, on his way back to Dublin, Moore visited a convent, whose Mother Superior, a friend of his sister's, had begged him to call. At her request he played a short air on the convent's new organ, then went into their little garden where the gardener was ready with a spade in order that Moore should plant a myrtle there. 'As soon as I had (awkwardly enough) deposited the plant in the hole prepared for it,' wrote Moore, 'the gardener, while filling in the earth, exclaimed "This will not be called *myrtle* any longer, but the *Star of Airin*!" Where is the English gardener that is capable of such a flight?'[6]

Where indeed, and to crown the joys of this triumphal visit was a letter he had received from Lord Lansdowne just before leaving Dublin, telling him that the new Whig government had awarded him a pension of £300 a year. He had immediately written to Bessy with the news, and when he got back to Dublin found her letter had crossed with his.

> Tuesday Night: My dearest Tom – Can it *really* be true that you have a pension of three hundred a year? Mrs, Mr, two Misses and young Longman were here today, and tell me it really is the case, and that they have seen it in two papers… Three hundred a year – how delightful! But I have my fears it is only a castle in the air. I am sure I shall dream of it and so I will get to bed, so that I may have this pleasure, at least, for I expect the next morning will throw down my castle.

And the next morning:

> Is it true? I am in a fever of hope and anxiety, and feel very oddly…How will you ever enjoy this quiet, everyday stillness, after your late reception, I hardly know. I begin to want you very much…How I wish I had wings for then I should be at Wexford as soon as you, & surprise your new friends…N.B. If this good news be true it will make a great difference in my *eating*. I shall then indulge in butter to my potatoes. *Mind* you do not tell this piece of gluttony to any one.[7]

It is an appealing, if slightly wistful glimpse of Bessy, so often a shadowy figure in Moore's journals but so central to his existence just the same. She was his bedrock; warm-hearted, energetic and practical, she smoothed his working life and sheltered him as best she could from family sorrows – even in *extremis*, when Anastasia was dying, her first thought had been to spare him the last agonising moments. Moore, the indulged and loving son, was an indulged and loving husband too, and in all his frivolities in London and elsewhere, it does not seem he was ever unfaithful to her. Charles Greville, in his diaries, describes a dinner where Luttrell was comparing Moore and Rogers – the poetry of Moore so licentious, that of Rogers so pure – and discussing the contrast between the *lives* and *works* of the two men: the former a pattern of conjugal happiness, the latter the 'greatest sensualist'[8] he had ever known. (Rogers' *amours*, as Moore once noted in his journal, were mostly of the commercial kind.)

The government pension had come in the nick of time. 'Never…' wrote Moore to Rogers, 'did a golden shower descend on a gentleman nearer what is called his "last legs" than I was at the moment when this un-asked for favour descended on me.'[9] He had never really caught up with the debts and interest payments he had incurred over the twin disasters of Bermuda and the Byron memoirs, and as well as the expenses of his own immediate family, was responsible for supporting his unmarried sister Ellen, and his mother-in-law. (His married sister Kate had died the year before.) Somehow, he was always running to stand still, and having parted with his most valuable copyrights – for *Lalla Rookh* and the *Irish Melodies* – had only his pen to rely on for the future. The pension, quietly masterminded by Lord Lansdowne and Lord John Russell, at last gave him a permanent income. In the summer of 1835, still bathed in the glow of his reception in Ireland, his financial prospects looked brighter than they had done since the success of *Lalla Rookh*.

Having virtually foresworn any further attempts at poetry – with the exception of a few songs and political squibs – Moore would spend the remaining years of his literary career on a massive history of Ireland. It was one of a series of national histories commissioned by Longmans: Sir James Mackintosh in three volumes on England, Walter Scott in two on Scotland. The first intention was that he should write the companion history in one volume, from the earliest times to the seventeenth century, the later period having already been covered by other historians. It soon became clear that he could not condense his material sufficiently to do so; the first volume, which appeared in 1835, went no further than the seventh century and would be followed by a further three. Once again it was a pioneering work, but the sheer weight of material bowed him down, and the fact that he had no Gaelic was an extra handicap. In the meantime, he was forced to turn down other, more attractive offers. 'Were it in my power, indeed,' he wrote to a would-be publisher, 'to reverse the present order of my operations, – to write Romance now, while there are still some few gleams of sunlight left me, and take to History when the night of old age sets in, it would be all very well; but bound as I am to my present task, I cannot conscientiously pledge myself to any other – at least one *de longue haleine* – till that is finished.'[10]

Despite this there were still some glimmerings of romance when, in 1839, he republished his novel *The Epicurean*, together with his unfinished and previously unpublished poem, *Alciphron*, written in Paris when he was first contemplating the subject in 1820. Turner, a good friend since they met in Rome, provided the illustrations, grandiose and romantically evocative, and for these alone the book is a collector's piece.

More substantial, and far more satisfying to Moore, was a collected edition of his entire poetical works. Power had now died, but Longmans bought back the copyright of the *Irish Melodies* from his widow for £1,000, offering Moore another £1,000 to write introductions to the various sections. The book was dedicated to Lord Lansdowne, though Moore at first was worried that the various squibs and satires it contained might make it embarrassing to accept. Lord Lansdowne's reply was typically gracious. He would be very sorry to decline the dedication on those grounds, he wrote. 'By receiving it I am not responsible for all that the volumes contain; and if I was, as I could only be made a party to anything that might be thought exceptionable, by being also a party to that far greater portion which all will join in admiring, I should be a gainer by it, independently of the value I attach to the expression of your friendship and kindness.'[11]

Bowood, where Moore had a special bedroom set aside for him, and where he had the free run of the library, was always a haven for Moore, and his delightful company was one of the attractions for the Lansdownes' guests. But as time went by, he went less and less to London, preferring the quiet 'still life' of Sloperton to the rush and hurry he encountered there. Of course this was largely his own fault. He still found it hard to refuse an invitation. Someone once asked Rogers where Moore could be found in London; impossible to say, he answered, since he was at that moment in three places at once.

Moore's greatest concern was now the future of his sons, Tom the eldest with all the gaiety and charm of his father, but with little of his application; Russell quieter and more serious, but alarmingly delicate. Both had been presented with places at Charterhouse, Tom's by Lord Grey, Russell's by Peel, but this was only the beginning of Moore's expenses. How fortunate he had been to be educated in Dublin, where he could live at home and the class system was more flexible. His sons were being educated as English public schoolboys, a costly process as he soon discovered. When Tom's headmaster suggested that Tom should go to university on an exhibition of £100 a year, adding that Moore need only give £150 more, Moore exploded to a friend: 'That is the *half* of the *only* income (my Pension) that I have ever possessed in my life without working hard for it aye, and sharing all my earnings, all the time, with almost everybody related to me. If *I* had thought but of "living like a *gentleman*" (as these … Tutors style it) what would have become of my dear Father & Mother, of my sweet sister Nell, of my admirable Bessy's mother?'[12]

When Tom's ambitions switched to the army, things were even worse. It cost £450 to purchase an ensigncy for the 22nd Foot, where after much anxious lobbying Moore found him a place. He entered the service in March 1838, joining his regiment in Cork, then transferring to Dublin in May. In between times he must have been in Belfast, for he was accused in *The United Services Gazette* of having insulted a young woman there. The story was repeated in the Ulster papers – delighted to blacken Moore's name at one remove – and though Tom put paid to it by threatening legal action, the episode was distressing enough to bring Moore over to Dublin. He found Tom 'looking very pale and ill',[13] though recovered enough to dance till two in the morning at a party of the Viceroy's soon after. On one evening the two of them went to the theatre in Ellen's box. When Moore was spotted the whole house rose to greet him as before. Years later, a member of the audience recalled the general reaction as the orchestra broke into a medley of Moore's airs:

> At each change from one well-known air, the audience poured forth a peal of unbridled applause…It was a delightful, and at the same time a melancholy moment. The remembrance came upon us of some who loved those tunes, now in the cold grave; of the hopes of freedom breathed by the bard yet unrealized; of the chains of slavery yet hanging around us. He spoke, – for the audience would have him speak – but he could say little; his gestures were more eloquent than the tongue of any man…Peal upon peal of applause followed…I shall never forget that night, or the effect of that proud swell of my country's music.[14]

It must have been hard for Tom to equate his father's brilliant position in public with his lack of means, harder still to keep up with his fellow officers on his army pay. The price of being a 'gentleman' came high.

Meanwhile, Moore had Russell's future to provide for, he too deciding on a military career – in this case in the East India Company's Army. At the age of sixteen he left Charterhouse, to study for a cadetship; and in April 1840, aged just eighteen set sail for India. Moore and Bessy went to Gravesend to see him off, the heartbroken Bessy following the course of his ship with a telescope until it disappeared from sight. It was not until December that they heard news of him from the Governor General, Lord Auckland, an old friend of Moore's, telling them that Russell had been seriously ill, and was staying with him at Government House till he was well enough to move; he would then be sent with a regiment into the dry climate of the upper provinces. 'This,' noted Moore in his journal, 'I look upon to be *thorough friendship*, and such, as if I live to the age of Methusalem, I could never forget.'[15] But though Russell sent a reassuring letter shortly after, both parents – remembering the loss of their three daughters – were in a torment of anxiety.

In 1841, Tom too was posted to India, involving his father in new expenses. Having sent him £40 for new equipment, he was appalled to get a letter from Bessy while he was in London, enclosing a bill for £112 from Tom, to pay for his overland journey to Cairo. 'I can hardly bring myself to send you the enclosed,' wrote Bessy. 'It has caused me tears and sad thoughts, but to you it will bring these and hard, *hard work*... My heart is sick when I think of you, and the fatigue of mind you are in.'[16] Somehow Moore found the money, only to receive a bill for £100 a few weeks later; on the arrival of Tom's regiment in Bombay, he had been forced to buy a new outfit to go on active duty. In three bills Tom had eaten up most of Moore's pension for the year.

In August 1841 Moore made what would be his last visit to Dublin to look at manuscripts in the Trinity Library. News of his arrival had got out, and he was greeted with cheers as he landed, but his reception was less triumphal than before. 'The old rail have died off or become indifferent, and to the young I am personally unknown – so that my progress here is not what it was in other days,'[17] he noted. But he was happy to see his sister Ellen and consoled, on going to the opera, when the audience raised 'a cheer for Tom Moore'.

For the rest of the year he concentrated on the Irish history. Consulting papers in the State Paper Office, he found a 'most curious letter' from the Duke of Sussex to Queen Elizabeth, offering to arrange the murder of Phelim O'Neill for a reward of a hundred marks a year. 'Showed this to my fellow workman, Tytler [who was writing a history of Scotland]...' he wrote, 'Tytler who has been well broken in to royal murders by his Scottish History (Cardinal Beaton's for instance, and he is now ferreting out another) was not quite so shocked by this discovery as I was.'[18] Amid such intriguing diversions, his work proceeded slowly. By December, now half way through the sixteenth century, he started his fourth volume. 'Whether I shall live to finish it,' he wrote, 'who knows.'[19]

25

'Oh who would inhabit
This bleak world alone?'

January 1842 started gaily, with a big party at Bowood, where Moore stayed for two nights: 'I sung a good deal as usual, and even the matter of fact looking Ex-Lord Chancellor [Lord Mounteagle] placed himself close to the pianoforte, and although it didn't quite amount to the "iron tears down Pluto's cheek" seemed very much pleased. I *think* it was he who mentioned that the nickname they've now got now got in Dublin for Peel is "the veiled Prophet", alluding to those promised revelations respecting his future policy for which the world is waiting.'[1]

He had scarcely returned home when a letter arrived from Lord Auckland telling them that Russell had been so ill that the doctors felt it was dangerous for him to remain in India; he would be sailing for England in the next three weeks. Lady Lansdowne, who had known the agony of losing a son herself, came over to see them immediately she heard the news. 'Nothing could be more feeling and affectionate than her manner – ', wrote Moore; 'kissed Bessy like a sister, on leaving us, and said to me, when I was putting her into her carriage, "she is a most marvellous person" – alluding of course to the deep but calm feeling with which my poor Bessy is making up her mind to the worst.'[2]

Four days later, a new blow fell. Tom had also fallen ill and was returning home on sick leave. 'His accounts of himself from Lower Scinde were such as a good deal to prepare us for this,' wrote Moore, 'but to say nothing of the anxiety and grief caused by it, how on earth am I to meet the additional expenses which the return of both boys will entail while I am still in debt too for most of the money which their first outfit, passage & c. required.'[3] Although he had received £1,000 for his *Poetical Works*, he was entitled to no royalties; his suggestion that Longmans might pay him extra for his work on the prefaces had fallen on deaf ears. He had been paid £750 for the first volume of his *History*, and £500 each for the subsequent three, but as usual had drawn on the money in advance. Considering the enormous sales of *Lalla Rookh* and later of the *Poetical Works*, Longmans could have been more generous; in Rogers' opinion they had behaved very shabbily. But Moore's great patron in the firm, Thomas Longman senior, was on the point of retiring in favour of his son, and his other faithful ally in the firm, Owen Rees, had died in 1837.

Some of Moore's worries were lightened when he heard that the East India Company would be paying Russell's fare home; and his old friend Thomas Hume (their quarrel over the duel long forgotten) promised he would help with Russell's other bills. 'This, after all (in a world where money is the universal touchstone) deserved eminently to be noted down as *true* friendship,'[4] noted Moore.

Meanwhile, in an attempt to raise money, he had been going through his letters from Byron with the idea of selling some of those he had already published in the *Life*: 'must...carefully expunge from autographs most of those passages for which I substituted stars,'[5] he noted in his journal. It was easy to see, from the samples he gives – excluded from Lord John Russell's edition – why asterisks were necessary. Lady Byron, for instance, is 'a mathematical Blue Devil'; Queen Caroline a '*Quim*'; Wordsworth (the subject of many tirades) a 'pedlar-praising son of a bitch'. Moore seems to have changed his mind about selling. Some time thereafter, in the confusion of his last sad years, the originals of Byron's letters disappeared – a loss, in its way, as tragic as that of the memoirs themselves.

Moore's troubles were now accumulating thick and fast. On 6 April, a letter dated from Hastings arrived from Russell, saying that he hoped to be at Sloperton that day. 'Our ears and eyes were of course on the watch for every carriage that approached', wrote Moore,

and at last we heard his own voice telling the fly-man *not* to drive into the gate – Our feeling at this remembrance of his mother's neat garden & his thoughtful wish not to spoil the gravel was hardly expressed by us when we saw the poor fellow himself getting slowly out of the carriage & looking as if the very next moment would be his last. It seemed indeed all but death. Both his mother and myself threw our arms about him and all three remained motionless for some time … It was very frightful nor shall I ever forget those few minutes at that gate.[6]

Russell had tuberculosis and though he seemed to rally for a while the doctors held out little hope of his recovery. He had scarcely returned home when the Moores received another crushing blow. Tom was not simply coming home on sick leave; he had fallen into debt and sold his commission. Having cost his father more than £1,500, he was now without resources or a career. 'Why do people sigh for children,' wrote Bessy sadly. 'They know not what sorrows come with them.'[7] Despite his parents' hope that he would be able to come and see Russell before he died, Tom got no further from India than France where, after some desperate string-pulling by his father, he obtained a commission in the French Foreign Legion – the first English officer to do so. He left for Algiers – having drawn on his father for a further £100 – at the beginning of 1843.

Before this Russell had died. Throughout the autumn of 1842 he had been gradually weakening, though in little pain. It was only in his last few days that he became conscious of his danger. On the morning of 23 November, he asked his mother for pen and paper to write a list of small bequests, to his father a ring, to Tom 'his dying love and a copy of Campbell's poems'. The vicar, Mr Drury, came to give him and his mother communion. When the ceremony was over Bessy asked him how he felt. 'Better and more comfortable.' 'Should you like Mr Drury to come again tomorrow?' 'Yes,' said the boy, 'if I'm alive.'[8] He died three hours later. He was nineteen, the youngest and perhaps the dearest of all Bessy's children.

As with the death of Anastasia twelve years before, Moore had been unable to face the final scene. It was only some weeks later that he could bear to record it in his journal, which from then on became increasingly sporadic and fragmented. The news from Tom was not encouraging. After less than two months in Algeria he was writing to say that 'he was twenty times worse off than in India';[9] a few months later he was sending a desperate appeal for £50 to keep him out of prison for debt. Of course his father sent it, 'though God knows,' he wrote, 'how I shall manage, in my present reduced state, to get on'.[10]

Meanwhile the *History* was a continuing burden. The piles of reference books overflowed from his study and were stacked in the back hall at Sloperton along with Bessy's piles of clothing for the poor. On his visits to

London he continued to spend hours among dusty manuscripts and anti-quarian books in the British Museum, working against the grain but bound by his contract and his dogged determination to see the project through.

There were still some good moments; at Bowood the unfailing kindness of the Lansdownes, who had swept up him and Bessy to stay when Russell died; in London invitations by the dozen though he had grown so forgetful that his engagements were often in confusion: 'If people will not send reminders, what is a much dinnered gentleman to do?'[11] As well as old friends there were new stars to meet: Dickens of whom he had been a warm admirer from the first; the young Disraeli who thought Moore's conversation the most brilliant he had ever heard. In August he made a long promised visit to Sydney Smith at his rectory at Combe Florey. The two men had been friends for nearly twenty years. Each could reduce the other to helpless laughter – Smith's wit, as recorded in Moore's uncut journals, far more Rabelaisian than Lord John Russell's edition allows. Each appreciated the other's courage and political integrity: Smith's battles on behalf of Catholic emancipation had cost him his chances of a bishopric. Moore spent a cheerful two days there; absent minded as usual on departure he was amused by a letter from Smith on his return: 'Dear Moore. – The following articles have been found in your room and forwarded by the Great Western – A right hand glove – an odd stocking – a sheet of music paper – a Missal – several letters, apparently from ladies – an Essay on Phelim ONeil… There is also a bottle of Eau de Cologne. What a careless mortal you are! God bless you.'[12]

Since Russell's death Moore disliked leaving Bessy alone for more than a few days; the brief visit to Combe Florey was a case in point. It suited his own inclinations more and more. 'A strange life mine,' he wrote at the end of 1843,

> but the best, as well as the pleasantest part of it lies at *home*. I told my dear Bessy, this morning while I stood at my study window, as she crossed the field, I sent a blessing after her – 'Thank you, bird', she replied 'that's better than money' – and so it is. 'Bird' is a pet name she gave me in our younger days, and was suggested by Hamlet's words, 'Hillo, ho, ho, boy! come bird, come' – being the call, it seems, which falconers use to their hawk in the air, when they would have him come down to them.[13]

Was Bessy too good to be true? Had she never complained of Moore's absences or his spending money in London while she economised at home?

She seems to have understood his 'evanescent temper' – the words are hers – and his need to shine in company too well for that. Perhaps she took refuge in her charitable activities – they gave her a status of her own – but she had never grudged him his successes. Like the falconer in *Hamlet*, she knew he would always come back to her.

Beset by his own private worries in 1843 and 1844, Moore's journals make little mention of the growing unrest in Ireland where O'Connell's monster meetings calling for the repeal of the Act of Union had led to his prosecution, with six other repealers, for 'conspiracy'. Moore had originally been against the Union – he had spoken against it, when it was only a possibility, as a Trinity student in Dublin. He was too tired now to become actively involved. But when O'Connell was found guilty in February 1844, and his sentence postponed for three months, he wound up his closing speech, as Moore noted in his journal, 'with the following anticipation of his fate from the Melodies':[14]

Far dearer the grave or the prison
Illumed by one patriot name
Than the trophies of all who have risen
On liberty's ruins to fame.

O'Connell was sentenced to a year's imprisonment that May.

In a way it was a mercy that when Ireland was struck by her greatest catastrophe, the failure of the potato crop and the mounting horrors of the Famine from 1845 to 1848, Moore was no longer fully capable of comprehending it. It was true that he struggled to the end of his *History* – his last tribute to Ireland – delivering it to the printers in May 1845, but abandoning the task of writing the Preface in despair. From Africa came a long melancholy letter from Tom's commanding officer saying that Tom was dangerously ill, and that if he recovered, he must return to England. Moore immediately sent what money he could, and after a long period of anxiety was cheered by a letter from Tom: he was improving, but could not leave Africa before spring because of a troublesome cough he had developed. 'We heard no more for some time,' wrote Moore in his retrospective journal for that year, 'and were kept in constant anxiety at the accounts in the newspapers. His poor mother tried not to agree with me, though her own feeling grew every day more sad and hopeless.'[15]

In February 1846 Moore's beloved sister Ellen died suddenly. Over the years since their mother had died she had become a regular visitor to

Sloperton, and had grown almost as dear to Bessy as to Moore. Then in March, wrote Moore, came a 'strange and ominous looking letter'. They opened it with trembling hands to find that Tom was dead.

'The shock was at first almost too much to bear,' wrote Moore; 'but on reading the letter again, we saw no reason to doubt the account it contained, and sent immediately to London and Paris to know if there was any truth in the rumour. It was, alas! but too true. The last of our five children is now gone, and we are left desolate and alone. Not a single relative have I now left in the world!'[16]

Whatever Tom's earlier misdemeanours, he had redeemed himself in Algeria. He had known beforehand what dangers and hardships awaited him and had encountered them cheerfully and courageously. He had taken an intelligent interest in North Africa; a notebook of his, preserved in Trinity College, Dublin, contains a careful and well-written summary of the history and geography of the area. His last letter home shows him commanding the guard under Arab fire; nights of sleeping out on the stones of the courtyard while under attack had exacerbated his cough, which had settled on his lungs. Still hoping to return home, he had worked out all his expenses, without making any further calls on his parents. 'You will really laugh to see me,' he concluded; 'I am only skin and bone, and might easily be mistaken for Don Quixote's eldest son.'[17]

Under the twin blows of Tom's and Ellen's deaths Moore's health collapsed. 'An illness of an alarming nature shook his frame,' wrote Lord John Russell, '& for a long time made him incapable of any exertion. When he recovered he was a different man.'[18] It was the start of a slow slide into senility. He rallied enough to update his journal for 1845 and the first half of 1846 with an account of Tom's and Ellen's deaths; thereafter there were signs of confusion in his narrative, and the entries for for 1847 were little more than jottings. They cease altogether in July. 'I am sinking here into a mere vegetable,'[19] he wrote to Rogers.

Bessy now took over. Relieved, though so tragically, of the expenses incurred by their sons, Moore's pension was enough for them to live on; the grinding money worries of the past were over. For a time Moore continued to have lucid moments. No longer constrained by work, he loved to browse for pleasure in the library at Bowood. Occasionally there were visitors. One of them, the painter William Creswick, found Moore in his garden among the laurels he and Bessy had planted: 'You find me reposing upon, or among, my laurels,' said Moore. When Creswick asked if he were writing any prose now, he shook his head dolefully. 'No, no! I have done with prose now and – what is worse! – with poetry too.'[20] Towards the end of 1849, after spending the afternoon with Lord Lansdowne and Lord John Russell, who had come over from Bowood to see him, he had some kind of fit. Whatever the medical explanation, it left him in a state of helplessness from which he never recovered. Bessy told Rogers that he could recognise her and could sometimes talk of Rogers and other friends, but that all the tragic events of the last few years were wiped from his mind. He lingered on for three more years, devotedly nursed by Bessy who allowed no-one else to look after him, or even to visit him in his pitiable state. On 26 February 1852, their neighbour, Mrs Starkey, wrote to Rogers: 'Mr Moore has been gradually sinking in the last few days, and yesterday evening, at six o'clock, he breathed his last.'[21]

Moore died, as he had lived, a Catholic, though since there was no Catholic mission nearby the funeral service was held in Bromham and conducted by the rector. Only his publisher, Thomas Longman junior, came down from London for the funeral, but the churchyard was filled with local people, their presence a tribute to the Moores' popularity in the neighbourhood. Most of Moore's closest friends, the Hollands, Sydney Smith and Jeffrey, were dead; Samuel Rogers, at eighty-nine, was too old to make the journey. Lord Lansdowne and Lord John Russell, the only notable absentees, were with Bessy very shortly after, and between them took charge of her affairs.

Thanks to Bessy's careful management during his last years, Moore had left no debts, but his pension of £300 stopped with his death. Lord Lansdowne immediately arranged a pension of £100 for her. Her other great resource was Moore's papers, and Moore in his will had directed that Lord John Russell should look over his journals and correspondence to see if they could be put to use for Bessy's benefit. He had never intended them to be published, but to be used as background material for anyone writing his biography. But when Thomas Longman offered Bessy £3,000 for Moore's journal and correspondence, provided Lord John Russell would edit them, she gratefully accepted. The money would provide an annuity that would enable her to go on living at Sloperton as before.

Lord John nobly agreed to undertake the task though he was fighting for his political life. Having been Prime Minister for the last four and three quarter years, he had been ousted by Palmerston in February 1852; he would return to office as Foreign Secretary and then President of the Council in 1853. No-one could have blamed him if he had said he was too busy, but

Lord John, as Sydney Smith once wrote, was utterly ignorant of all moral fear: 'There is nothing he would not undertake. I believe he would perform an operation for the stone – build St Peter's – or assume (with or without ten minutes' notice) the command of the Channel Fleet; and no-one would discover by his manner that the patient had died – the Church tumbled down – the Channel Fleet been knocked to atoms.'[22]

Lord John's edition of Moore's letters and journals and letters, published in eight volumes between 1853 and 1856, was generally agreed to be a botched and hurried job. It also caused considerable offence, for though he had announced his intention of expunging any passages that might wound living people, he was careless in his cuts, and enough was left behind to stir up the animosities of Moore's enemies. The most virulent of these was the aged Tory John Wilson Croker who, though not mentioned by name (Lord John had substituted a dash) felt himself aggrieved by a disparaging reference in the journal some twenty years before. In a seventy-one-page review in the *Quarterly Review* he proceeded to tear Moore's character to shreds. The journals, he wrote were a mass of vanity, trivia and inaccuracies, Moore's financial dealings dubious, his politics disgraceful. Most wounding of all was the slyly sympathetic way he commiserated with Bessy, so often left alone while Moore enjoyed himself, and never referred to more uxoriously than 'just before or just after some *escapade* from home'. Even Croker did not hint that Moore was actually unfaithful, but the charges of neglect cannot be altogether dismissed; 'all that can be said about them', as Terence de Vere White remarks, 'is that Moore's wife did not love him any the less on their account.'[23]

'What a bitter, unfeeling man he is!'[24] was Bessy's only comment. Lord John reacted indignantly with a letter to the *Times*, and other papers, especially in Ireland, sprang to Moore's defence. But the journals no longer aroused the interest they would have done a few years earlier. Except in the case of the *Irish Melodies*, Moore's reputation was already in decline. His poems were no longer fashionable, his picture of aristocratic Whig society out of date for a new generation of Victorians. It is only with time that the historical and social value of the journals – as witnessed by the countless historians who have drawn on them – has come to be appreciated. Today, thanks to Professor Dowden's discovery and publication of the original notebooks, we can enjoy them in their entirety, though Lord John's edition, with its romantic vignettes and green board covers stamped with an Irish harp, will always have a special charm.

Bessy lived on at Sloperton till 1865, often in ill health, but greatly helped by her neighbours and old friends. Lord John gave her a pony when walking became difficult, the young Lady Lansdowne (her mother-in-law had died in 1851) was a frequent visitor. She was buried in Bromham churchyard beside her husband and two of their three youngest children, Tom's name being also inscribed on the simple slab that marked their grave.

In 1857, thanks to the efforts of Lord Lansdowne, Thomas Longman and others, a memorial statue of Moore by the sculptor Christopher Moore was erected on College Green in Dublin. It was not a satisfactory work and being made of some inferior metal rather than bronze soon acquired a dull, matt texture in the Irish weather. The siting of a public lavatory nearby was a further misfortune. Bloom, passing under 'the roguish finger of Tommy Moore' in *Ulysses*, reflects on its appropriate placing: 'They did right putting him up over an urinal: the meeting of the waters.'

A happier memorial was a richly coloured stained-glass window on the west wall of Bromham Church, put there to celebrate Moore's centenary in 1879, with contributors including Tennyson, Longfellow and Wilkie Collins. It looks down the nave to another, with stained glass by Burne Jones, given in memory of Bessy by her sister's son, Charles Murray. For the parishioners of Bromham, where Bessy had been a well-loved figure for almost fifty years, it must have been a welcome gift.

The final tribute was a tall Celtic cross in dark Irish granite, erected above Moore's grave in 1907. It is inscribed on one side with Byron's famous phrase, 'the poet of all circles and the idol of his own', on the other with the opening lines of Moore's farewell to the *Irish Melodies*:

Dear Harp of my country! in darkness I found thee,
The cold chains of silence had hung o'er thee long,
When proudly, my own island harp I unbound thee,
And gave all thy chords to light, freedom and song...

'He will live in his "Irish Melodies",' said Byron; 'they will go down to posterity with the music; both will last as long as Ireland, or as music and poetry.'[25]

NOTES

Quotations from Thomas Moore's journal are from the six-volume edition, edited by Wilfred S. Dowden, 1983–1991, unless otherwise noted. Quotations from Moore's letters, from the two-volume edition, edited by Wilfred S. Dowden, 1964, unless otherwise noted. Quotations from Moore's poetry from *The Poetical Works of Thomas Moore* (with notes and prefaces by Moore), 1864. Quotations from Byron's *Letters and Journals* (*LJ*) from the twelve-volume edition, edited by Leslie A. Marchand, 1872–1982. Quotations from Byron's poetry from the *Poetical Works of Lord Byron* (with notes by Moore and others), 1863. Quotations from newspapers and journals as given in the text, or from the Moran Collection in the British Library.

INTRODUCTION

1 Byron, *LJ*, 22 November 1813
2 Moore, *Letters*, 23 November 1837
3 Moore, *Journal*, January 1839 (To me, for many years, your patriotic poetry has seemed to express not only the sorrows of Ireland, but the sufferings of all oppressed peoples.)
4 Blessington, 185
5 Speech at a dinner for Lord John Russell, 10 November 1835, Moran MSS
6 Moore, *Life and Death of Lord Edward Fitzgerald*, vol 1, 306
7 Betjeman & Taylor, ed., *English Love Poems*, 8
8 Moore, *Journal*, 18 February 1839
9 Flannery, quoted on book cover

CHAPTER 1

1 Moore, *Journal*, 13 August 1835
2 Russell, I, 2 (*et seq*)
3 Ibid, 1
4 Ibid, 22
5 Moore, *Life of Sheridan*, I, 3
6 Russell, I, 17
7 Ibid, 38
8 Ibid, 26

9 Ibid, 13 (*et seq*)
10 Moore, *Journal*, 31 October 1825
11 Russell, I, 21
12 Moore, *Poetical Works*, 87
13 Jordan, I, 15
14 Russell, I, 50
15 Strong, 39
16 Russell, I, 24

CHAPTER 2

1 Russell, I, 69
2 Moore, *Life of Byron*, 65
3 Russell, I, 68
4 Ibid, 59
5 Ibid, 68
6 Ibid, 49
7 Lecky, VII, 96
8 Moore, *Life and Death of Lord Edward Fitzgerald*, I, 261
9 Grattan, IV, 223
10 Strong, 51
11 Moore, *Poetical Works*, 88
12 Russell, I, 49
13 Moore *Poetical Works*, 89
14 Russell, I, 47
15 Moore, *Life and Death of Lord Edward Fitzgerald*, II, 300
16 Russell, I, 59
17 Russell, I, 56

18 Strong, 51
19 Moore, *Poetical Works*, 90
20 Russell, I, 57
21 Ibid, 58

CHAPTER 3

1 Moore, *Poetical Works*, 91
2 Russell, I, 64 (*et seq*)
3 Ibid, 66
4 Moore, *Poetical Works*, 93
5 There was not, in any city... O'Faolain, 38
6 Russell, I, 60
7 Ibid, 70
8 Ibid, 72

CHAPTER 4

1 Russell, I, 73
2 Ibid, 74
3 Moore, *Letters*, 29 April 1799
4 Russell, I, 75
5 Moore, *Letters*, 14 December 1799
6 Moore, *Journal*, 20 October 1838
7 Moore, *Letters*, 14 December 1799
8 Ibid, April or May, 1799
9 Mumford Jones, 53
10 (Music before all things... and all the rest is literature.) Paul Verlaine, *Art Poètique*, 1874
11 Moore, *Letters*, 4 August 1800
12 Moore, *Memoirs of Captain Rock*, 346
13 Moore, *Letters*, 28 March 1800
14 Ibid, 3 January 1801
15 Ibid, 18 July 1802
16 Coleridge, II, 477

CHAPTER 5

1 Rennie, 171
2 Burke, 218
3 Ibid, 219
4 Russell, VIII, 41–42
5 Moore, *Letters*, 20 January 1802
6 Ibid, 20 May 1803
7 Kee, I, 168
8 Moore, *Letters*, September 1803
9 Russell, I, 130
10 Moore, *Letters*, 22 September 1803
11 Moore, *Journal*, 12 August 1834
12 Moore, *Letters*, 10 October 1803

13 Moore, *Poetical Works*, 340 (*et seq*)
14 Moore, *Letters*, 7 November 1803 (*et seq*)
15 Ibid, 19 March 1804
16 Ibid, 17 February 1804
17 Zwill, 26
18 Jordan, I, l0l
19 Moore, *Letters*, 19 March 1804

CHAPTER 6

1 Moore, *Letters*, 11 May 1804
2 Ibid, 7 May 1804
3 Ibid, 13 June 1804 (*et seq*)
4 Moore, *Poetical Works*, 315
5 Ibid, 335
6 Randall, III, 119
7 Moore, *Letters*, 13 June 1804
8 Mumford Jones, 84
9 Moore, *Letters*, 13 June 1804
10 Ibid, 10 July 1804
11 Ibid, 17 July 1804
12 Ibid, 24 July 1804
13 Moore, *Poetical Works*, 340
14 Moore, *Letters*, 20 August 1804
15 Ibid, 16 September 1804
16 Ibid, 12 November 1804
17 Ibid, November 1804
18 Russell, I, 23
19 Moore, *Letters*, 30 March 1805
20 Russell, I, 185
21 Moore, *Letters*, 6 February 1806
22 Ibid, May 1806
23 Ibid, July 1806

CHAPTER 7

1 Russell I, 204
2 Ibid, 201
3 Ibid, 202
4 Ibid, 203
5 Moore, *Letters*, August 1806
6 Russell, I, 204
7 Moore, *Letters*, August 1806
8 Russell, I, 205
9 Moore, *Letters*, 17 August 1806
10 Russell, I, 212
11 Moore, *Letters*, December 1806
12 Ibid, 2 February 1807
13 Ibid, 4 December 1806
14 Ibid, February 1807

CHAPTER 8

1 Moore, *Letters*, March 1807 (He gives me the cuffs and I have no shirt.)
2 Ibid, 27 April 1807
3 Mumford Jones, l05
4 Moore, *Poetical Works*, 140
5 Moore, *Journal*, 15 June 1831
6 Johnson, 62
7 Berlioz, 518
8 Moore, *Letters*, August 1808
9 Ibid, 3 January 1810
10 Mumford Jones, 121
11 Ibid, 123
12 Moore, *Journal*, 29 August 1823

CHAPTER 9

1 Mumford Jones, 125
2 Ibid, 340
3 Jordan, I, 181
4 Moore, *Journal*, 10 July 1820
5 Moore, *Letters*, 1 January 1810
6 Russell, I, xi
7 Moore, *Letters*, 11 September 1811 (*et seq*)
8 Medwin, 176

CHAPTER 10

1 Byron, *LJ*, 9 June 1820
2 Byron, *Poetical Works*, 417
3 Byron, *LJ*, 27 October 1811
4 Moore, *Life of Byron*, 143
5 Moore, *Letters*, 29 October 1811
6 Byron, *LJ*, 29 October 1811
7 Moore, *Letters*, 30 October 1811
8 Byron, *LJ*, 30 October 1811
9 Ibid, 2 November 1811
10 Ibid, 22 October 1815
11 Moore, *Life of Byron*, 145 (*et seq*)
12 Ibid, 149
13 Byron, *LJ*, 6 November 1811
14 Moore, *Letters*, 14 April 1830
15 Moore, *Life of Byron*, 163
16 Ibid, 152
17 Byron, *LJ*, 29 January 1812
18 Moore, *Life of Byron*, 152
19 Ibid, 159
20 Ibid, 149
21 Moore, *Poetical Works*, 530
22 Moore, *Letters*, 19 May 1812
23 Ibid, 6 March 1812

24 Byron, *LJ*, 15 October 1821–18 May 1822
25 Morgan, II, 200
26 Byron, *LJ*, 25 March 1812
27 Ibid, 19 May 1812
28 Ibid, 20 May 1812
29 Moore, *Letters*, December 1812 (*et seq*)
30 Ibid December 1812
31 Ibid, December 1812
32 Ibid, December 1812

CHAPTER 11

1 Moore, *Letters*, June, 1813
2 Ibid, 16 March 1813
3 Ibid, March 1813
4 Ibid, 8 April 1813 (*et seq*)
5 Ibid, June 1813
6 Moore, *Life of Byron*, 180 (*et seq*)
7 Ibid, 183
8 Moore, *Letters*, June 1813
9 Ibid, May, 1813
10 Byron, *LJ*, 28 August 1813
11 Byron, *Poetical Works*, 63
12 Byron, *LJ*, 8 December 1813
13 Ibid, 24 November 1813
14 Ibid, 13 July 1813
15 Ibid, 22 August 1813
16 Ibid, 22 November 1813

CHAPTER 12

1 Byron, *LJ*, 6 January 1814
2 Moore, *Letters*, 13 January 1814
3 Byron, *LJ*, 8 February 1814
4 Moore, *Letters*, 28 February 1814
5 Ibid, 28 February 1814
6 Byron, *LJ*, 3 March 1814
7 Marchand, I, 377
8 Byron, *LJ*, 12 March 1814
9 Byron, *Poetical Works*, 63
10 Marchand, I, 449
11 Moore, *Life of Byron*, 253
12 Byron, LJ, 14 June 1814
13 Moore, *Letters*, 28 June 1814
14 Ibid, 18 August 1814
15 Ibid, 29 August 1814
16 Byron, *LJ*, 10 January 1815
17 Hunt, I, 31 February 1814
18 Moore, *Poetical Works*, 3
19 Byron, *LJ*, 30 September 1814
20 Ibid, 7 October 1814
21 Moore, *Life of Byron*, 269
22 Moore, *Letters*, December 1814

23 Moore, *Life of Byron*, 272
24 Moore, *Letters*, 25 January 1815
25 Ibid, 1 January 1815

CHAPTER 13

1 Moore, *Letters*, 15 June 1815
2 Ibid, 3 July 1815
3 Ibid, 22 August 1815
4 Ibid, 19 September 1815
5 Ibid, 19 October 1815
6 Ibid, 30 June 1816
7 Ibid, 13 January 1816
8 Ibid, February 1811
9 Ibid, January 1816
10 Moore, *Life of Byron*, 291
11 Moore, *Letters*, January 1816
12 Russell, II, February 1816
13 Moore, *Letters*, January or February 1816
14 Ibid, February 1816
15 Byron, *LJ*, 29 February 1816
16 Moore, *Letters*, March 1816
17 Byron, *LJ*, 8 March 1816
18 Moore, *Letters*, March 1816
19 Moore, *Life of Byron*, 207
20 Russell, VIII, April, 1816
21 Moore, *Letters*, May 1816
22 Moore, *Life of Sheridan*, II, 454
23 Moore, *Letters*, 23 May 1816
24 Ibid, 24 December 1816
25 Jordan, I, 258
26 Moore, *Letters*, 24 September 1816
27 Moore, *Poetical Works*, 4
28 Moore, *Letters*, 8 January 1817
29 Ibid, 18 January 1817
30 Ibid, 11 March 1817

CHAPTER 14

1 Moore, *Life of Byron*, 306
2 Moore, *Letters*, 24 December 1816
3 Byron, *LJ*, 25 March 1817
4 Ibid, 24 December 1816
5 Ibid, 26 March 1817
6 Moore, *Letters*, 26 March 1817
7 Ibid, 13 May 1817
8 Moore, *Poetical Works*, 5
9 Moore, Ibid, 6
10 Ibid, 6
11 Ibid, 7
12 Byron, *LJ*, 15 September 1817
13 Ibid, 10 July 1817

14 Ibid, 2 February 1818
15 Moore, *Letters*, 23 November 1837
16 Haydon, 23 June 1817
17 Moore, *Letters*, 7 August 1817
18 Moore, *Poetical Works*, 443
19 Moore, *Letters*, 20 September 1817
20 Ibid, 11 October 1817

CHAPTER 15

1 Moore, *Letters*, 9 December 1817 (*et seq*)
2 Moore, *Letters*, 8 December 1817
3 *Cambridge History of English Literature*, XII, 102–103 (*et seq*)
4 Moore, *Letters*, 6 February 1818
5 Moore, *Journal*, 1 September 1818
6 Ibid
7 Moore, *Letters*, 23 December 1817
8 Byron, *LJ*, 1 June 1818
9 Strong, 221
10 Moore, *Letters*, 2 April 1818 (*et seq*)
11 de Vere White, 80
12 Moore, *Letters*, 6 May 1818
13 Keats, *Letters*, (footnote), 259
14 Keats, *Letters*, 16 December 1818–4 January 1819
15 Ibid, 3 May 1818
16 Moore, *Letters*, 18 June 1818
17 Ibid, 14 May 1821
18 Ibid, 7 October 1818
19 Ibid, 29 October 1818

CHAPTER 16

1 Hazlitt, *Works*, V, 151
2 Hazlitt, *The Spirit of the Age*, 327
3 Hazlitt, *Works*, VIII, 166
4 Moore, *Journal*, 11 January 1819
5 Ibid, 25 March 1819
6 Ibid, 31 January 1819
7 Byron, *LJ*, 19 January 1819
8 Mumford Jones, 159
9 Moore, *Journal*, 1 February 1819
10 Ibid, 29 September 1818
11 Ibid, 27 April 1819
12 Ibid, 13 June 1819
13 Ibid, 7 July 1819
14 Ibid, 15 July 1819
15 Ibid, 13 July 1819
16 Ibid, 16 July 1819
17 Ibid, 17 August 1819
18 Ibid, 3 September 1813
19 Ibid, 6 September 1819

20   Ibid, 11 September 1819
21   Ibid, 22 September 1819
22   Ibid, 29 September 1819
23   Ibid, 2 October 1819
24   Ibid, 5 October 1819

CHAPTER 17

1   Moore, *Journal*, 8 October 1819
2   Ibid, 7 October 1819
3   Ibid, 7 October 1819
4   Moore, *Life of Byron*, 410–ll
5   Ibid, 416
6   Ibid, 422
7   Ibid, 422 (*et seq*)
8   Ibid, 423 (*et seq*)
9   Byron, *LJ*, 29 October 1819
10   Moore, *Journal*, 11 October 1819
11   Morgan, II, 117–118
12   Moore, *Journal*, 8 October 1819
13   Russell, *Early Correspondence*, Sec 14, 1819
14   Moore, *Journal*, 15 November 1819
15   Ibid, 11 December 1819
16   Ibid, 30 December 1819 (*et seq*)
17   Ibid, 4 January 1820
18   Ibid, 5–8 January 1820
19   Moore, *Poetical Works*, 211
20   Ibid, 180
21   Moore, *Journal*, 8 April 1820

CHAPTER 18

1   Moore, *Life of Byron*, 317
2   Moore, *Journal*, 24 October 1820
3   Ibid, 25 October 1820
4   Ibid, 27 October 1820
5   Ibid, 28 April 1820
6   Byron, *LJ*, 9 December 1820
7   Moore, *Journal*, 28 September 1821
8   Ibid, 2 October 1821
9   Ibid, 23 October 1821
10   Ibid, 23 October 1821
11   Ibid, 11 February 1822
12   Moore, *Letters*, 30 September 1821
13   Ibid, 9 February 1822
14   Hazlitt, *Works*, VII, 378
15   Moore, *Journal*, 17 October 1823
16   Ibid, 28 December 1823
17   de Vere White, 170
18   Moore, *Journal*, 17 October 1823
19   Ibid, 28 July 1823
20   Jordan, II, 370
21   Moore, *Journal*, 31 July 1823

22   Ibid, 11 August 1823

CHAPTER 19

1   Moore, *Memoirs of Captain Rock*, 99
2   Ibid, 121
3   Ibid, 165
4   Ibid, 251
5   Russell, *Early Correspondence*, I, 235
6   Byron, *LJ*, 27 December 1823
7   Moore, *Journal*, 14 May 1824
8   Ibid, 15 May 1824
9   Langley Moore, 30
10   Moore, *Journal*, 15 May 1824 (*et seq*)
11   Ibid, 16 May 1824
12   Ibid, 17 May 1824 (*et seq*)
13   Langley Moore, 34
14   Moore, *Journal*, 17 May 1824 (*et seq*)
15   Moore, *Journal*, 18 May 1824 (*et seq*)

CHAPTER 20

1   Pushkin, *Letters*, second half of November 1825
2   Russell, IV, 192
3   Moore, *Life of Byron*, 654
4   Moore, *Journal*, 20 May 1824
5   Ibid, 18 May 1824
6   Ibid, 22 May 1824 (*et seq*)
7   Ibid, 12 July 1824
8   Ibid, 2 June 1825
9   Ibid, 6 September 1825
10   Langley Moore, 269
11   Moore, *Journal*, 7 October 1825
12   Ibid, 8 October 1825
13   Moore, *Life of Sheridan*, II, 94
14   Ibid, II, 430
15   Moore, *Journal*, 29 October 1825
16   Russell, I, vi
17   Moore, *Journal*, 31 October 1825
18   Ibid, 8 November 1825
19   Ibid, 12 December 1825

CHAPTER 21

1   Moore, *Journal*, 16 December 1825
2   Ibid, 19 December 1825
3   Ibid, 23 December 1825
4   Vail, 184
5   Moore, *Journal*, 16 January 1826
6   Moore, *Letters*, 17 January 1826
7   Langley Moore, 274
8   Moore, *Journal*, 29 May 1826
9   Ibid, 26 May 1826

10   Ibid, 29 May 1826
11   Ibid, 27 May 1826 (*et seq*)
12   Moore, *Letters*, 21 April 1828
13   Jordan, II, 479
14   Moore, *Journal*, 18–19 January 1838
15   Ibid, 1 July 1827
16   Langley Moore, 277
17   Moore, *Letters*, 30 November 1827
18   Moore, *Journal*, 7 February 1828
19   Ibid, 11 February 1828
20   *Byron Journal*, 1992, 53

CHAPTER 22

1   Moore, *Journal*, 5 February 1829
2   Ibid, 9–12 February 1829
3   Ibid, 19 February 1829
4   Ibid, 18 February 1829
5   Ibid, 22 March 1829 (*et seq*)
6   Ibid, 1 April 1829
7   Ibid, 15 October 1829
8   Ibid, 13 December 1829
9   Ibid, 24 December 1829
10   Ibid, 1–3 January 1830
11   Moore, *Life of Byron*, 296
12   Ibid, 655
13   Mary Shelley, *Letters*, 19 January 1830
14   Langley Moore, 291
15   Hobhouse's entries in Moore's *Life of Byron*
16   *The Tatler*, January 1831
17   Langley Moore, 331
18   Moore, *Letters*, 27 May 1831

CHAPTER 23

1   Moore, *Letters*, 22 April 1829
2   Moore, *Lord Edward Fitzgerald*, II, 195
3   Moore, *Journal*, 16 December 1830
4   Ibid, 20 January 1831
5   Ibid, 13 February 1831
6   Ibid, 17 February 1831
7   Russell, I, xxxvi
8   Moore, *Journal*, 12 May 1832
9   Moore, *Journal*, 2 November 1834
10   Russell, I, xxxiv
11   Moore, *Letters*, 8 November 1832
12   Moran MSS
13   Moore, *Journal*, 30 March 1832
14   Ibid, May 6, 1832

CHAPTER 24

1   Gosse, 172
2   Moore, *Journal*, 15 August 1835
3   Ibid, 25 August 1835
4   Ibid, 26 August 1835
5   Ibid, 27 August 1835
6   Ibid, 28 August 1835
7   Ibid, 29 August 1835
8   Greville, 16 December 1835
9   Moore, *Letters*, 6 October 1835
10   Ibid, 14 November 1836
11   Moore, *Journal*, 3 July 1840
12   Hall, 17
13   Moore, *Journal*, 13 September 1838
14   Jordan, II, 585
15   Moore, *Journal*, 1–3 December 1840
16   Ibid, 26 August 1841
17   Moore, *Journal*, 26 August 1841
18   Ibid, 17 November 1841
19   Ibid, 1–3 December 1841

CHAPTER 25

1   Moore, *Journal*, 1 January 1842
2   Ibid, 10 January 1842
3   Ibid, 11–13 January 1842
4   Ibid, 25 March 1841
5   Ibid, 1–2 March 1841
6   Ibid, 1–3 April 1842
7   Ibid, 1–3 July 1841
8   Ibid, 1–31 December 1842
9   Ibid, 24–25 February 1843
10   Ibid, 19 December 1843
11   Ibid, 5 June 1843
12   Ibid, 12–13 August 1843
13   Ibid, 30–31 December 1843
14   Ibid, 16 February 1844
15   Ibid, March 1846
16   Ibid, March 1846
17   Ibid, May 1846
18   Russell, VIII, 7
19   Moore, *Letters*, 23 June 1846
20   Jordan, II, 628
21   Mumford Jones, 320
22   Pearson, 284
23   de Vere White, 269
24   Mumford Jones, 322
25   Medwin, 176

BIBLIOGRAPHY

All titles are published in London, unless otherwise stated.

Auden, W.H., *Foreword and Afterwords* (essay on Pope), 1973

Betjeman, John, *High and Low* ('Ireland's Own or the Burial of Thomas Moore'), 1967

Betjeman, John and Geoffrey Taylor (ed.), *English Love Poems*, 1964

Berlioz, Hector, *Memoirs*, tr. Rachel and Eleanor Holmes, revised by Ernest Newman, 1964

Blessington, Countess of, *Conversations of Lord Byron*, 1834

Burke, James, *The Life of Thomas Moore*, Dublin, 1879

Byron, Lord, *Letters and Journals*, ed. Leslie Marchand, 12 vols, 1972–1982

The Poetical Works of Lord Byron, 1863

Cambridge History of English Literature (essay on Moore by George Saintsbury), Cambridge, 1915

Chenevix Trench, Charles, *The Great Dan: A Biography of Daniel O Connell*, 1984

Christiansen, Rupert, *Romantic Affinities*, 1988

Clayden, P.W., *Rogers and his Contemporaries*, 1889

Clifford, Brendan, ed., *The Life and Poems of Thomas Moore*, 1984

Coleridge, Samuel Taylor, *Collected Letters*, ed. E.L. Griggs, Oxford, 1932

Cullen, Fiona and Foster, Roy, *Conquering England: Ireland in Victorian London*, 2005

David, Saul, *Prince of Pleasure: The Prince of Wales and the Making of the Regency*, 1998

Dictionary of National Biography, 1885–1900

Elliott, Marianne, *Robert Emmet*, 2003

Flannery, James W., *Dear Harp of my Country* (with two CDs), Nashville, 1997

Foster, Roy, ed., *The Oxford History of Ireland*, 1989

Friel, Brian, *The Home Place*, 2005

Gilmour, David, *The Making of the Poets: Byron and Shelley in their Time*, 2002

Gosse, Edmund, *Leaves and Fruit* (essay on Tom Moore in Wiltshire), 1927

Grattan, Henry, *Memoirs of the Right Hon. Henry Grattan*, vol iv, 1802

Greville, Charles, *Memoirs*, vol iii, 1875

Grosskurth, Phyllis, *Byron: The Flawed Angel*, Toronto, 1997

Gwynn, Stephen, *Thomas Moore*, 1905

Hall, Samuel Carter, *A Memory of Thomas Moore*, 1879

Haydon, Benjamin, *Diaries, 1808–1846*, ed. John Jolliffe, 1990

Hazlitt, William, *The Collected Works of William Hazlitt*, ed. A.R.Waller and A.Glover, 12 vols, 1902–1904

The Spirit of the Age, Foreword by Michael Foot, introduction by Robert Woof, Grasmere, 2004

Holmes, Richard, *Shelley – The Pursuit*, 1974

Hunt, Leigh, *Correspondence*, ed. by his eldest son, 1862

Lord Byron and Some of his Contemporaries, 1828

Johnson, Graham, *Britten, Voice and Piano: Lectures on the Vocal Music of Benjamin Britten*, 2003

Jones, H. Mumford, *The Harp that Once: Tom Moore and the Regency Period*, Harvard, 1937

Jordan, Hoover H., *Bolt Upright: The Life of Thomas Moore*, Salzburg, 1975

Keats, John, *The Letters of John Keats*, ed. M. Buxton Foreman, Oxford, 1952

Kee, Robert, *The Green Flag: Vol I, The Most Distressful Country*, 1972

Kelly, Linda, *Richard Brinsley Sheridan*, 1997

Lecky, William, *The History of England in the Eighteenth Century*, vol vii, 1890

MacCarthy, Fiona, *Byron: Life and Legend*, 2002

Macaulay, Thomas Babington, *Critical and Historical Essays* (review of Moore's *Life of Byron*), 1943

McGann, Jerome J., ed., *The New Oxford Book of Romantic Period Verse*, Oxford, 1993

Marchand, Leslie A., *Byron*, 3 vols, 1957

Medwin, Thomas, *Conversations with Lord Byron*, 1824

Mitchell, Leslie, *Holland House*, 1980

Moore, Doris Langley, *The Late Lord Byron*, 1961

Moore, Thomas, *The Epicurean*, 1827

The History of Ireland (4 vols), 1852

The Journal of Thomas Moore, ed. Wifred S. Dowden, 6 vols, 1983–1991

The Letters of Thomas Moore, ed. Wildred S. Dowden, Oxford, 1964

The Life and Death of Lord Edward Fitzgerald, 1831

The Life, Letters and Journals of Lord Byron, 1920

Memoirs of Captain Rock, 1824

Memoirs, Journal and Correspondence of Thomas Moore, ed. Lord John Russell, 8 vols, 1856

Memoirs of the Life of the Right Honourable Richard Brinsley Sheridan, 1825

The Poetical Works of the late Thomas Little Esq, 1801

The Poetical Works of Thomas Moore, 1862

Travels of an Irish Gentleman in Search of a Religion, 2 vols, 1831

Morgan, Lady, *Memoirs*, 1862

O'Faolain, Sean, *The Story of Ireland*, 1943

O'Sullivan, the Rev. Mortimer, *A Guide to an Irish Gentleman in his Search for a Religion*, Dublin, 1833

Pakenham, Thomas, *The Year of Liberty*, 1969

Pearson, Hesketh, *The Smith of Smiths*, 1934

Pushkin, A.S., *Letters*, tr. and ed. by J.T. Shaw, Indiana, 1967–1968

Quennell, Peter, *Byron: The Years of Fame*, 2001

Randall, Henry S., *The Life of Thomas Jefferson*, 1858

Rennie, Elizabeth ('A Contemporary'), *Traits of Character*, 1860

Russell, Lord John, *Early Correspondence of Lord John Russell 1805–1840*, ed. R. Russell, 1913

Seymour, Miranda, *Mary Shelley*, 2000

Shelley, Mary, *The Letters of Mary Wollstonecroft Shelley*, ed. Betty T. Bennett, 2 vols, 1983

Strong, L.A.G., *The Minstrel Boy: A Portrait of Tom Moore*, 1937
Vail, Jeffery, *The Literary Relationship of Lord Byron and Thomas Moore*, 2001
de Vere White, Terence, *Tom Moore: The Irish Poet*, 1977
Watson, J. Steven, *The Reign of George III*, Oxford, 1992
Woof, Robert, *Byron – A Dangerous Romantic*, Grasmere, 2003
Wordsworth, Jonathan and Jessica, ed., *The New Penguin Book of Romantic Poetry*, 2001
Zwill, William, ed., *Tom Moore s Bermuda Poems and Notes*, Bermuda, n.d.

CATALOGUES AND EXHIBITIONS

National Portrait Gallery, *Conquering England: Ireland in Victorian London*, 2005
Royal Irish Academy, *Thomas Moore*, 2002
Victoria & Albert Museum, *Byron*, 1974
Wordsworth Trust, Grasmere, *Byron – A Dangerous Romantic*, 1989

JOURNALS AND PAMPHLETS

Byron Journal, 1992 (article by Thérèse Tessier, 'Byron and Thomas Moore: A Great
    Literary Friendship')
Edinburgh Review (dates of issues as given in the text)
Croker, Thomas Crofton, *Notes from the Letters of Thomas Moore to his Music Publisher*,
    James Power, New York, 1854
Quarterly Review (review of Moore's journals by John Wilson Croker), July 1856

ARCHIVES AND COLLECTIONS

British Library, Moran MSS (Egerton 2149–2153). Collection for the illustration of
    the *Life and Works of Thomas Moore*, consisting of cuttings, engravings etc., 5 vols
John Murray archive. Letters from Thomas Moore to Lord Byron and others
National Library of Ireland. Books and periodicals from the holdings of the Library
    (including the Joly Collection) relating to Thomas Moore
Trinity College, Dublin. Collection of papers relating to Thomas Moore, MS 2009
Transcription of Hobhouse's entries in Doris Langley Moore's copy of Moore's *Life
    of Byron*, now in the collection of Mr Jack Wasserman (courtesy of Dr Peter
    Cochrane)

INDEX

Note: Works by Thomas Moore (TM) appear directly under title; works by others under author's name

Abbotsford, 190–191
Addington, Henry (*later* 1st Viscount Sidmouth): premierships, 46; and Pitt's death, 62
Aeschylus, 175
Alciphron (TM), 226
Allen (Lord Holland's librarian), 153
Amiens, Peace of (1802), 47
Anacreon: TM translates, 17, 31–2, 35–39, 41, 57
Anthologica Hibernica (literary magazine), 10–11, 17
Arkwright family, 107
Ashbourne, Derbyshire *see* Mayfield Cottage
Atkinson, Joseph, 35, 41, 47, 80
Auckland, George Eden, 1st Earl of, 228, 230
Auden, Wystan Hugh: admires TM, 4
Austen, Jane: *Emma*, 121
Austerlitz, battle of (1805), 62
Avoca, vale of (Ireland), 223
Azores, 49

Bannow (Ireland), 223–224
Barry, Charles, 200

Bartolini, Lorenzo, 161
Basil, St, 114
Beau Monde (magazine), 70
Bedford, John Russell, 6th Duke, and Georgiana, Duchess of (*née* Gordon), 154–155
Beethoven, Ludwig van, 77, 126
'Believe me, if all those endearing young charms' (TM), 78
Beresford, John, 19
Berlioz, Hector, 77–78
Bermuda: TM appointed Registrar to Naval Prize Court in, 48–49, 51–53; TM summoned over Goodrich's misappropriation of prize money in, 143–144, 151–154; TM's debt settled, 168–169
Berry, Mary, 36
Bessborough, Henrietta Frances, Countess of, 138
Betjeman, Sir John: praises *Lalla Rookh*, 1; admires TM, 4; 'Ireland's Own or the Burial of Thomas Moore', 221
Bishop, Sir Henry Rowley: arranges music for *Irish Melodies*, 151, 220

Blackwood s Magazine, 136
Blessington, Marguerite, Countess of, 215–216
Blue Stocking, The (TM) *see M.P. or the Blue Stocking*
Bonaparte, Jerome, 54
Borrowes, Lady, 10, 80
Boston, HMS, 53, 54, 57, 59
Bowles, Rev. William, 141, 176
Bowood, Wiltshire, 138, 141, 147, 154, 188, 227, 230, 233, 235
Bowring, John, 200
Boyce, Mr (TM's host on Irish journey), 223–224
Brighton Pavilion, 132
British Critic, 70, 210
British Review, 127, 176
Britten, Benjamin, 77
Bromham, near Bowood, Wiltshire: Sloperton Cottage, 139, 140–2, 148, 168, 170–171, 227; pictured, 206; cottage repaired and lease extended, 207; church memorial window to TM, 238
Brougham, Henry, Baron Brougham and Vaux: co-founds *Edinburgh Review*, 64; criticises Byron's *Hours of Idleness*, 84; friendship with TM, 90; and TM's

custody of Byron's memoirs, 178
Brown, Tom, 46
Bunting, Edward, 14, 21, 73
Burdett, Sir Francis, 154, 183–184
Burke, Edmund: on Catholic laws in Ireland, 13; founds Historical Society at Trinity, 21; in TM's life of Sheridan, 189
Burne-Jones, Sir Edward, 238
Burns, Robert, 56, 73
Burrowes, Revd Robert, 16
Burston, Beresford, 15, 18, 32
Byrne, Hannah, 10
Byron, Allegra (Byron-Claire Clairmont's daughter), 160
Byron, Annabella, Lady (née Milbanke): Byron courts, 112; marriage to Byron, 116–117; separation from Byron, 122–123, 208; in Byron's Don Juan, 151; refuses to read Byron's memoirs, 166–168; and disposal of Byron's memoirs, 178–180, 186; prospective marriage to Cunningham, 190; opposes TM's biography of Byron, 195, 200; Campbell defends in review of TM's Life of Byron, 210; disparaged in Byron's letters, 231; 'Remarks on Mr Moore's Life of Lord Byron', 208–209
Byron, Augusta Ada (later Lovelace; Byron's daughter): birth, 122
Byron, George Gordon, 6th Baron: friendship with TM, 1, 91, 95, 99, 105, 113–114, 116,

121–2; on TM's conversation, 2; memoirs burned at Murray's, 3–4, 181–2, 185; TM's biography of, 3, 110, 157, 195–197, 199, 201–203, 208–211, 215; pictured, 60; TM challenges to duel, 84–85, 95; TM writes conciliatory letters to on return to England, 91, 92–94; reads and praises TM's Thomas Little poems, 92; dieting, 94; TM meets, 94–95; deceived by maid Susan, 96; fame and reputation, 96, 169; and Lady Caroline Lamb, 99–100, 110, 112; quarrel with Colonel Greville, 99; visits Leigh Hunt in prison, 106; admires TM's Irish Melodies, 109; affair with Lady Oxford, 110; letters to TM, 110, 130–131, 142–143, 177; liaison with half sister Augusta, 110, 112, 208–209; attacked by Tory press, 111–112; courts Annabella, 112; lends journal to TM, 114; praises TM's review of Church fathers, 114; literary earnings, 116; marriage to Annabella, 116–117, 122; birth of daughter Ada, 122; separation from Annabella, 122–123, 208–209; leaves England, 123–125; in Venice, 130; popularity as poet, 132, 163; on success of Lalla Rookh, 137; on Sheridan, 142; indiscretion in letter to Murray, 152; TM visits

in Italy, 156–160; appearance, 157–158; liaisons in Italy, 157; on scandals and exile from England, 159; gives manuscript of memoirs to TM, 160, 166–168; Wordsworth accuses of plagiarism, 166; and settlement of TM's Bermuda case debt, 168; collaborates with Leigh Hunt on The Liberal, 169–170; TM dedicates Fables for the Holy Alliance to, 172; death in Greece, 177–178, 185; disposal of memoirs after death, 178–180, 195; funeral, 187; Scott on, 190–191; TM's farewell poem to, 194–195; Leigh Hunt attacks, 200–201; TM collects letters for biography, 202; homosexual practices, 209–210; letters disappear, 231; on enduring quality of TM's Irish Melodies, 238; Cain, 169; Childe Harold, 37, 95–96, 116, 130; The Corsair, 111–113; Don Juan, 151–152, 169, 180, 190; English Bards and Scotch Reviewers, 84–85, 92, 94–95, 99; The Giaour, 107–108, 111; Heaven and Earth, A Mystery, 169; Hours of Idleness, 84, 92; 'Lines to a Lady Weeping', 111; 'Sympathetic Address to a Young Lady', 98

Camden, John Jeffreys Pratt, 2nd Earl and 1st Marquess of, 19–20
Campbell, Lady (Lord Edward Fitzgerald's

daughter), 212,
214–215
Campbell, Thomas, 94,
109, 137, 149, 187, 210
Canada: TM travels in,
57–60
'Canadian Boat Song, A'
(TM), 58, 70
Canova, Antonio, 161
Captain Rock (TM) *see*
Memoirs of Captain Rock
Caroline, Queen of
George IV, 231
Carpenter, James
(publisher), 46, 74, 79,
102–103, 116
Castlereagh, Robert
Stewart, Viscount, 145,
151
Catholic Association
(Ireland), 174, 176
Catholic emancipation:
discussed and deferred,
2, 15, 19, 30, 37, 46,
73–74, 85, 174, 198,
203; agreed, 203–204,
212–213, 215
Catholic Relief Bill (1829),
203–204, 213, 217
Catholics: status in
Ireland, 10, 12–13;
admitted to Trinity
College, 14; law
openings limited, 39–40;
appointment of Irish
bishops, 85–86; TM's
views on, 217–218
Chantrey, Francis, 161–2
Charlemont, Francis
William Caulfeild, 2nd
Earl of, 145
Charlotte, Princess (Prince
Regent's daughter), 98
Chatsworth House,
Derbyshire, 114,
117–119
Chaworth, Mary, 200
Chrysostom, St, 114
Clare, John Fitzgibbon,
2nd Earl of, 25, 199
Cockburn, Captain (*later*
Admiral) George, 49–50

Codd, Joyce (TM's uncle),
49, 63; death, 79
Codd, Tom (TM's maternal
grandfather), 223
Coleridge, Samuel Taylor:
declines to contribute
to anthology including
TM poem, 41–2;
pictured, 60; Byron on
as poet, 109; poverty,
126; *Christabel*, 126
Colman, George, the
younger, 46
Congreve, William, 83
Copenhagen, battle of
(1801), 81
Corruption (TM), 74, 79
Corry, James, 98, 105, 140
Courier (newspaper), 112
Cowper, Emily Mary,
Countess (*née* Lamb),
195
Crabbe, George, 142, 216
Craddock, Dean, 17
Crampton, Dr Philip, 193
Creevey, Thomas, 152
Creswick, William, 235
Critical Review, 70
Croker, Crofton, 82–83
Croker, John Wilson,
83–84, 237
Cromwell, Oliver, 175
Curran, John Philpot, 187,
189
Curran, Sarah, 96–97

Dalby, Rev. John, 45, 79
Dalby, Mary, 104, 114,
216
Dallas, R.C., 112
Dalton, James, 120
'Dear Harp of my
Country' (TM), 118,
238
'Delusive dream' (TM), 17
Dennie, Joseph, 56
Devonshire, William
George Spencer
Cavendish, 6th Duke of,
114
Dibdin, Charles: *Peeping
Tom*, 81

Dickens, Charles, 54;
Bleak House, 78
'Did Not' (TM), 18
Donegal, Barbara,
Dowager Marchioness
of: friendship with TM,
45, 61, 63, 64, 70, 80,
184, 196; and TM's
aborted duel with
Jeffrey, 68; and TM's
giving up writing love
poems, 74; and death
of TM's uncle Joyce
Codd, 79; letter from
TM on absence from
London, 79; friendship
with Bessy, 89; and
TM's views on Ireland,
119; TM and family
stay with, 139; and
TM's lawsuit over
Goodrich, 143;
criticises TM's *Tom
Crib s Memorial to
Congress*, 150; shocked
at TM's *Loves of the
Angels*, 171; death, 216
Donington Park (and Hall),
near Derby: TM visits,
36, 40, 45, 47, 73,
79–80, 87, 100, 114
Donovan (Latin usher), 13
Douglas, Rev. Archibald,
170
Douglas, Captain (*later
Rear-Admiral*) John,
53, 59, 79, 121
Dowden, Wilfred S., 3,
146, 237
Doyle, Colonel Francis
Hastings, 179–182, 186
Doyle, Wesley, 12
Driver, HMS, 51
Dublin: character, 8; in
1798 rising, 28;
importance declines
after Union, 30; TM
revisits, 70–71, 79–80,
87, 119–20, 168, 223,
228–299; theatre in, 80;
TM visits to research
life of Sheridan, 145;

TM's memorial statue in, 238
Duff, John R., 83
Duff, Mary Anne (née Dyke; Bessy's sister), 83
Duigenan, Patrick, 25–26
Dyke, Bessy see Moore, Bessy
Dyke, Mr (Bessy's father), 83
Dyke, Mrs (Bessy's mother), 226, 227

'Echo' (TM), 164
Edinburgh, 191
Edinburgh Review: founded, 41, 63; reviews TM's Epistles, Odes and Other Poems, 64–66, 70, 92, 136; criticises Byron's Hours of Idleness, 84; TM writes for, 114–115, 199; reviews Coleridge's Christabel, 126; praises Scott's novels, 163; Hazlitt reviews TM's Loves of the Angels in, 171; Sydney Smith praises TM's Captain Rock in, 176; Macaulay reviews TM's Life of Byron in, 211
Eliot, George, 198
Elizabeth I, Queen, 229
Emmet, Robert: death, 2, 21, 71, 97, 134; at Trinity College, 21; friendship with TM, 21, 23; absence from Trinity during 1798 rising, 25; return to Ireland, capture and execution, 47–48; engagement to Sarah Curran, 96–97
Emmet, Thomas Addis, 22, 24
Epicurean, The (TM), 198–199, 226
'Epistle from Tom Crib to Big Ben' (TM), 120

Epistles, Odes and Other Poems (TM), 62–63, 70
Evenings in Greece (TM), 194
Examiner, The (journal), 103, 106

Fables for the Holy Alliance and Rhymes for the Road &c. (TM), 172
Fincastle, George Murray, Viscount (later 5th Earl of Dunmore), 66, 68
Fionnuala (swan princess), 77
Fitzgerald, Lord Edward: TM's life of, 2–3, 20, 212–215; in 1798 rising, 24–25; death, 27
Fitzgerald, Henry, 212
Fitzgerald, Vesey, 203
Fitzherbert, Maria Anne, 36
Fitzpatrick, General Richard, 68
Fitzwilliam, William Wentworth, 2nd Earl, 19–20
Flannery, James, 5
Florence, 161
Forbes, Lady Adeline, 110
Fouqué, Friedrich Heinrich Karl de la Motte, Baron, 136
Fox, Charles James: supports French Revolution, 13; in Ministry of All the Talents, 62; death, 90; Byron on, 142–143; in TM's life of Sheridan, 147
Fox Talbot, William Henry, 142
France: war with England, 12; and Irish rising (1798), 20, 24, 27; attempted invasion of Ireland (1796), 21; rebel leaders emigrate to, 28; renews war with

Britain (1803), 47; war ends (1815), 113
French Revolution, 12–13, 120
Friel, Brian: The Home Place (play), 5
Fudge Family in Paris, The (TM), 138, 140, 142, 144–145, 150, 164
Fudges in England, The (TM), 223

Galignani's Messenger (journal), 155
Garrick, David, 187
Gautier, Théophile, 199
George III, King: anti-Catholicism, 19, 30, 74, 85; and Ministry of All the Talents, 62; declared insane, 87, 89
George IV, King (earlier Prince of Wales and Prince Regent): TM dedicates Anacreon translation to, 37, 39, 103; TM meets, 39, 61; questions TM on social background, 44; compliments TM on Epistles, Odes and Other Poems, 63n; moral libertinage, 65; adopts Tory sympathies, 89, 97, 106; Leigh Hunt libels, 89; TM turns against, 89–90; TM satirises, 97–98, 103, 118, 120, 150; Moira breaks with, 98; and Leigh Hunt's imprisonment, 106; and Brighton Pavilion, 132; converted to Catholic emancipation, 204; death, 213
Gifford, William, 180
Gipsy Prince, The (TM; operatic afterpiece), 40–41
'Give me a harp of epic song' (TM), 40

Gloucester, William Frederick, Duke of, 186

Goddard, Rev. William, 142, 207

Godfrey, Mary: friendship with TM, 45, 61, 65, 80; and TM's return to Ireland, 70–71; friendship with Bessy, 89; and TM's disparagement of *The Blue Stocking*, 90; and Moira's break with Prince Regent, 98; and TM's view of Mrs Ready, 106; and TM's reaction to publication of Byron's *The Giaour*, 107; and TM's view of end of war with France, 121; and Byron's separation, 122

Goodrich, Edward, 153

Goodrich, John William: as TM's registrar in Bermuda, 84; and court case for misappropriation, 143, 153

Gosse, Sir Edmund, 223

Grattan, Henry, 8–9, 12, 19–20, 86, 152

Gregory Nazianizen, St, 114

Grenville, William Wyndham Grenville, Baron, 89

Greville, Charles, 215, 225

Greville, Colonel (manager of Argyle Rooms), 99

Grey, Charles, 2nd Earl, 89–90, 213, 227

Grierson, George Abraham, 32

Griffin, Gerald and Daniel, 218–219

Grosskurth, Phyllis, 5

Guiccioli, Contessa Teresa, 157–160, 200

Gwynn, Stephen, 4

Haggard, Sir H. Rider: *She*, 199

Halifax, Nova Scotia, 57, 59–60

Hall, Bond, 18–19

Hamilton, Colonel (British consul in Norfolk, Virginia), 50–51

Hamilton, Dacre, 25

Hamilton, Mrs (Colonel's wife), 51, 54

Hannah (maidservant), 140, 152

'Harp that once through Tara's Halls, The' (TM), 76

Harrington, Charles Stanhope, 3rd Earl of, 61

Hastings, Warren, 189

Haydn, Joseph, 126

Haydon, Benjamin Robert, 137

Haymarket Theatre, London, 46

Hazlitt, William, 149–150, 170–171; *The Plain Speaker*, 170

Heaney, Seamus, 5

Hertford, Isabella, Marchioness of, 98

History of Ireland (TM): writing, 226, 229, 232, 234; payment for, 231

Hobhouse, John Cam: and Byron's meeting with TM, 94–95; accompanies Byron to Dover on leaving England, 123; doubts on publication of Byron's *Don Juan*, 151; and disposal of Byron's memoirs, 178–183, 186, 191, 195; and Byron's funeral, 187; and TM's request to write life of Byron, 195, 200; and TM's reconciliation with Murray, 196; jealousy over Byron's preference for TM, 200;

Doris Langley Moore on, 202; comments on TM's life of Byron, 210

Hodgson, Francis, 85, 93

Holland, Elizabeth, Lady, 90, 147, 152, 166, 185, 187, 200, 236

Holland, Henry Richard Vassall Fox, 3rd Baron: praises TM's pamphlet on Irish Catholics, 86; status, 90; Byron attacks in *English Bards and Scotch Reviewers*, 95; at Kemble's farewell dinner, 137; as source for TM's biography of Sheridan, 152; and TM's flight abroad after Bermuda court case findings, 153; TM shows manuscript of Byron's memoirs to, 166; and TM's life of Byron, 200; views on TM's life of Fitzgerald, 212–214; as Chancellor of Duchy of Lancaster, 213; death, 236

Holland House, Kensington, 90, 188

Holland, Stephen Fox, 2nd Baron, 212

Hopkins, W. (prompter), 189

Horner, Francis, 67, 69

Hornsey, 129, 131, 139

Horton, Wilmot, 178–182, 186

Hudson, Edward, 21–2, 24, 28–29, 57

Hume, Thomas: friendship with TM, 36, 46, 55; as TM's second in duel, 66–67, 69–70, 82; breach with TM, 70, 82; and TM's supposed immorality, 81; helps settle Russell Moore's bills, 231

Hunt, John, 103, 106

Hunt, Leigh: imprisoned for libelling Prince Regent, 89, 103; reviews TM's *The Blue Stocking*, 90; TM and Byron visit in prison, 106; attempts to introduce Keats and TM, 146; supports subscription for TM after Bermuda court case, 153; in Italy, 169–170; hostility to TM, 170; TM attacks for disparaging Byron, 201; on TM's 'loving a lord', 210; 'The Feast of the Poets', 89; *Lord Byron and Some of his Contemporaries*, 200–201

'I wish I was by that dim lake' (TM), 177
Intercepted Letters; or, the Twopenny Post-Bag (TM), 102–103, 112, 116
Intolerance (TM), 74, 79
Ireland: cultural identity, 2, 13–14; 1798 rising, 2, 20, 24, 27–29; Union with Britain (1801), 2, 30; independent parliament, 8, 13; sectarian differences and religious bigotry, 12–13, 74, 86; music collected and preserved, 14, 21, 73; attempted French invasion (1796), 21; repressive measures in, 22; TM revisits, 70–71, 79, 87, 119–20, 212, 214, 223–224; TM satirises English attitudes to, 80–81; Catholic Church in, 86; poverty and injustices in, 173–176; TM accompanies Lansdownes on tour of estates in, 173–174;

unrest in, 214, 234; TM writes history of, 226, 229, 232–234; potato famine, 234
Irish Melodies (TM): success and popularity, 1–2, 4–5, 74, 78, 80–81, 89, 109, 165, 223, 238; and Irish nationalism, 30–31; Jefferson reads and praises, 56; gestation and writing, 71–2, 73; parts published, 74–78, 86, 96, 105, 109, 113, 118, 127, 131, 142, 147, 150, 164, 176–177, 221; Stevenson arranges music for, 75–76; music, 76–77; preface, 76; qualities, 77; set by other composers, 77; Byron admires, 109; Hazlitt disparages, 150; Bishop arranges music, 151, 220; influence on Irish liberty, 219; payments for, 220–221, 226
Irving, Washington: pictured, 60
'It is not the Tear at this Moment shed' (TM), 56
Italy: TM travels in, 155–161

Jackson, John, 161–2
Jefferson, Thomas, 55
Jeffrey, Francis: co-founds *Edinburgh Review*, 6; reviews TM's *Epistles, Odes and Other Poems*, 66, 92; TM's abortive duel with, 66–68, 84–85, 112; apologises to TM and establishes friendship, 69; pays TM for writing for *Edinburgh Review*, 115; and TM's offer to review Coleridge's *Christabel*, 126; praises *Lalla*

Rookh, 136; offers loan to TM after Bermuda court case, 153; death, 236
Jersey, Sarah, Countess of, 200
Johnson, Graham, 77
Johnson, Samuel, 162, 191
Jones, Howard Mumford, 4, 74
Jordan, Hoover H., 4, 136
Joyce, James: *Dubliners*, 165
Joyce, Stanislaus, 165

Kean, Edmund, 115
Kearney, John (*later* Bishop of Ossory), 16, 31–2, 37
Keats, John: destructive reviews of, 115; on banquet for TM in Dublin, 146; on Hazlitt's lectures, 149; in Shelley's *Adonais*, 199
Kegworth, Leicestershire, 98, 104
Kelly, Joe, 12, 37
Kelly, Michael, 12, 37, 40–41, 90
Kemble, John Philip, 137
Kenmare, Valentine Browne, 2nd Earl of, 174
Kilkenny Theatre, 80–81
Kinnaird, Charles, 8th Baron, 156, 170
Kinnaird, Douglas, 178–180

Lalla Rookh (TN): contemporary success, 1; Schumann bases *Das Paradies und die Peri* on, 77; writing and research, 90, 98, 100, 107–108, 113, 115, 119, 128, 132; and Byron's *The Giaour*, 107–108, 112; publisher's payment for, 115–116, 128–129, 226; publication, 129, 130;

structure and themes, 132–135; success, 132, 136, 163, 231; qualities, 135; translated, 136; TM predicts fading interest in, 137; adapted as opera, 145; Hazlitt criticises, 149–150

Lamb, Lady Caroline: Byron's affair with, 99–100, 112

Lamb, William (*later* Viscount Melbourne), 90, 152

Langley Priory (house), Leicestershire, 102

Lansdowne, Emily Jane, Marchioness of (*née* de Flahault), 238

Lansdowne, Henry Petty-Fitzmaurice, 3rd Marquess of: praises TM's pamphlet on Irish Catholics, 86; TM meets, 90; and TM's move to cottage in Wiltshire, 138–141; public appointments, 141; stands godfather to TM's son, 148; offers help to TM after Bermuda court case, 154, 167–168; TM shows manuscript of Byron's memoirs to, 166, 185; TM accompanies on tour of Irish estates, 173–174; confirms Byron's death, 178; friendship with TM, 196, 233, 236; as Lord President of the Council in Grey's government, 213; and TM's biography of Fitzgerald, 214; and Reform Bill (1832), 216; informs TM of award of pension, 224–226; TM's collected poetical works

dedicated to, 227; and TM's death, 236

Lansdowne, Louisa Emma, Marchioness of (*née* Fox-Strangways), 173, 207, 230, 238

Lawrence, Sir Thomas, 161, 208

Lecky, William, 19

Lefanu, Elizabeth (*née* Sheridan), 146

Leigh, Augusta Mary (Byron's half sister): pregnancy and child, 110, 112–113; and disposal of Byron's memoirs, 179–181, 186; TM meets, 188; opposes TM's biography of Byron, 195, 200

Leinster, Augustus Frederick Fitzgerald, 3rd Duke of, 212, 214–215

Leinster, Emily Mary, Duchess of (*later* Ogilvie), 212

Leinster, James Fitzgerald, 1st Duke of, 212

Leinster Journal, 80–81, 86

'Letter to the Roman Catholics of Dublin, A' (TM), 86

Lewis, Matthew Gregory, 42, 45

Liberal, The (magazine), 170, 171

Life and Death of Lord Edward Fitzgerald (TM), 214–215

Life, Letters and Journals of Lord Byron, The (TM), 93, 202, 208–211, 213

'Lines on the Death of Sheridan' (TM), 172

Literary Chronicle, 176

Literary Fund *see* Royal Literary Fund

Little, Thomas: as TM pseudonym, 41; immorality criticised,

66; *see also Poetical Works of the late Thomas Little, The*

London: TM arrives in, 32, 33–34; TM's social life in, 35–36, 44, 61–2, 89–90, 227, 233

London Journal, 80

Longman, Thomas (publisher): publishes TM's *Lalla Rookh*, 115, 128–129, 132, 137; and *The Fudge Family in Paris*, 145; offers advance to TM after Bermuda court case, 154; TM writes *Rhymes on the Road* for, 155; and Byron's memoirs, 167, 180, 182; holds Lansdowne's gift to settle TM's Bermuda case debt, 167; publishes TM's *Loves of the Angels*, 171; TM borrows from, 177, 183, 194, 202; publishes TM's life of Sheridan, 188–189, 194; and TM's agreement with Murray's to publish life of Byron, 196, 202; publishes TM's *The Epicurean*, 198; publishes TM's life of Lord Edward Fitzgerald, 212; suggests TM write long poem, 223; commissions history of Ireland from TM, 226; buys copyright of *Irish Melodies* from Power's widow, 227; declines extra payments to TM, 231

Longman, Thomas, junior, 236

Lorne, George William Campbell, Marquess of, 147

Louis XVIII, King of France, 113

Loves of the Angels, The
  (TM), 169, 171–2, 223
'Love's Young Dream'
  (TM), 96
Luttrell, Henry, 136,
  179–183, 186, 225

Macaulay, Thomas
  Babington, Baron, 90,
  211
McColl, Seamus, 4
McCormack, John, 5
Mackintosh, Sir James,
  132, 226
Maclise, Daniel: 'The
  Origin of the Harp'
  (painting), 29
Macmahon (apothecary),
  35
Macpherson, James
  ('Ossian'): forgeries,
  13–14
Malone (schoolteacher), 9
Masterton family, 32, 34
Masterton, Sally, 34
Matthews, Captain
  Thomas, 147
Mayfield Cottage,
  Ashbourne, Derbyshire,
  106–107, 114, 121
Maynooth: seminary
  established, 12
'Meeting of the Waters,
  The' (TM), 4, 223
*Melalogue on National
  Music* (TM), 86
Melbourne, Elizabeth,
  Viscountess (*née*
  Milbanke): Byron
  admires, 110; Byron's
  letters to, 195–196, 200
*Memoirs of Captain Rock,
  The* (TM), 174,
  175–176
Mendelssohn, Felix, 77
Mercier (Dublin
  bookseller), 10
Merry, Mr and Mrs
  Robert, 49–50, 55
Middle Temple: TM at,
  32, 34
Milan, 156

Ministry of All the
  Talents, 62, 73, 85
'Minstrel Boy, The' (TM),
  1, 77, 108–109
Missolonghi, Greece, 177
Mitchell, Admiral Sir
  Andrew, 52
Moira, Francis Rawdon
  Hastings, 2nd Earl of
  (*later* Marquess of
  Hastings): TM meets,
  35–36; TM stays with
  at Donington, 40, 47,
  73, 100, 141; public
  appointments, 46–47,
  62; gains post for TM
  in Bermuda, 48; TM
  dedicates *Epistles, Odes
  and Other Poems* to, 62;
  demands on patronage,
  63, 102; helps TM's
  father to post in
  Dublin, 63, 70; and
  TM's dismay at bad
  reviews, 70; unable to
  find post for TM, 71,
  73, 98, 100–101; retires
  from office, 74, 89;
  kindness to Bessy, 88;
  introduces TM to
  Hollands, 90; breach
  with Prince Regent, 98;
  appointed Governor-
  General of Bengal,
  100; TM ends relations
  with, 101; sails for
  India (1813), 102
Montreal, 58–59
Moore, Anastasia Mary
  (TM-Bessy's daughter):
  birth, 103–104; health
  decline and death, 201,
  203–205, 207
Moore, Anastasia (*née*
  Codd; TM's mother):
  background, 8; and
  TM's upbringing and
  education, 9, 14–15;
  singing and
  entertaining, 11–12;
  and TM's appointment
  to Bermuda, 48–49;

and TM's social life in
  London, 62; not told of
  TM's marriage, 87; and
  TM's breach with
  Moira, 101; and TM's
  visit to Dublin (1815),
  119; and publication of
  TM's *Lalla Rookh*, 129;
  TM tells of death of
  daughter Barbara, 138;
  TM visits (1821), 168;
  and TM's visit to
  Ireland with
  Lansdownes, 173;
  offered widow's
  pension, 194; illness,
  214; death, 216
Moore, Barbara (TM-
  Bessy's daughter):
  birth, 98; at Oakhanger
  Hall, 105; illness in
  Dublin, 120; illness and
  death after fall,
  138–140; moves to
  Sloperton Cottage,
  Bromham, 140
Moore, Bessy (*née* Dyke):
  TM meets and courts,
  81, 87; background and
  character, 83–84,
  87–88; marriage to
  TM, 87, 233–234;
  social shyness, 87, 154;
  depicted, 88; birth of
  children, 98, 103–104,
  114, 148, 172; Byron
  praises, 100; prefers
  Rogers's house to
  Moira's, 100; at
  Oakhanger Hall,
  104–105; at Mayfield
  Cottage, 107; avoids
  visit to Chatsworth,
  117; and death of
  daughter Olivia, 119,
  140; visits Dublin with
  TM, 119–20; ill health,
  121; and death of
  daughter Barbara, 138,
  140; enjoys London
  pleasures, 138; moves
  to Sloperton Cottage,

Bromham, Wiltshire, 139, 140; at Bowood, 141; friendship with Crabbe, 142; visit to Scotland, 152–153; and TM's flight to continent, 154–155, 161–2; breaks nose, 162–163; joins TM in France, 162–163; and settlement of TM's Bermuda case debt, 168; returns to Sloperton from Paris, 170; Lady Lansdowne praises, 173; offers help to TM's widowed mother, 194; and daughter Anastasia's illness and death, 204–205, 207; on award of pension to TM, 225; and son Russell's death, 232; on sons' troubles, 232; charitable activities, 234; in TM's final years, 235–236; granted widow's pension, 236; sells TM's papers to Longmans, 236; Croker on, 237; death and funeral, 238

Moore, Christopher: memorial statue of TM, 238

Moore, Doris Langley, 202

Moore, Ellen (TM's sister): birth, 8; on dying father, 193; circumstances on father's death, 194; informs TM of mother's illness, 214; TM visits in Ireland, 223, 229; TM supports, 226, 227; death, 234–235

Moore, John (TM's father): grocery business, 7; family background, 8; and TM's appointment in Bermuda, 48; Moira helps to position as Barrack Master, 63; moves to Abbey Street, Dublin, 70; not told of TM's marriage, 87; TM visits in Dublin, 119; retires on half pay, 128; toasted at Dublin banquet, 146; and TM's visit to Ireland with Lansdownes, 173; decline and death, 193

Moore, Kate (TM's sister) see Scully, Kate

Moore, Olivia Byron (TM-Bessy's daughter): birth, 114; death in infancy, 119, 140

Moore, Russell (TM-Bessy's son): birth, 172; childhood, 207; Hobhouse offers cadetship at Addiscombe, 210; education, 227; career in India, 228–229; returns on sick leave from India, 230–2; death, 232–233

Moore, Thomas: friendship with Byron, 1, 91, 94–95, 99, 105, 110, 113–114, 116, 121–2; conversation, 2; as performer and singer, 2, 11, 17–18, 36, 45, 86–87, 89, 105, 215–216; journals, 3–4, 28, 146, 157, 204, 233–234, 236–237; reputation, 4–5; birth, 7; childhood and upbringing, 8, 10–12; amateur dramatics and acting, 9–10, 80–81; political opinions and involvement, 9, 12–13, 22–23, 74; schooling, 9; juvenile verse, 10–11; musical interests, 11, 17, 31, 34–35; at Trinity College, Dublin, 13–15, 16–18; religious indifference, 13; appearance and small size, 16, 44; protests at Fitzwilliam's dismissal, 20; on repression in Ireland, 22; and 1798 rising, 25–27, 28, 31; translates Odes of Anacreon, 31–2, 35–39, 57; university degree, 31; leaves for Middle Temple, London, 32–34; social life in London, 35–36, 44, 61–2, 89–90, 227, 233; financial difficulties, 39, 46, 61, 79, 102, 229, 230; gives up legal studies, 39; condemned for immorality in 'Thomas Little' poems, 41–43; charm, 44; private discretion, 46; seeks patronage, 46–47; sells copyrights, 46; appointed Registrar to Naval Prize Court in Bermuda, 48–49, 51–53; in USA and Canada, 48–51, 54–60; attachment to Hester Tucker, 52–53; in Mottram group portrait, 60; operation for tumour, 63; *Edinburgh Review* accuses of licentiousness, 65, 70; challenges Jeffrey to duel, 66–68, 84, 112; Jeffrey apologises to and establishes friendship with, 69; obscure movements between 1807 and 1809, 79; meets and courts Bessy Dyke, 81, 83, 87; reputation for immorality, 82–83; challenges Byron to duel, 84–85; contract with John William Goodrich, 84; marriage to Bessy, 87; retainer from Power brothers, 87, 102, 151; Whig sympathies, 89–90; letters to Byron on return to England, 92–94; sees proofs of Byron's *Childe Harold*, 95–96; birth of children, 98, 103–104, 114, 148, 172; and Byron's affair with Lady Caroline Lamb, 99; ends relations with Moira, 100–101; moves to Mayfield Cottage, Ashbourne, 106–107; Byron praises poetry of, 109–110; letters from Byron, 110, 130–131, 142–143, 177; Byron dedicates *The Corsair* to, 111–112; writes for *Edinburgh Review*, 114–115, 199; payment for *Lalla Rookh*, 116, 129; receives payment from Bermuda agent, 116; and Byron leaving England, 123–125; supports Sheridan in decline, 125; on Sheridan's death and funeral, 126; at Kemble's farewell dinner, 137–138; and death of daughter Barbara, 138–140; visits Paris, 138; moves to Sloperton Cottage, Bromham, Wiltshire, 139, 140; summoned to settle Goodrich's Bermuda obligations, 143–144, 151–154; Hazlitt lectures on,

149–150; accused of snobbery, 152, 170, 210; loses Bermuda court case, 153; flight to France after Bermuda court case, 154; visits Byron on trip to Italy, 157–161; Byron gives manuscript of memoirs to, 160; bust by Bartolini, 161; stays in Paris with Bessy, 162–163, 166, 168; Bermuda case debt settled, 168–169; returns to Sloperton from Paris, 170; learns of Byron's death, 177–178; and question of disposal of Byron's memoirs, 178–183, 195; declines payment for Byron's memoirs, 182–183, 186; on content of Byron's lost memoirs, 185–186; trip to Scotland, 190–2; visits Ireland to see dying father, 193; Gilbert Newton portrait of, 196–197; satirical verse in *Times*, 197–198; and death of daughter Anastasia, 204–205, 207; Lawrence portrait of, 208; interest in theology, 217–218, 223; declines nomination as Parliamentary candidate, 218–219; home life, 218–220; self-deprecation, 224; awarded pension by Whig government, 225–226; writes history of Ireland, 226, 229, 232–234; collected poetical works published, 227; pays for sons' careers, 227–229; and death of son

Russell, 232; and death of son Tom, 235; health decline, 235–236; death and funeral, 236; memorials to, 238
Moore, Thomas Lansdowne (TM-Bessy's son): birth, 148; childhood illnesses, 148, 208; education, 227; military career, 228–229; illness in India, 230; falls into debt, sells commission and joins French Foreign Legion, 232; activities and illness in North Africa, 234–235; death, 235
Morgan, Sir Charles, 161
Morgan, Lady *see* Owenson, Sydney
Morning Chronicle, 98, 100, 120, 150, 178
Morning Post, 37
Mottram, Charles: group portrait, 60
Mounteagle, Lord (former Lord Chancellor), 230
Mozart, Wolfgang Amadeus, 126
M.P. or the Blue Stocking (TM; operetta), 90
Mulgrave, Henry Phipps, 3rd Baron, 128
Murray, Ann (*née* Dyke; Bessy's sister), 83, 87, 152, 191, 216
Murray, Ann (singer), 5
Murray, Charles (Bessy's nephew), 238
Murray, John: publishes Byron's *Childe Harold*, 95; opposes Byron's dedication of *The Corsair* to TM, 111; offers payment to TM for *Lalla Rookh*, 115; and review of Coleridge's *Christabel*, 126; TM praises Byron's *Childe Harold* to, 130;

Byron praises *Lalla Rookh* to, 137; invites TM to write biography of Sheridan, 142; doubts on publication of Byron's *Don Juan*, 151–2; TM on social status of, 152; TM leaves manuscript of Sheridan biography with, 154; and TM's stay with Byron in Venice, 160; and payment to TM for manuscript of Byron memoirs, 167, 177–178, 182–183; and blasphemy in Byron's *Cain*, 169; and disposal and burning of Byron's memoirs, 179–182, 186; and payment for TM's life of Sheridan, 188; and TM's biography of Byron, 196, 199, 201–2, 204, 209, 211; TM's reconciliation with, 196; suggests TM write commentary for collected edition of Byron's works, 223

Murray, William, 191

'Musings of an Unreformed Peer' (TM), 217

Napier, Colonel (Lord Edward Fitzgerald's cousin), 212

Napoleon I (Bonaparte), Emperor of the French: Egyptian campaign, 27, 164; abdicates, 113; flight from Elba, 119; defeat at Waterloo, 120; downfall, 145

National Airs (TM; collection), 142, 144, 150, 164, 188, 199

Nelson, Admiral Horatio, Viscount, 62, 81

New Monthly, The (journal), 210

New York, 54, 57

Newton, Gilbert Stewart: drawing of Bessy, 88; portrait of TM, 196–197

Niagara Falls, 58

Nicholas I, Tsar, 136

'Nonsense' (TM), 43

Norfolk, Virginia, 49–51, 54–55

North, Christopher *see* Wilson, John, 136

Oakhanger Hall, Cheshire, 104, 106

O'Connell, Daniel: campaign for Catholic emancipation, 30, 174, 176; and appointment of Irish Catholic bishops, 86; at Dublin banquet for TM, 145; on TM's *Loves of the Angels*, 172; TM meets in Ireland, 174; defeats Fitzgerald in 1828 election, 203; and achievement of Catholic emancipation, 204; praises influence of TM's *Irish Melodies*, 219; and TM's declining to stand for Parliament, 219; demands repeal of Act of Union, 234; imprisoned, 234

O'Connor, Arthur, 24

Odes of Anacreon (translated TM), 37–41, 46, 57, 64

O'Driscoll, John, 173

O'Faolain, Sean, 30

'Oft in the Stilly Night' (TM), 5, 144

Ogilvie, William, 212

Ogle, Sukey, 152

'Oh Blame Not the Bard' (TM), 1, 33, 86

'Oh, Breathe not his Name' (TM), 2, 48, 71, 76

'Oh! had we some bright little isle of our own' (TM), 108

'Oh ye Dead' (TM), 165

O'Neill, Phelim, 229

'Origin of the Harp, The' (TM), 28–29

Orlando, Jean, 187

O'Sullivan, Rev. Mortimer, 223

Owenson, Robert, 80

Owenson, Sydney (Lady Morgan), 99, 161; *The Wild Irish Girl*, 80

Oxford, Elizabeth Jane, Countess of, 110

Palmerston, Henry John Temple, 3rd Viscount, 236

Paris: TM visits, 138; TM flees to after Bermuda court case, 154–155; TM stays in with Bessy, 162–163, 166, 168

'Parody of a Celebrated Letter' (TM), 97

Parr, Dr Samuel, 148

'Pastoral Ballad by John Bull' (TM), 198

Peel, Sir Robert, 227, 230

Perry, James, 115–116, 153

'Petition of the Orangemen of Ireland, The' (TM), 198

Phaeton, HMS, 49–50

Philadelphia, 56–57

Pitt, William, the younger: writes no verse, 9; defers Catholic emancipation, 19, 30, 85; resigns, 30, 46; death, 62

Poe, Edgar Allan, 177

Poetical Works of the late Thomas Little, The (TM), 41–44, 46, 62, 92, 151

Poetical Works (TM), 132, 227, 231

Pope, Alexander, 175

Porchester, Henry John George Herbert,

Viscount (*later* 3rd Earl of Carnarvon), 188

Port Folio (US magazine), 56

Portland, William Henry Cavendish Bentinck, 3rd Duke of, 74

Power, James: payments for *Irish Melodies*, 73; and publication of *Irish Melodies*, 73, 105, 127, 131–2, 164; pays annual retainer to TM, 87, 102, 151; witness at TM's wedding, 87; and TM's thwarted hopes of patronage from Moira, 100–101; discusses publication of *Sacred Songs*, 120; and TM's financial support for parents, 128; breach with brother William, 151; offers loan to TM after Bermuda court case, 153; relations with TM, 153; and TM's farewell poem to Byron, 195; TM writes glees for, 199; deducts Bishop's payments for *Irish Melodies* from TM's account, 220–221; death, 227

Power, Richard, 80, 119

Power, William, 73, 79, 102, 151

Press, The (newspaper), 22

Priestley, Joseph, 141

Prometheus (Greek mythical figure), 176

Pushkin, Alexander, 185

Quarterly Review, 115, 237

Ready, Mrs (of Oakhanger Hall), 104–105, 106

Rees, Owen, 116, 168–169, 177, 221, 231

Reflector, The (journal), 89

Reform Bill (1832), 216–218

Rhymes on the Road (TM), 155, 164, 170

'Rock, Captain' (mythical Irish rebel figure), 174–175

Rogers, Samuel: pictured, 60; TM meets, 61; on Jeffrey, 66; and TM's duel with Jeffrey, 68; praises Bessy, 88; introduces TM to Hollands, 90; as intermediary between TM and Byron, 91, 93–95; sees proofs of Byron's *Childe Harold*, 95; friendship with TM, 99, 196; on Lady Caroline Lamb, 99; and TM's breach with Moira, 101; in Thurlow's poem, 105–106; Byron on as poet, 109; Byron dedicates *The Giaour* to, 111; and TM's invitation to Chatsworth, 114; published by Longmans, 115; TM praises Jane Austen's *Emma* to, 121; and Byron's friendship with TM, 125; supports Sheridan in decline, 125; invites TM to Paris, 138; and TM's relations with Lansdownes, 141; and Byron's *Don Juan*, 151; offers loan to TM after Bermuda court case, 153; and TM's return from abroad, 168; and TM's custody of Byron's memoirs, 178; and TM's refusal to take payment for Byron's memoirs, 186; attends Byron's funeral, 187; on Sheridan, 187; and TM's view of biography, 197; TM interviews for life of Byron, 200; and Murray's publication of Byron papers, 201; Luttrell compares TM's poetry with, 225; on TM's social life in London, 227; and TM's health decline, 235–236

Rome, 160–161

Rousseau, Jean-Jacques, 162, 170, 185

Royal Literary Fund: helps Coleridge, 126

Russell, Lord John (*later* 1st Earl): edits TM's journals, 3–4, 28, 146, 200, 233, 236–237; on TM's happy marriage, 87; accompanies TM on flight to France, 154–155; visits Bessy at Sloperton, 154; in Rome, 159, 161; stands godfather to TM's youngest son, 172; on TM's *Captain Rock*, 176; on content of Byron's memoirs, 185; and TM's political views, 212; as Paymaster-General in Grey's government, 213; opposes TM's biography of Fitzgerald, 214; introduces Reform Bill (1832), 216; arranges pension for TM, 226; on TM's health decline, 235–236; premiership and political offices, 236; and TM's death, 236; gives pony to Bessy, 238

Sacred Songs (TM), 119, 126–127

St Lawrence river, 58

Saintsbury, George, 4, 140

Satirist, The (journal), 83

Sceptic, The (TM), 80

Schumann, Robert, 77
Scotland: TM visits, 190–2
Scott, Alexander, 158–159
Scott, Captain Sir James, 49–50
Scott, Sir Walter: TM visits, 12, 190–2; on TM's charm, 15; and Prince Regent's amusement at TM's satirical description, 97; Byron praises poetry, 109; published by Longmans, 115; popularity, 163; writes history of Scotland, 226; *Rokeby*, 115
Scully, John, 194
Scully, Kate (*née* Moore; TM's sister): birth, 8; learns piano, 11; TM sends piano to, 46; marriage, 120; TM visits in Ireland, 120, 173; death, 226
Sheddon, Robert, 143, 153, 168
Shee, Martin Archer, 35
Shelley, Mary, 199–200, 209
Shelley, Percy Bysshe, 170, 199; *Adonais*, 199
Sheridan, Charles, 143, 152, 188
Sheridan, Elizabeth (*née* Linley; RBS's first wife), 147
Sheridan, Richard Brinsley: TM's biography of, 3, 142, 145–148, 150, 152, 164, 186–190, 215; related to Samuel Whyte, 9; schooling at Harrow, 11, 187; social life in London, 35, 90; charm, 44; pictured, 60; and Bessy Moore in theatre, 83; friendship with TM, 99; decline, death and funeral, 125–126, 188; elopement, 147;

political career, 189–190; *Duenna*, 3
Sirr, Major, 212
Sloperton Cottage *see* Bromham, near Bowood
Smith, Sydney: co-founds *Edinburgh Review*, 64; praises music of *Irish Melodies*, 76–77; friendship with TM, 90; praises TM's *Captain Rock*, 176; on Newton's portrait of TM, 196; TM visits at Combe Florey, 233; death, 236; on Lord John Russell, 237
Society of United Irishmen *see* United Irishmen
Southey, Robert: pictured, 60; Byron on as poet, 109; in Byron's *Don Juan*, 151; *The Curse of Kehama*, 107; *Thalaba*, 107
Spencer, William: friendship with TM, 45, 61; lends duelling pistols to TM, 67; reveals TM's duelling plans, 68
Stanhope, Colonel Leicester (*later* 6th Earl of Harrington), 187
Starkey, Mrs (TM's neighbour), 236
Stevenson, Sir John: sets TM's poems to music, 36, 40, 43, 45; TM collaborates on operatic pieces with, 46; and TM's proposals for *Irish Melodies*, 71, 73; collaborates on *Irish Melodies*, 75–76; arranges TM's *Sacred Songs*, 126; with TM in Paris, 138; supports William in Power brothers' quarrel, 151;

TM dedicates final volume of *Irish Melodies* to daughter, 223
Stockdale's (publisher), 36
Strangford, Percy Clinton Sydney Smythe, 6th Viscount: friendship with TM, 45–46, 61; TM sends poem to, 50; and TM's duel with Jeffrey, 67
Strong, L.A.G., 4, 143
Strutt family, 107

Talbot, W.H. Fox *see* Fox Talbot, William Henry
Tavistock, Francis Russell, Marquess of, 155
Tennyson, Alfred, 1st Baron: on 'Oft in the Stilly Night', 145
Tessier, Thérèse, 202
Theatre Royal, Dublin, 83
Thierry, Jacques, 1
'This Earth is the Planet' (TM), 127
Thurlow, Edward Hovell-Thurlow, 2nd Baron, 105, 114
Tierney, George, 48
'Time I've lost in Wooing, The' (TM), 117
Times, The (newspaper), 176, 197
''Tis the Last Rose of Summer' (TM), 1, 108–109
'To Zelia on her charging the author with writing too much on Love' (TM), 10
Toller (TM's proctor), 151–153
Tom Crib s Memorial to Congress (TM), 150
Tone, Wolfe, 13–14, 21, 28
'Torch of Liberty, The' (TM), 172
Tories: and appointment of Irish Catholic bishops, 86; Prince Regent supports,

89, 97–98; TM satirises, 120

Trafalgar, battle of (1805), 62

Travels of an Irish Gentleman in Search of a Religion, The (TM), 217–218, 223

Trinity College, Dublin: TM studies at, 13–15, 16–18; Bishop Marsh's library, 17, 31, 217; political discussions, 20–21, 23; and 1798 rising, 25

Trollope, Frances, 54

Tucker, Hester, 52

Tucker, William, 52

Turner, J.M.W.: in Rome, 161; illustrates TM's *The Epicurean*, 199, 226

Twopenny Post-Bag, The (TM) see *Intercepted Letters*

Tytler, Patrick Fraser, 229

Ulm, battle of (1805), 62

Union, Act of (1801), 2, 30, 214, 234

United Irishmen, 13, 19–24, 27–28

United States of America: TM visits, 49–51, 54–57; native Indians

in, 57

Vail, Jeffry, 5

Venice, 158–160

Vilamil family, 163

Warens, Françoise de la Tour, baronne de, 162

Warren, Billy, 11, 17, 36

Washington, DC, 55–56

Waterloo, battle of (1815), 120

Weber, Anton, 77

Wellesley, Richard Colley, Marquess of, 193–194

Wellington, Arthur Wellesley, 1st Duke of, 203, 218

Wesley, Charles, 196

Wexford: in 1798 rising, 27; TM visits, 223–225

'When first I met thee' (TM), 117, 216

Whig party: and Catholic emancipation, 19; and appointment of Irish Catholic bishops, 86; loses Prince Regent's support, 89–90; TM's sympathies with, 89; social style, 90; return to power (1830), 213

White, Terence de Vere, 4, 237

Whyte, Samuel, 9, 11, 14

Wilks, Colonel Mark, 132

William IV, King: accession, 213

Willis, E.P., 215

Wilson, John ('Christopher North'), 136

Woolriche, Stephen, 66

Wordsworth, Mary (*née* Hutchinson), 166

Wordsworth, William: pictured, 60; Byron on as poet, 109; published by Longmans, 115; TM meets in Paris, 166; slighting comment on TM's poetry, 224; disparaged in Byron's letters, 231; *Lyrical Ballads* (with Coleridge), 37

'Written aboard the Phaeton frigate, off the Azores, by moonlight' (TM), 50

Yeats, William Butler: disparages TM, 4; as Irish voice, 77; 'Innisfree', 108

York, Prince Frederick Augustus, Duke of, 97

'Young May Moon, The' (TM), 108